MIKE MACLAY
APPLICATIONS
SAIC LTD.

Total Management Thinking

Left	**Right**
Competition	Environment
Total quality	Quest for quality
Benchmarking	Improvement
Re-engineering	Concern for people
Measurement	Self appraisal
Decision-making	Empowerment
The learning organization	Quest for knowledge
Team performance	Teaming
Customer focus	Service excellence
Technology	Creativity

An insight into the changing business world

Total Management Thinking

Sultan Kermally

This book is dedicated to:
- My wife Laura and my children Jenny, Susan and Peter.
- To all those business executives/employees who have gone through
  and are going through the traumas and perhaps pleasures of change
  and those who have become casualties of organizational
  transformation.

Butterworth-Heinemann
Linacre House, Jordan Hill, Oxford OX2 8DP
A division of Reed Educational and Professional Publishing Ltd

A member of the Reed Elsevier plc group

OXFORD BOSTON JOHANNESBURG
MELBOURNE NEW DELHI SINGAPORE

First published 1996
© Reed Educational and Professional Publishing Ltd

British Library Cataloguing in Publication Data

Kermally, Sultan
 Total management thinking
 1. Management   2. Organizational change   3. Strategic planning
 I. Title
 658.4

ISBN 0 7506 2614 3

Typeset by Avocet Typeset, Brill, Aylesbury, Bucks
Printed and bound in Great Britain

Contents

Acknowledgements

This book would have not been possible without the help of the individuals, organizations and publishers who have given me permission to reproduce conference presentations and extracts from journals and books. My thanks go to:

* All my students and those executives with whom I have come in contact at training sessions and conferences who planted the idea of this book.
* Henri Aebischer of Apple Computer Europe.
* David Allen-Butler, business operations manager, Digital Systems, Digital Equipment Co.
* American Management Association, USA.
* The Anglo-German Foundation for the Study of Industrial Society, London. (Extract from the report, Managing in Britain and Germany.)
* BBC Worldwide Ltd.
* The Boston Consulting Group. ('The Myth of Horizontal Organization' and 'Reengineering Bumps Into Strategy.')
* Martin Brackenbury, Thomson Travel Group.
* *Business Week*: How to make your Company Quality Master (Dec, 1992) and Benchmarking at Work: Improving Procurement (Dec, 1993).
* Nick Butcher, managing director, DHL Int (UK) Ltd.
* Butterworth-Heinemann, Oxford, UK.
* Roger Davies, manager of operational performance, British Airways.
* Department of Trade and Industry, UK.
* Digital Equipment Co., Reading, UK.
* The Economist Conferences, 15 Regent Street, London, UK.
* The Economist Intelligence Unit, UK.
* European Foundation for Quality Management. Avenue des Pleiades 19, 1200 Brussels.
* Harbridge Consulting Group, London. In particular Phil Lowe, senior consultant.
* Harvard Business School Publishing: Gene Hall, Jim Rosenthal and Judy Wade, How to Make Re-engineering

Really Work. Nov-Dec, 1995. Robert Kaplan and David P. Norton, Putting the Balanced Scorecard to Work. Sept-Oct 1993.

- Richard Haydon, Artemis International, Slough, UK.
- International Institute for Management Development, Lousanne, Switzerland.
- Clive Jeanes, managing director, European Division, Miliken Industrials Ltd.
- Sune Karlsson, customer focus co-ordinator, ABB, Manheim, Germany.
- John Kelly, managing director, European Quality Publications Ltd, London (Extracts published by kind permission, © 1995. European Quality Publications Ltd/UK Publications Ltd.)
- Lloyd's Register Quality Assurance Ltd, Croydon, UK.
- McGraw-Hill Inc. (Extract from *Quality Without Tears* by P. Crosby.)
- Trevor Mills, general manager, The Solution Centre, ICL, Bracknell, Berks.
- 3M United Kingdom PLC. (Conference presentation, The Lateral Alternatives, by Paul M. Davies, manager, HRD, Europe.)
- The Open University Business School, Milton Keynes, UK. (Material from Course B889: Performance Measurement and Evaluation.)
- Prentice-Hall Inc. for permission to reproduce a diagram from *Principles of Marketing* by Philip Kotler.
- Gareth Reece, chief executive officer, Kinsley Lord Ltd, London.
- Graham Witney, partner, Coopers & Lybrand, London.
- Royal Mail, UK.
- Simon & Schuster Inc. for permission to reproduce Figure 2.2 from *Competitive Advantage: Creating and Sustaining Superior Performance* by Michael E. Porter and Figures 1.1 and 3.1 from *Competitive Strategy: Techniques for Analysing Industries and Competitors* by Michael E. Porter.
- The Times Newspaper, London.
- *The European Management Journal*. Cases on Hall Mark, Rank Xerox, UK, Taco Bell and Wal-Mart. Reprinted from *The European Management Journal*, **13**, 1, March, 1995. Article entitled Re-engineering and Organizational Change

by Ascari, Rock and Dutta, with kind permission from Elsevier Science Ltd, The Boulevard, Langford Lane, Kidlington, Oxford OX5 1GB, UK.
* The McKinsey Quarterly, UK. Reprinted by special permission from Frank Ostroff and Douglas Smith. The Horizontal Organization. The McKinsey Quarterly, 1992. No. 1 Copyright © 1992. McKinsey & Co. All rights reserved.
* Wally Welling, quality manager, TSB, UK.

I am particulary indebted to Jacquie Shanahan for her encouragement and direction and for giving me an opportunity to write this book and Jonathan Glasspool for his guidance and perseverance. Both Jacquie and Jonathan are from Butterworth-Heinemann.

Finally my thanks and affection go to my wife Laura for her support and encouragement and for letting me hide in my study to write this book.

Sultan Kermally

Introduction: about the book

The title of the book contains three significant words, namely, 'Total', 'Management' and 'Thinking'.

Total: This suggests the totality of application of management ideas and theories, not only from the point of view of organization, structures and processes but also individuals working in the organizations and customers. The term does not refer to all management thinking.

Management Thinking: The book explores some key management thinking and theories presented by various 'gurus' and consultants in the last 25 years.

> **Management has always been beset by fads and fashions, gurus and demagogues. But never before has there been such a sheer volume of new approaches.**
>
> Professor Edward Lawler of the University of Southern California School of Business Administration

Why this book?

I have been involved in management development and training for a number of years. I have a passion for new management thinking and its *applicability* in the business world we work in and live in.

In my present job as a senior vice president and the director of the Economist Conferences and in my previous job as senior group director at Management Centre Europe, Brussels, I have come across thousands of business executives who have attended leading edge management conferences and training programmes.

The topic of conversation always boils down to the following key aspects of business:

- We cannot cope with the various management fads and thinking that are proliferating in the business world.
- One needs to spend a lot of money and read at least 15 to 20 books and numerous articles to keep track of what is happening.
- As it is, it is difficult to manage our time. The problem is accentuated by working with less people due to restructuring and downsizing.
- Do these management ideas work in practice and what types of organizations have applied them?
- Wouldn't it be nice to have all these issues addressed in one book?

Similar views have been expressed by my MBA students over the years.

As we live in a customer-focused world, I have decided to take these issues on board and meet the demands of customers. I have used presentations made at the Economist Conferences, articles published in professional journals and management reviews, and tried to present the topics in a simple and pragmatic way.

I have also addressed the various concerns and issues raised by the casualties of corporate restructuring and those employees who work in a new environment.

How have the topics been chosen?

All businesses operate within the external environment consisting of sociological, technological, economic and political factors (the **competitive environment**). To respond to these external as well as internal environments, organizations have embarked upon improving the quality of products, processes and people (**total quality management**). To become a quality-driven organization, efforts have to be made to adopt best practice (**benchmarking**). The focus of being the best in class is to deliver service excellence (**customer focus**) and to continually monitor performance in order to sustain best practice (**performance management**).

The race has developed to abandon 'status quo' and adopt

radical thinking in order to eliminate non-value adding activities and be responsive to customer needs (**business process re-engineering**). In such an environment workers have to be given power to solve problems and make decisions (**empowerment**). Streamlining structure due to re-engineering has led to flat organizations (**the horizontal organization**), in which employees now strive to acquire new knowledge and skills (**the learning organization**) and work in groups (**teams and teaming**). Finally the application of all these concepts and thinking will lead to organizations becoming knowledge-driven within the context of the information society. Entering the **knowledge era** will mean that organizations will need to underpin their strategies, processes and structure with **computer technology** and the **convergence of various communications systems**.

Right and left sides of the brain

We are told by experts that as far as brain hemispheres are concerned, the left part of the brain controls a significant proportion of analytical mental functions and logical and rational capabilities, whereas the right part of the brain controls much of the intuitive capabilities. The left hemisphere tends to process information in a sequential manner whereas the right hemisphere tends to deal with simultaneous relationships.

People in business (top management as well as low levels of management and employees) have to be adept at using the right and left sides of their brain. **The new management thinking reflects not only logic and rational thinking but it also incorporates emotions, trust and intuition**. Practising both sides of the brain will bring about alignment between organizational development and goals on the one hand, and aspirations of employees and satisfaction of customers on the other (see Figure I.1).

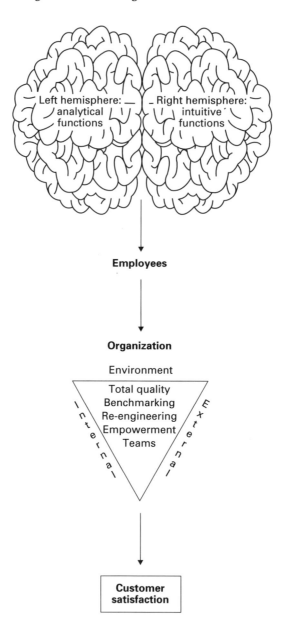

Figure I.1   Brain hemispheres, organizational development and customers

Message to readers

There are many echoes in the world but few original voices.

Unknown

By the time you read this book your organization may have benchmarked many aspects of its business, the processes may have been re-engineered and you may be working as an empowered member of a high-flying, high-performing, multi-skilled team.

Some of you still await such experience. For those of you who have been baptized in change initiatives, do compare your experiences with the experience of other organizations. Is your experience the same as the experience of one business executive who said 'Our organization has gone through a lot of changes but very little improvement'?

This book is written for you and its main objective is to explain how different management thinking has influenced the business world. I would welcome comments on your experience and suggestions for improvement. Please do write to me through Butterworth-Heinemann.

Thank you

Prayer

God grant me courage to change the things I can,
The patience to accept the things I cannot change,
And the wisdom to know the difference.

Poets' prayer

Prologue: Memo from the chief executive officers to all employees

To: All employees (converts, believers, agnostics and atheists)
From: Chief executive officers
Subject: Managing and living with change

....

The business world is changing very dramatically and we have to change accordingly if we want to survive in an intensely competitive climate. We would like to take this opportunity to outline for you the various change initiatives our companies have adopted so that you understand the reasons behind certain decisions and actions.

Total quality management

All companies are facing fierce competition. To win and retain customers we have to deliver quality goods and services. Total quality management is not a fad; it is a business reality.

We have to improve the quality of products, processes and people. Everyone in the company is responsible for total quality.

Benchmarking

We will initiate projects to benchmark different aspects of business. Some of you will be involved in benchmarking customer service, some in financial operations, marketing and sales and human resources. The main objective of bench-marking is to adopt best practice.

Customer service

Your salaries are paid by customers not companies. The way we deal with our customers and the way we treat them is going to be the key differentiating factor. We urge you to adopt an attitude, 'treat others as you would wish them treat you'.

We have put in place various mechanisms to listen to our customers and to treat our suppliers as our partners. We also expect you to establish long-term reletionships with our key customers.

Business process re-engineering

The latest management thinking is to focus our attention on our processes, that is the way we develop new products, the way we fulfil our orders and so on. We have formed teams to look at various processes and to suggest ways to eliminate activities that do not add value. Re-engineering could lead to job losses but in our view it is better to lose a few jobs now than to lose the whole business if we do not re-engineer.

Performance measurement

We have decided to review our measurement philosophy and approach. We will be measuring the effectiveness of all our processes and the way our people perform various roles within the companies.

Empowerment

We have recently made 200 managers and supervisors redundant in order to flatten our organizational structure. You now have to work in teams and in each team you will have a freedom to address various problems and make key decisions.

In order to enable you to perform specialized as well as general functions within teams we have asked our human resource departments to recommend training programmes and to present the budget with their recommendations. In the absence of vertical career ladders we will institute ways of moving employees horizontally across the company so that you build portfolios of skills.

You are our greatest asset. If you can understand the reasons for various changes and the rationale behind them, we feel you will be able to give us your full commitment.

We, in turn, will try to be as open and honest in our communications with you. However, you have to understand that our board from time to time may recommend cost-cutting exercises, in which case we may have to reduce the numbers in our work force. We do, however, value your service and commitment.

1 Snapshots of the competitive environment

It is only when you are pursued that you become swift.

Anonymous

Summary

- The profile of the business world is changing dramatically.

- Businesses are affected by the external environment within which they operate. The variables in the external environment are categorized into sociological, technological, economic and political (STEP) factors. Factors within each category influence business strategy.

- In addition to external environment, forces within the industry affect the competitive positions of the firms. These forces are categorized by Michael Porter as barriers to entry and exit, substitutes and bargaining power of suppliers and buyers. It is important for an organization to conduct an industry analysis.

- If an organization wants to gain and retain competitive advantage it should not only study competitive environment but it must track its key competitors and their performance. Without such tracking an organization will not have performance targets to benchmark against.

- In preparing its action plan, an organization should look at outsourcing as a strategic option.

- Finally in order not only to survive in the changing business climate of the 1990s but also to be an organization of the twenty-first century, it is recommended that organizations re-think the philosophy and the role of marketing. Some experts advocate relationship marketing in order to gain, satisfy and retain customers. It is also proposed that 'business excellence' should be the focus and the core of business.

Introduction

This chapter is not about management theories or about total management thinking as such. All organizations have to operate and make decisions within the national and international or global environment. Management gurus and writers have advocated adopting new management thinking in order to respond effectively to the changing sociological, economic, technological and political envirinment. In addition, organizations constantly have to review their positions in the competitive arena in which they are players.

It is important to get an insight into changing business profile in order to appreciate **corporate fears** and the emergence and adoption of 'new' management ideas. According to Peter Drucker some new management ideas and new management thinking is 'recycled conventional wisdom'.

Corporate casualties

According to Professor D. Quinn Mills today's 'status quo' is change. The profile of the business world is changing dramatically. The history of enterprise is littered with household names which have gone out of existence. In 1986 IBM was one of the most admired companies. In 1993 IBM made a loss of $48.1 billion. The book *In Search of Excellence* by Peters and Waterman was published in 1982. It became the all-time business bestseller in America. Almost half of the 43 companies selected for the 'excellence' class no longer deserve the classification. What went wrong?

The following are some of the reasons which contributed to the downfall of some of the 'excellent' companies:

- Failure to read market signals.
- Arrogance.
- Rigid organizational culture.
- Bureaucracy.
- Obsession with analysing own performance to the neglect of customers.
- Ego trips.

Household names like Philips, Digital Equipment, Caterpillar, General Motors, Matsushita and the like had to restructure their organizations in order to survive. Survival in the 1990s means that organizations have to be able to adapt. Organizations have to pay attention not only to a changing competitive environment but also to keep an eye on their competitors from all over the world.

Organizational effectiveness depends on how well changes in the micro-environment and macro-environment are responded to. The micro-environment consists of the industrial structure within which companies operate. The macro-environment consists of social, technological, economic and political factors (**STEP factors**) affecting business operations and strategies (see Figure 1.1).

Figure 1.1   Micro- and macro-environmental factors

Strategic decisions are influenced by the behaviour of the competitors, the nature of the industry within which companies operate and changes in the STEP factors.

STEP factors

1. Social factors

Social factors relate to changes taking place in a society. These changes apply to social attitudes, social values, changes in the educational system, life styles, structure of household, the family unit, the role of women and minorities, and so on. All these changes impact upon industrial structure and organizational strategies. Demographic changes such as birth rates, population size, age structure and population mobility affect human resources and marketing strategies of companies.

Impact of demography
If we consider the demographic factors alone it is estimated that the world population is going to grow to six billion before the end of the century. Asia will remain by far the most populous continent. Many countries will experience a trend towards smaller families as a result of changes in socio-economic conditions. Mortality rates in all countries will fall and in regions such as the USA and Europe, the population will become increasingly aged.

Ageing populations present the global challenge. In 1990 almost 500 million people (more than 9 per cent of the world's population) were more than 60 years old. The World Bank estimates that by 2030 the number will be 1.4 billion and that most of the growth will take place in developing countries and specifically in Asia.

The World Bank points out that while it took more than 100 years for the share of the population over 60 in Belgium to double from 9 to 18 per cent, the same transition will take only 34 years in China and 22 years in Venezuela. Developing countries will have elderly demographic profiles at much lower levels of per capita income than the leading industrialized countries.

In India with a population of over 900 million (1994), economic growth will lead to the creation of an urban middle-class with both the ability and desire to buy consumer goods and services. Over 50 per cent of India's gross domestic product (GDP) is currently accounted for by 180 million urban dwellers. Of these, 30-40 million have consumption patterns similar to those of the West.

Speaking at the Pharmaceutical Conference organized by the Economist Conferences in October 1994 in London, Richard Sykes, CEO of Glaxo Holdings plc, said 'the basic demand for healthcare remains sound. New needs are being created by demographic change. Our understanding of the disease process, and hence, our ability to meet the challenges is expanding at an unprecedented rate. The ability to bring together different scientific disciplines, apply them to specific disease states and deliver products which meet the needs of patients and the doctors is a unique and a socially-valued capability for those than can compete.'

The Green revolution
Society is also concerned about the environmental and ecological factors such as emission and safety standards, recycling and pollution levels. Products are coming to the market which are labelled as 'environmentally friendly' in order to respond to the desires of the customers. In the early 1990s some computer printer manufacturers started to market environmental aspects of their products such as recycled paper and the use of toner containers capable of being burned.

Some organizations consider environmental indicators as one of the key measures of their performance. At the second World Industry Conference on Environmental Management held in Rotterdam in April 1991, there were more than 700 leading industrialists present to discuss key environmental issues for industry. The environment is becoming just another part of a business manager's legitimate day-to-day concern.

The introduction of the Eco-Audit Management Scheme (EMAS) throughout the European Union has added an extra dimension for companies seeking to use management systems in order to raise environmental awareness and improve business performance. EMAS is a voluntary scheme aimed at improving the environmental performance of companies. To achieve recognition companies must develop an environmental management system and prepare a public environmental statement. Both must be then validated by an independent accredited certification body.

BS 7750 is the UK standard for defining the scope and contents of an organization's Environmental Management System (EMS). It is currently the only EMS standard available and applicable world-wide. The standard is voluntary and consists of the following five elements:

- Developing an environmental policy
- Evaluating environmental effects.
- Setting overall goals and specific measurable targets.
- Establishing management control.
- Reviewing the system regularly.

BS 7750 is applicable world-wide whereas EMAS applies only to organizations within the European Union.

The *Financial Times* on 31 May 1995 reported Vauxhall, the UK arm of the US company General Motors, as the first recipient of an award for environmental management. Vauxhall's Ellesmere Port plant has become the first car factory to receive the BS 7750 award for the environment management from the British Standards Institution. It acknowledges the management's environmental awareness. Shopfloor staff were trained and the environmental responsibility was shifted to the senior staff. Ten environmental auditors were appointed to monitor environmental progress. Most of the changes involved eliminating waste and reducing energy consumption.

The article Greening the bottom line, published in *Management Today* in July 1995, describes how Nissan, the Japanese car company, is attempting to become environmentally friendly: 'the most vivid example of Nissan's policy in action is the way that money saved by recycling plastic off-cuts from the manufacture of Micra and Primera fuel tanks is paying for the switch to environmentally friendly (but more expensive) water-based paints on the Micra to reduce solvent emissions.'

The same article goes on to say that several of the most environmentally conscious companies have been using their clout to try to encourage environmental friendliness in their suppliers. According to KPMG, one of the leading management consultancies, in 1994, 34 per cent of the *Financial Times*' top 100 companies produced separate environmental reports, compared with only 20 per cent in 1993.

What do business executives think about the environment?
In early 1995 Management Centre Europe carried out the survey on Business and the Environment. Participants who were attending seminars were surveyed. Seven per cent of the

sample were under 30; 34 per cent between 30 and 39, a further 33 per cent between 40 and 49, 23 per cent between 50 and 59 and just 2 per cent over 60. Eleven per cent were chief executives, 43 per cent top managers, 32 per cent middle managers and the rest specialist functions.

Asked the question: 'Regarding environmental issues, how would you describe your personal attitude?' the response was:

Concerned and active:	16 per cent
Concerned but passively involved:	68 per cent
Mixed/undecided:	12 per cent
Totally disinterested:	1 per cent
No response/don't know:	2 per cent

When asked 'Regarding environmental issues, how would you describe the attitude of the organization you work for?' the following was the response:

Concerned and very active:	28 per cent
Concerned and active:	32 per cent
Concerned but passively involved:	26 per cent
Mixed/undecided:	12 per cent
Totally disinterested:	2 per cent

The response seems to show that organizations are ahead of individuals in the active contribution they are prepared to make. (*Source*: Business and the Environment Survey, 1995. Management Centre Europe.) It will be interesting to examine a survey undertaken in 1998 and see to what extent business executives' views converge towards environmentalists' perspectives.

National differences
Within the sociological factors also come differences in national cultures. Understanding the national characteristics and histories of particular societies have also become important in managing at cross-border level. In every culture authority, bureaucracy, creativity, empowerment and downsizing are experienced in different ways. Often management techniques with standardized jargons taken from one culture fail when they are taken across borders.

The most widely known research in the field of culture is the pioneering work of Geert Hofstede. His research covered 53 countries within a single organization, IBM. He concluded that there are four work-related dimensions in which cultures differ. These dimensions were power/distance (distribution of power in society), uncertainty avoidance, individualism versus collectivism and masculinity versus femininity (society's endorsement of masculine and feminine qualities).

Another description of how cultures differ has been developed by a Dutch economist and consultant, Fons Trompenaars. His research revealed seven dimensions of culture. His findings facilitate the most practical way for managers to consider how cultural differences influence their organizations.

Cultural differences
Understanding differences in national cultures help organizations become effective in negotiations, selection, team work, performance management, empowerment and adopting an appropriate management style.

In a recent report published by the Anglo-German Foundation, the findings highlight differences in managing in Britain and in Germany. German managers desire control over uncertainty and they rely on inter-personal formality, punctuality, consistency and order, dependability and trust, team spirit and co-operation. In Britain the managers focus on commitment, initiative, ownership, responsibility, personal sense of accomplishment and coaching.

If one takes an example of negotiation, for example in Japanese and American contexts, the Japanese team will consist of many delegates (focus on collectivism), they arrive at decisions by consensus, they are generally polite and value trust. The American team on the other hand, will consist of few delegates, the decisions will be made by majority vote, they will be assertive and focus on legal agreement.

According to Michael Porter (1985), 'National differences in character and culture, far from being threatened by global competition, prove integral to the success of it.'

2. Technological factors

New technologies and skills are becoming increasingly diffused world-wide and more and more businesses are becoming high tech. For example, South Korean companies were renowned for producing cheap shoes and textiles. Now they are becoming leading producers of high-tech goods. The push is led by Samsung, Hyundai and Daewoo.

Advances in telecommunications and computing

Technological developments are taking place at breathtaking pace specifically in the telecommunications and entertainment industries. Advances in technologies such as personal communications systems/personal communications networks (PCS/PCNs) and low grade orbiting satellite systems (LEOs) will intensify competition. Faster switching is allowing almost unlimited quantities of information to travel at an accelerating speed.

Optical fibres are circling the globe enabling the realization of the global information infrastructure. Satellite technology is creating a 'global broadcasting system'. It is predicted that almost all the major countries in the Asia-Pacific region will be linked by optical fibre submarine cable systems by the end of this century.

Several dominant technologies are converging which is shaping the telecommunications industry. These technologies are fibre optic radio, ATM (asynchronous transfer mode) and low cost computing. These technologies are being deployed concurrently. The convergence of computing, communications and information will lead to a global information superhighway which will expand markets, develop new businesses and increase competition. Some say 'the future is not what it used to be'.

Advances in general purpose computing are allowing users to create and use extremely sophisticated applications. Such applications create new capabilities and opportunities. More and more people now use PCs in the workplace and at home. In the European Union alone $76 billion investment is planned over the next five years for advanced network and interactive video services. Computing is decreasing time to market and increasing the ability of service providers to innovate and offer flexibility so essential in a changing business climate.

Everyone is familiar with the Internet and yet a decade ago it was unthinkable that an international network could grow from 1 million to 30 million users in less than four years. New technologies and their falling costs have become the important catalysts in changing the way business is being organized. We are now witnessing collaborative technological projects being undertaken with rivals. For example, Texas Instruments and Hitachi Ltd, NEC and AT&T and Intel and Sharp. According to Lawrie Philpott of Coopers & Lybrand 'individually and corporately we will have to learn how to deal in a marketspace rather than marketplace'. One must also not forget that the faster rate of technological breakthroughs makes organizational uniqueness obsolete very fast.

Technology has also been the main driver behind flexible working. It is estimated that the cost of providing an office-based desk in the UK is about £6000 per annum. Many organizations such as Anderson Consulting and Digital Equipment Co. are investigating more cost-effective ways of managing their organizations.

According to the survey commissioned by Digital, more than half of their salespeople, service staff and consultants spend less than 40 per cent of their time in the office. Facts like this are prompting organizations to analyse how people work within their organization. Equipped with modems, fax machines and mobile telephones, some employees are involved in flexible work practices. Some practices develop environments where work is performed in the most effective way at home, in community offices and in 'tele-cottages'.

Flexible working will increase in the twenty-first century. It is important to consider a careful integration of business needs, people needs and technology. More and more people will opt for home-based working and advances in multimedia is facilitating such needs.

3. Economic factors

The economic landscape is also changing dramatically. Key economic variables such as wealth, purchasing power, inflation, unemployment, interest rates, exchange rates, growth, investment and savings are all key determinants of demand. One of the most sensitive issues for many businesses today is the level of interest rates. The late 1980s and early 1990s saw a high level of interest rates in many European countries. Interest rates increase as soon as there is an indication of the inflation rate increasing. Interest rates affect servicing of loans, level of capital expenditure, housing finance, movement of 'hot' money, savings and investment.

Another key economic factor impacting on competition is exchange rates. Fluctuations in exchange rates affect exports and imports. Arguments and discussions are still going on in relation to the fixing of exchange rate fluctuations within the European Union and an introduction of the single currency.

The past two decades have also seen a revolution as domestic financial markets have been opened up to create a massive global capital market. This change has contributed to the explosive growth of the financial markets. A free capital market ensures that savings are directed to the most productive investments without regard for national boundaries.

Most economists predict that the fastest growing economies will be South East Asia and Japan. Economic growth in Europe and the USA is likely to remain sluggish. The annual percentage increase in the gross domestic product of the UK, Italy, France and Germany, for example, is forecasted to be under 3 per cent in 1997. The North American Free Trade Association (NAFTA) and the completion of the GATT Uruguay Round will provide a boost to world trade volumes. The high spots for growth in the European economy are in Central and Eastern Europe. In Hungary, Poland, the Czech Republic and Slovakia, a rapid growth is already establishing itself.

As far as the Asian economies are concerned Korea, Taiwan, Singapore and Hong Kong are expected to gain a significant increase in the world manufactured exports. The share of the world output held by all the Asian developing economies is likely to increase from one fifth in 1990 to nearly one third by 2010. Many analysts believe India is poised to become economically one of the key 'Asian tigers' by the end of the century. Her open policy on inward motor industry investment has attracted the US's General Motors, Germany's Daimler Benz, Fiat of Italy and Peugeot of France to a market expected to grow from 350 000 in 1994 to at least 600 000 by 2004.

4. Political factors

Politically the climate is changing from conflict to co-operation. Geographic boundaries are ceasing to be barriers to competition. State-owed businesses are being sold and markets are being liberalized. Many countries are emulating the success of the UK's and USA's privatization and deregulation policies. Privatization and deregulation are becoming the major internal sources of new competition.

Since the fall of the Berlin Wall and the abandonment of communism there have been steady streams of acquisitions, alliances, strategic partnerships and supplier networks. The global shrinkage is the result not only of advances in technology and communication but also of changing political ideologies. Former communist and socialist countries are opening up their markets and are creating an infrastructure to compete with industrially advanced countries. On 26 July 1995, an international accord on liberalizing trade in financial services was completed after Japan and South Korea joined other countries in committing themselves to improving access to the markets. This accord (the Geneva accord) will cover an estimated 90 per cent of the financial services market. Indonesia, Thailand, Malaysia and other Asian countries offered attractive prospects in life and health insurance with China and Vietnam among those which would develop later.

China has initiated the creation of a socialist market economy. In March 1993 the overall concept of socialist market economy was embedded in China's constitution. In such a market structure central management of the economy is replaced by market forces. Special economic zones were created in which liberalized policies are tried. The first securities exchanges opened in Shanghai and Shenzen. Nation-wide electronic trading systems for securities including treasuries were also initiated. In 1993 the Central Committee of the Communist Party of China in its 'Decision on Economic Structure' reaffirmed the commitment to a wide spectrum of market-based economies.

Vietnam in 1991 at the Vietnam Communist Party VIIth

Congress adopted the socio-economic development strategy towards 2000. The targets were related to significant improvement in social and economic development. Vietnam is expected to attract more trade and investment and perform better since the lifting of the US embargo.

The Republic of Cuba is changing its laws to attract foreign capital in all sectors of industry and in some cases inducing joint ventures. The Cuban Foreign Minister announced very recently that his government would implement an open-market policy with no limits on the entry of foreign capital regardless of its origin. This decision also applies to expatriate Cuban capital. This was made clear in Havana in April when exiles and Cuban officials met for the first time since 1978.

Speaking at the Economist Conferences in Havana in June 1994, the Minister of Basic Industry said, 'In the last 30 years Cuban industry achieved a high level of integration with the former socialist countries'. The disintegration of the USSR 'posed a challenge to reconvert the industry to compete in quality and price in the world market for which technologies, capital sources and partners are needed who can appreciate the opportunities offered by the Cuban economy, its potentialities and to jointly do sound business'. At present the Mitsubishi Corporation of Japan is assessing the market in Cuba for a range of private cars and buses.

President Fidel Ramos of the Philippines on 24 July 1995 made a State of the Nation Address in which he said, 'We cannot enter the twenty-first century with one foot in the feudal era ... In its present condition our bureaucracy is saddled with a structure fit only for a bygone age ... we must press on with deregulation and liberalization and bring down the last of our self-imposed barriers left over from the days of protection.'

Influence of STEP factors on business organizations

- Changing political ideologies and a climate of co-operation have facilitated 'borderless organizations'. Thomson, a French consumer electronics giant, is making TV tubes in Poland. Ireland's Waterford Wedgewood plc is producing its

crystals in Hungary. German businesses are shifting some
of their operations to Slovakia and Slovenia. Audi has
operations in Hungary, Siemens in Poland and Volkswagen
has a 25 per cent stake in the Czech car maker Skoda.
NEC, the largest semiconductor manufacturer in the
world, is opening a plant in Scotland. In June 1994
Hyundai Electronics announced plans to invest $1.3 bil-
lion in a semiconductor plant in Oregon. Intel has opened
a semiconductor plant in Ireland and is now expanding
production in California, Arizona and New Mexico. And the
story of 'borderless' organizations and production continues.

- Central Europe is becoming the manufacturing zone for
European businesses. The workers in these countries are
hitting quality and productivity standards on a par with
their Western counterparts. Central European countries
are aligning their trade, legal and economic systems to
those of the West.

- Toyota, Japan's leading car maker, announced in July
1995 that it wants to double its total production outside
Japan by the end of the century. The main growth in overseas production will come in North America and South
East Asia. Toyota also hopes to establish more plants in
Canada, Argentina, the UK, Thailand, the Philippines and
hopefully in China and Vietnam.

- Of all Sanyo brand TV sets sold in Japan in 1994, 75 per
cent were manufactured in the Philippines and Mexico.

- Toshiba has plants in South East Asia and China. In both
China and Vietnam, joint ventures are becoming the order
of the day for multinationals. BP Petco for example, in
Vietnam, is 65 per cent owned by BP and 35 per cent by
Petrolimax, the local state-owned oil company.

- Pepsi expects to have $1 billion committed to China by
2000. Pepsi also bought three of the top eight brands in
China and has commitment to bottle up to 30 per cent
local brands at its joint venture bottling plants.

- In November 1994 Ciba Geigy opened its fifteenth operation in China. The company at present has 1050 staff in
China and $270 million in capital commitments.

- Royal Dutch Shell, the Anglo-Dutch oil company, plans to
move a regional HQ to Beijing by the end of 1997, the year

in which Hong Kong is due to be handed back to China.
* Philips is moving more and more of its electronics business
  to South East Asia. Hoechst, a German chemical company,
  has shifted the bulk of its genetic research to the USA.
  Electrolux has a research laboratory in Finland, a development centre in Sweden and a design group in Italy. Skills
  and knowledge are now being managed across borders.
* Agreements have been finalized between Hindustan Motors
  and Mitsubishi of Japan to make Mitsubishi's Lancer
  model in India by 1997.

The latest cross-border globalization story is that of Texas
Instruments' high speed telecommunications chip which was
conceived by engineers from Ericsson Telephone Co. in
Sweden, designed in Nice with software tools the company
developed in Houston. According to *Business Week* (7 August
1995), 'Today's TCM 9055 chip rolls off production lines in
Japan and Dallas, gets tested in Taiwan and is wired into
Erricson line-cards that monitor phone systems in Sweden,
the US, Mexico and Australia'.

In response to STEP factors organizations are becoming
increasingly 'borderless' and such ventures will continue
throughout the 1990s. According to Professor Quinn Mills
(1985), 'The new competition is contributing to a renaissance
in the fundamentals of management'.

Changing competitive climate favours 'the survival of the
fittest'. To become the fittest, organizations have to be agile
and responsive to customers' needs. Even when they think
they have the right strategy they need constantly and continuously to review their operation. As someone said 'Being on
the right track is not enough. If you do not move fast and in
the right direction you will be taken over or run over'.

A good example to illustrate how organizations respond to
market needs is to examine the decision of AT&T to disinte-
grate in order to enhance its responsiveness to market needs.
On 20 September 1995, AT&T chairman Robert Allen
announced that the corporation's different businesses will be
split and listed on the New York Stock Exchange. One entry
will be AT&T Communications and will include the card service and systems integration businesses. A second entry will
cover AT&T's research and development arm, while the third

covers the corporation's network and business communications system and microelectronics.

AT&T is also pulling out of the manufacture of personal computers as part of a bid to scale back its global information systems division and spin it off. According to Robert Allen, transformation of AT&T is due to customer needs, technology and public policy. The move to demerge makes a sharp reversal of policy for a company that has preached the virtues of 'big is beautiful' for more than 100 years.

World competitiveness, 1995

On 6 September 1995, the World Economic Forum issued a report on world competitiveness. The report caused some controversy in terms of the methodology used and the interpretations but it does give an insight into world competitiveness. Below is an extract from the report. However, the following definitions should be kept in mind in reading it:

- **Domestic economic strength**: The overall evaluation at a micro level.
- **Internationalization**: The extent to which a country participates in international trade and investment flows.
- **Government**: The extent to which government policies are conducive to competitiveness.
- **Finance**: Performance of capital markets and quality of financial services.
- **Infrastructure**: The extent to which resources and systems are adequate to serve the basic need of business.
- **Management**: The extent to which enterprises are managed in an innovative, profitable and responsible manner.
- **Science and technology**: Scientific and technological capacity, together with the success of basic and applied research.
- **People**: The availability and qualifications of human resources.

Getting the feel of world competitiveness

The world of competitiveness is changing very quickly. In 1994, after a very long time, the US regained the top rank in the World Competitiveness Report, a place occupied by Japan for nine years. In 1995, the gap is widening even more between the US, which is still in the lead, and Japan, now in 4th position and continuing to slide ...

Two winners are ahead of the pack
The US and Singapore are not only ahead of every other nation this year, but they are also increasing their lead in competitiveness.

The US ranks 1st in Domestic Economic Strength, Internationalization and Management, a unique position which reflects the US's ability to thrive on a buoyant and large domestic market while maintaining a strong presence in international markets. The aggressiveness of industry in the US is especially noticeable in new technologies such as computers, software telecommunications, etc. Not surprisingly, the country also ranks first in Science and Technology. On the other hand, devaluation of the dollar continues to increase the attractiveness of the US as a location for both investment and procurement activities. Some weaker points do remain, however: Government (6th position) and especially People (9th position). The question that arises is: how high will the social cost of such a remarkable comeback be?

Singapore continues its outstanding performance. It ranks 1st in Government, Finance, and especially People, thus aspiring to be a blueprint for the development of competitiveness in the industrializing world. Singapore is also the 2nd in Domestic Strength and Industrialization, thereby underlining a pattern found in most Asian countries, where a strong growth in the local economy is combined with a significant orientation toward the outside world. Singapore also emerges with a formidable level of self confidence, as shown by its 1st position in the Executive Opinion Survey, another trend commonly found in East Asia.

Japan is struggling with itself
Japan, which dominated the competitiveness league so strongly in the past, has still not been able to solve its problems. Being only in 4th position this year is certainly disappointing. The unprecedented economic crisis of the past two years explains the country's ranking 4th in Domestic Economic Strength and 6th in Finance. But the confidence crisis being experienced in the country is most evident in its

ranking 27th in Government – a long drop from the 2nd position in 1991 – and it is 6th in People, which had a long-standing leading position in the past. Japan's sufferings seem to be socially rather than just economically related, which means that the challenge will lie in the country's ability to reform itself. Meanwhile, the confidence level has fallen to an all-time low (23rd in the Executive Opinion Survey).

Europe continues to diverge
In the 1995 ranking, the European countries are more dispersed than ever, thus underlining the difficulty they are experiencing in their efforts to converge their economies, a prerequisite of the Maastricht Treaty.

Switzerland (5th), followed by Germany (6th) are still forerunners, perhaps because they are able to resist shocks better than others and maintain a balanced economic structure. Both perform very well in Science and Technology (4th and 3rd) and in Finance (3rd and 8th). However, they differ in Internationalization (18th and 5th) where Switzerland continues to appear isolated, and in Management (3rd and 14th) where Germany has a surprisingly bad performance. This poor showing is compounded by the People factor, where Germany ranks 9th this year (3rd in 1994), an indication of growing tension in industrial relations.

The Northern European countries are doing rather well, with the first group comprising The Netherlands (7th), Denmark (9th) and Norway (10th), followed by a second group with Austria (13th), Sweden (15th) and Finland (26th). Joining the European Union gave these last three countries a very positive boost in their confidence level. Iceland (25th), which is included in the rankings for the first time this year, is comparable to this group with very good position in Infrastructure (8th) and People (5th), but differs from them by having a low performance in Internationalization (38th).

France (17th) and the UK (18th) continue their tight contest. Both countries perform very well in Internationalization (6th and 8th), thus departing from their former image of being rather self-centred countries. However, they seem to suffer from having a certain distrust in Government. France has an extraordinarily bad ranking (35th position, reflecting the situation before the latest elections), while the UK is less critical (14th). Management is also considered to have some shortcomings in both countries (21st and 20th). More disquieting perhaps, is the bad ranking given to the People factor (15th and 24th), which is also vital for the long-term future of a country.

Belgium/Luxembourg (19th) and Ireland (22nd) are two smaller countries which share a similar pattern of strong Internationalization (7th and 10th), while still struggling with a Government performance which is less satisfactory (49th and 29th), undoubtedly reflecting the high debt level in both countries.

The Southern European countries continue to struggle. Spain (28th), Italy (30th) and Portugal (31st) are in a group of their own, while Turkey (40th) and Greece (43rd) are declining compared to 1994. These countries share a disappointing ranking in the Executive Opinion Survey (e.g. Italy 40th, Greece 41st), which indicates a strong feeling of disillusionment among the people. They perform especially badly in the Government factor with Spain (40th), Turkey (41st), Italy (46th) and Greece (47th).

Finally, Central Europe is showing some progress in the transformation of its economy. However, the results are still too scattered to have any real overall impact, although they constitute a sound basis for the future. The Czech Republic (38th) is clearly ahead, followed by Poland (45th) and Hungary (46th).

The Asian tigers still have big teeth
The dynamism of East Asia remains staggering. Next to Singapore, Hong Kong (3rd) is showing a surprisingly strong performance, reflected especially by its high position in Internationalization (3rd) and Government (2nd). However, with the 1997 deadline approaching, some uncertainties remain regarding the future.

Taiwan also has gained an excellent ranking – 11th position this year, a 7-place jump from last year. Malaysia is less impressive in 21st position, but these two countries perform very well in Domestic Economic Strength (7th and 5th). The more distant rankings of Korea (24th), Thailand (26th), Indonesia (33rd) and the Philippines (35th) underline again, the inevitably more difficult task of developing the competitiveness of heavily populated countries. All together, the four above-mentioned countries account for 356 million people!

And Latin Americans are also growing some teeth
Latin America seems to be more and more in the world competitiveness picture, although the various countries are recovering from their past problems at different speeds.

Chile (20th) and Argentina (29th) are undoubtedly the stars of the day. But Peru (32nd), Colombia (36th) and Brazil (37th) are closing the gap and have embarked on a series of reforms which are showing encouraging results. Mexico (44th) and Venezuela (47th) have a disappointing performance. In the case of Mexico, the political crisis experienced by the country – which has pushed its Government ranking to 39th (compared to 10th position last year), as well as the devaluation of the peso have shattered the country's confidence level. It now ranks 43rd in the Executive Survey instead of 24th, as in 1994!

The development of regional economic agreements such as Mercosur, and access to NAFTA, have opened new growth opportunities. In North America, the growth of the USA as well as of Canada (in 12th position this year compared to 16th last year), provide a huge potential for accessing wealthy markets with excellent technology and management know-how.

New Zealand, Australia and South Africa: southern stars?
New Zealand, in 8th position this year, continues to be impressive with its remarkable comeback from 18th position in 1991. Recovering from a severe slowdown in its domestic economy, New Zealand has an outstanding result in Government (3rd) and in Management (6th). The deregulation policy undertaken by the Government and the reform of the labour relation laws are being scrutinized by experts around the world. The negative effect on the People factor is slowly being absorbed – that ranking has improved, reaching 12th position this year (compared to 17th in 1991).

Australia, in 14th position, has a very balanced performance. Like New Zealand, it performs very well in Government (9th) and obviously in Infrastructure (4th), which also includes natural resources. Australia, however, does not rank so well in Internationalization (31st), thus indicating the necessity for the country to determine its markets more efficiently.

South Africa in 42nd position (35th last year), suffers from the entry of several new countries in the report, five of which ranked higher. The respectable ranking of South Africa in Finance (20th) and in Infrastructure (19th) underlines the country's strong assets. Its transition toward democracy is also well perceived, bringing about a slight improvement in Government (38th), despite the new countries included. South Africa's bad ranking in People (48th) stresses a priority area for future development and underlines the need for a long-term outlook on certain facets for achieving competitiveness.

A first for the Middle East
For the first time this year Israel (23rd), Egypt (27th) and Jordan (41st) are included in the report. Although these countries are very different in their economic structure (Egypt being ten times larger in population than Israel or Jordan), they probably share a common fate due to the peace process. A large amount of international aid has been earmarked for this region, and an improvement in infrastructure and in the business environment can be expected.

China, India and Russia: in a class by themselves
These three mega-markets together represent 2250 million people,

almost half the entire human race. Obviously, the magnitude of the problem, but also the opportunities, encountered in these countries put them in a different class.

China (34th) and Russia are ranked in the report for the first time this year. However, their respective situations are very different. China enjoys an especially strong growth in Domestic Economic Strength (12th), which is both supported by more demand at home and its being very attractive for foreign investments (4th), as seen in the Internationalization factor. China, nevertheless, has a less satisfactory ranking in Infrastructure (45th), thus showing there are many areas for improvement.

India, in 39th position, loses five slots compared to last year (34th); four of them, however, are due to the newly included countries which rank higher. Like China and Russia, India's performance is especially low in Infrastructure (43rd). However, the size of the market, the availability of competent managers, having a skilled although too limited workforce, numerous engineers and a government policy which is committed to liberalizing the economy should provide a better perspective for the future.

Russia (48th) ranks last in every factor except People (46th). This ranking does indicate that, despite the massive problems encountered by the country in trying to move from a centrally planned to a market economy, the potential is still there. The transition is undoubtedly a painful one, as seen in the Executive Opinion Survey, where Russia not only ranks last, but is far below its predecessor.

Source: IMD-World Economic Forum, The World Competitiveness Report, 1995.

Benchmarking world competitiveness

The World Competitiveness Report 1995 is produced in full in order to enable the readers to use it as a base so as to examine the changes in the competitive situation as we approach the millennium.

Hindsight analysis
Look at the situation in 1999 and answer the following questions:

• How dramatic have the changes been between 1995 and 1999 compared to changes that took place between 1991 and 1995?
• How wide is the gap between three blocs of developed

countries namely, the USA, Europe and Japan.?

- Has the East Asian economy maintained or increased its dynamism?
- Have reforms in Brazil, Colombia, Peru and Mexico made any impact on their competitiveness?
- Has South Africa made any major advances as the experts predicted?
- How has China fared after taking over Hong Kong in 1997? Have its Infrastructure and People attributes improved?
- Has peace in the Middle East improved competitive ranking?

STEP factors and your business

Analysing your business

Under each category – namely, social, technological, economic and political – identify key variables and assess their probability of change and the consequent impact of that change on your operations in terms of cost or revenue or profitability (see Figure 1.2). All the factors in the high-high box should be analysed in detail and taken on board to formulate your business strategy.

As an example Figure 1.3 shows the relationship between STEP factors and the computer industry. Similar analysis could be done in relation to your industry.

The industry analysis

Forces of competition

Apart from analysing changes taking place in STEP factors, organizations also have to analyse the industrial and the competitive environment within which they operate and make decisions. The effective scanning of the business environment enables timely identification and quick strategic response.

Michael Porter (1980) postulated that there are five basic sets of forces governing competition in industry (see Figure 1.4). The interaction of these factors is reflected in the ultimate sur-

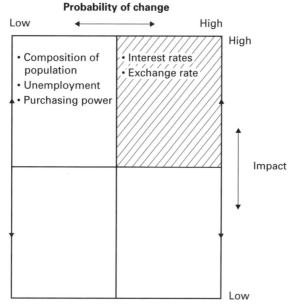

Figure 1.2 Impact analysis (economic factors)

vival or success. Under each force there are significant factors which need to be analysed in detail to conduct competitive analysis. For example within the industrial sector itself one needs to look at the number of players involved, the relative size of each player and their relative market share and how good they are in terms of exercising various strategic options, their cost structure and so on. As far as barriers to entry and exit are concerned one needs to analyse economies of scale, product differentiation, brand management, access to distribution channels, experience curve and so on. Figure 1.5 shows the key factors under each force.

According to Porter (1980), 'Competitive strategy involves positioning a business to maximize the value of the capabilties that distinguish it from its competitors. It follows that a central aspect of strategy formulation is perceptive competitive analysis. The objective of a competitor analysis is to develop a profile of the nature and success of the likely strategy changes each competitor might make, each competitor's probable response to the range of feasible strategic moves other firms could initiate and each competitor's probable reaction to the array of industry changes and broader environmental shifts that might occur.'[1]

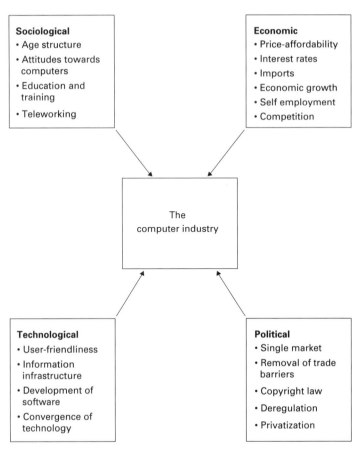

Figure 1.3 Example of the relationship between STEP factors and the computer industry

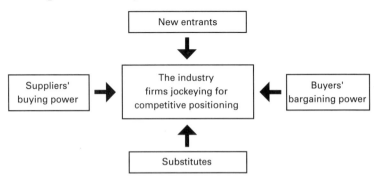

Figure 1.4 Forces governing competition

1. (see p. 23). Reprinted with permission of The Free Press, an imprint of Simon & Schuster, from *Competitive Strategy: Techniques for Analyzing Industries and Competitors* by Michael E. Porter. Copyright © 1980 by The Free Press.

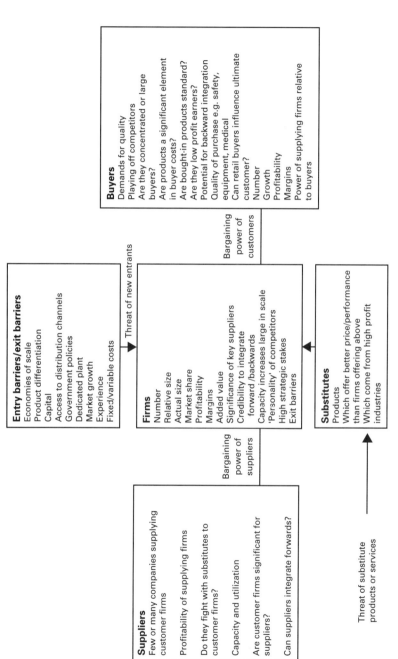

Entry barriers/exit barriers
Economies of scale
Product differentiation
Capital
Access to distribution channels
Government policies
Dedicated plant
Market growth
Experience
Fixed/variable costs

Threat of new entrants

Buyers
Demands for quality
Playing off competitors
Are they concentrated or large buyers?
Are products a significant element in buyer costs?
Are bought-in products standard?
Are they low profit earners?
Potential for backward integration
Quality of purchase e.g. safety, equipment, medical
Can retail buyers influence ultimate customer?
Number
Growth
Profitability
Margins
Power of supplying firms relative to buyers

Bargaining power of customers

Firms
Number
Relative size
Actual size
Market share
Profitability
Margins
Added value
Significance of key suppliers
Credibility to integrate forward /backwards
Capacity increases large in scale
'Personality' of competitors
High strategic stakes
Exit barriers

Bargaining power of suppliers

Suppliers
Few or many companies supplying customer firms

Profitability of supplying firms

Do they fight with substitutes to customer firms?

Capacity and utilization

Are customer firms significant for suppliers?

Can suppliers integrate forwards?

Substitutes
Products
Which offer better price/performance than firms offering above
Which come from high profit industries

Threat of substitute products or services

Figure 1.5 Industry analysis and forces of competition

Competitive analysis enables organizations to learn about customers, distributors, suppliers and technology as well as finding out about the performance of their organization in relation to their strategy and vulnerability. Porter also put forward the framework for analysing competitors shown in Figure 1.6.

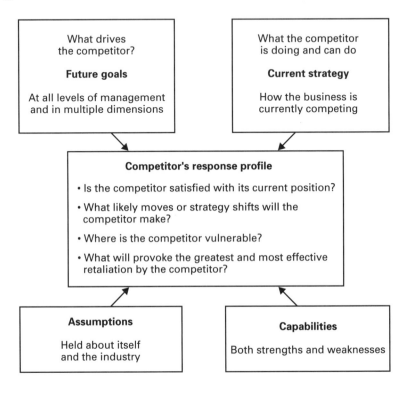

Figure 1.6   A framework for competitive analysis. Reprinted with permission of The Free Press, an imprint of Simon & Schuster, from *Competitive Strategy: Techniques for Analyzing Industries and Competitors* by Michael E. Porter. Copyright © 1980 by The Free Press

The basics of tracking your competitors

Having analysed the competitive environment the next step for an organization is to identify its key competitors and track their performance. Doing intelligence work on competitors involves the systematic collection, collation, evaluation and use of intelligence about competitors.

Conducting competitor analysis: a five-stage process

1. **Plan**: Decide what it is you are after. Appoint a project leader at this stage to determine what is required.
2. **Collect**: Gather information on your competitors. Information can be obtained from annual reports, investment analysts' reports, company literature, competitor advertising, trade associations, customers, suppliers, sales force, conferences and so on.
3. **Process**: At this stage process the information gathered.
4. **Evaluate**: Do detailed evaluation of the information processed in terms of its reliability and usefulness.
5. **Communicate**: Communicate your findings to all groups of employees.

Once you have gathered all the information, a comparative performance can be presented as shown in Table 1.1:

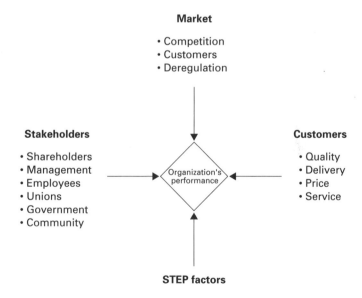

Figure 1.7 Pressures from various stakeholders

Table 1.1   Analysing competitor performance

Aspects of performance	Your organization	Competitor A	Competitor B	Comments
Product portfolio:				
Product line				
Product functionality				
Product quality				
Maintenance				
etc.				
Market share				
Marketing				
Advertising				
Promotion				
R&D				
Costs				
Financial performance:				
Return on investment				
Gross margin				
Profit per employee				
etc.				
No of employees				
Quality				
Technology				
Style of management				
International reach				
Alliances/networks				

After conducting this analysis an organization is in a position to prepare a competitive action plan. It is imperative that all groups of people are involved in conducting competitor analysis. It is also important to remember that while conducting such an analysis, organizations have pressures coming from different directions. These are pressures from competitors, colleagues, managers, shareholders and customers. In other words, from all the stakeholders.

Strengths and weaknesses of conducting competitor analysis

Strengths

- Companies are kept on their feet.
- Companies become aware of what competition is like and

what their competitors are doing.
- Companies find out how their competitors are performing compared with their own performance.
- Helps the organization refine and fine tune their corporate strategy.
- It provides focus to corporate strategy.
- Information can be used to conduct benchmarking in order to adopt best practice.

Weaknesses

- Some companies get bogged down into getting too much information and not doing anything with it.
- Some get too involved in analysing infomation gathered to the extent that they neglect their own business.
- Some undertake competitor analysis as a window-dressing exercise.
- Some collect very good information but do not follow it up with action plans and subsequent implementation.

Use of the value chain concept

Another way to conduct competitor analysis is to do it through the value chain. The value chain is the activities the competitor engages in in order to produce products and deliver service. This involves competitors' infrastructure, human resource management, technology, procurement, inbound logistics, operations, outbound logistics, marketing and sales and service. The concept of the value chain was made popular by Michael Porter in 1985.

Organizations aim to achieve optimization of each element of the value chain. In analysing various elements, for example, inbound logistics (material handling, inspection, just-in-time delivery), operations (assembly, testing, processes, physical plant operations), outbound logistics (order processes, transport), marketing and sales (product development, pricing, promotion, distribution), service (on-site and off-site, spare parts, customer care), organizations stand to gain insight not only into their own abilities but also of their competitors' capabilities and competencies. Based on the analysis done, the organization is then ready to assess its own strengths and weaknesses and move forward to prepare an action plan.

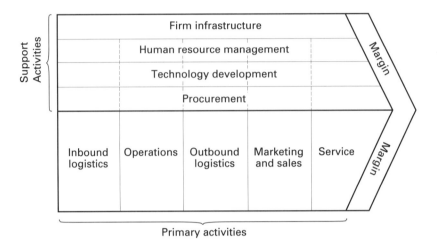

Figure 1.8   Value chain analysis. Reprinted with the permission of The Free Press, an imprint of Simon & Schuster, from *Competitive Advantage: Creating and Sustaining Superior Performance* by Michael E. Porter. Copyright © 1985 by The Free Press

STEP factors – conclusion

Analysing the external environment consists of examination of STEP factors and competitive environment followed by doing intelligence work on competitors. Such an analysis enables organizations to assess their own strengths and weaknesses and explore opportunities and threats. The action could lead to instituting either incremental or radical changes and empowering employees. The comprehensive framework of project management is shown in Figure 1.9.

Too much analysis leads to paralysis

However, organizations should not become too obsessed with analysing the competitive environment and competitors because the business is changing all the time. Totally unexpected competitors can enter the market and frustrate their strategies. AT&T never considered oil haulier Williams Co. to be a competitor until one day Williams Co. decided to use their pipelines to carry fibreoptic cables. Many big organizations like Marks & Spencer, for example, offer financial services. Should banks consider them as key competitors? It is said that General Motors is really a bank that uses cars as incentive. Now some mortgage lenders offer expensive cars as incentives if you take out loans with them. Too much internal analysis can lead to the organization's downfall. Remember 'The downfall of a magician is the belief in his own magic'.

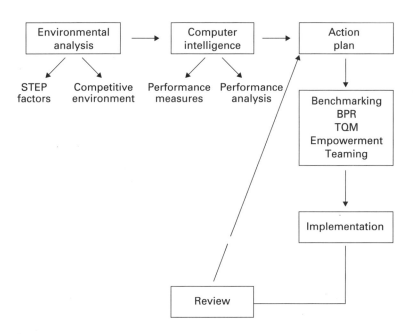

Figure 1.9   Project management framework

Having done the analysis of competition and competitors, organizations have then to take necessary actions to position themselves in the global marketplace. IBM in 1994 decided to restructure its world-wide marketing and sales, manufacturing and engineering operations in order to take advantage of global markets. Other companies who have undertaken similar reorganizations to position themselves in a competitive global markets were Bristol-Meyer Squibb Co., Ford, General Electric, AT&T, Hewlett-Packard, Toyota and even ABB, which carved its global operations into three super-regional groups for Europe, the Americas and Asia, thus folding six industrial divisions into four. According to Percy Barnevik, the CEO of ABB, organizations these days have to manage 'perpetual revolution'.

Another action plan would be to focus on core activities and processes and outsource other functions. Outsourcing nowadays has become an important way of enabling organizations to remain responsive to market needs. According to Tom Peters, everything can be outsourced. Outsourcing at present takes place in the activities such as catering, cleaning, computing, logistics, and so on. Some companies even outsource the research and development function. Outsourcing R&D is more common among Japanese companies than US or European companies.

Outsourcing is not taken for purely 'outloading' reasons. Companies now make outsourcing decisions on a strategic basis. Few companies can cope with the increasing costs of keeping up with a large number of different technologies. Outsourcing of any function or operation should be a part of an overall strategic framework that takes into account corporate objectives. Outside such a strategic framework, outsourcing will remain an ad hoc response to circumstances driven by cost minimization and downsizing.

Reviewing the marketing philosophy

Finally in the light of changing business profile and the ways organizations respond to the changing environment, the time has come for organizations to review their marketing function. Like organizations, **marketing needs to reinvent itself**. It was Peter Drucker who a long time ago said that marketing is not an appendix to an organization. **Marketing is business and business is marketing**. Why is it then that we are reluctant to move from the old concept of marketing?

The basic definition and functions of marketing have remained unchanged in many educational and training syllabi. Marketing is about understanding and meeting customer needs and maintaining customer loyalty. This is as true today as it was in the 1950s and 1960s when we were studying marketing. What, however, has changed is the nature of the customers.

Today's customers
Customers now have a wide variety of choice. They have become educated and sophisticated. Japanese products did well in the West because the customers found out that Japanese goods did not mean shoddy goods. Consumers became discriminating customers. Japanese companies truly understood how to win customers globally, whereas in the West the concept of marketing has not changed but most importantly the approach has not changed much either. In an effort to make companies and organizations market-focused, organizations are undergoing total quality management, delayering, downsizing, restructuring, re-engineering and transformation. Some organizations have embarked upon relationship marketing. Employees are being grouped into multi-tasking teams and empowered, and we are told top management is becoming more enlightened.

The road to business excellence

Organizational restructuring – focusing attention on products, processes and people
The core objective of marketing should still be to understand and to satisfy customers but today's marketers should be highly conversant with the ways to win and retain customers and enable organizations to deliver this objective. The marketing department should be abolished and in its place we should have a department of business excellence. This department would focus its attention on three Ps – product, processes and people.

An aspect of this department should look at the products that customers want and those that customers could want. Attention should be paid to creativity and innovation. The other aspect should be the processes which organizations undertake in order to produce these products. The department should focus on value-adding activities in each process. The people aspect should be divided into employees and customers. The department will be responsible for fostering very good inter-personal relationships within the organizations. This aspect will take on board selection, training, communication and 'internal customers' perspectives. Finally external customers would include suppliers, distributors and customers.

The core of the organization structure should be the business excellence department consisting of multi-skilled individuals. The board of management should be dominated by business excellence champions. The main functions of the director of business excellence should be to align the operational and people objectives to corporate objectives and customer needs to corporate strategy.

Relationship marketing

The term 'relationship marketing' has been talked about and written about for a number of years. Various articles have appeared in the professional journals focusing attention on creating customer value.

Relationship marketing calls for customer-orientated production and delivery of services and products. Database technology enables companies to gather huge amounts of data on individual customers' needs and preferences. Companies that create relationships with their customers will be able to retain them for a very long time. 'Keeping customers for life' seems to be the main marketing cry today.

According to Fredrick Reichheld of Bain & Co., 'Raising customer retention rates by five percentage points increases the value of an average customer by 25 per cent to 100 per cent'. Also the retained customer costs less to service than the cost of acquiring new customers, though winning new customers is important as well.

What is the difference between relationship marketing and traditional marketing?
Adrian Payne, Martin Christopher, Moira Clark and Helen Peck have written a very readable book entitled *Relationship Marketing for Competitive Advantage* (1995). They have con-

trasted traditional marketing which they call the 'transactional approach' from relationship marketing. The following is an extract from their book:

Transactional focus	**Relationship focus**
Orientation to single sales	Orientation to customer retention
Discontinuous customer contact	Continuous customer contact
Focus on product features	Focus on customer value
Short time scale	Long time scale
Little emphasis on customer service	High customer service emphasis
Limited commitment to meeting meeting customer expectations	High commitment to meeting customer customer expectations
Quality is the concern of production	Quality is the concern of all staff

Examples of relationship marketing

- Mr Bloggs bought a multimedia computer for £2500 from distributor 'A'. Two months later 'A' got in touch with Bloggs to find out if he was satisfied with the purchase and to inform him not to hesitate to contact them if there was any problem or if he wanted more information. The store also assured him not to worry and keep in touch with them even after expiry of the warranty.
- The store kept in touch with Bloggs. After two years Bloggs decided to upgrade the system. He dealt with 'A'. What is more he encouraged all his relatives and friends to deal with 'A' thus generating additional revenue for 'A'.
- A manufacturer of cat food has all the details of its customers including the number of cats, their names and their birthdays on its database. The company sends birthday cards to their key customers' cats. They thus maintain a good relationship with their customers.

In his interview with the editor of the *European Management Journal*, December 1994, Philip Kotler said, 'companies have shifted their focus from customer attraction to customer retention. Customer retention requires knowing much more about a customer, as might be captured in a marketing database. The company's task is not to make a sale but to build loyal customers. Marketing is the company's manufacturing department and relationship marketing is the key.'

For relationship marketing to succeed organizations must have:

(a) capacity to deliver;
(b) information on their customers; and
(c) staff who understand the value of relationships with their customers.

In other words, the main drivers of relationship marketing are a good database, personalized approach, integrated functions and a customer-focused mindset. The four Ps of traditional marketing (product, place, promotion and price) have to be replaced with four Cs – customer, communication, conviction and commitment – in order to retain customers and sustain their loyalty.

Do organizations have a choice?

There have been dramatic changes in the STEP factors. Companies must reorient their entire business to face the market. In the past few years many organizations have undergone transformation in order to be responsive to market needs. Various functions have become integrated in order to break out from 'compartmentalized thinking'. Marketing requires new philosophy and marketers have to adopt a new mindset.

According to Mack Hanan, a consultant, 'Marketing has been advertised as an instrument of warfare against our competitors, rather than an instrument of welfare helping customers'.

The rest of the book examines how companies have operationalized management theories and thinking in order to be close to their customers and survive in a fierce competitive climate.

Selected reading

Joseph L. Bower (1986). *When Markets Quake*. Harvard Business School Press.

Joan Cannie and Donald Caplin (1991). *Keeping Customers for Life*. American Management Association.

Peter F. Drucker (1986). *The Frontiers of Management*. Butterworth-Heinemann.

Peter F. Drucker (1992). *Managing for the Future*. Butterworth-Heinemann.

Peter F. Drucker (1995). *Managing in a Time of Great Change*. Butterworth-Heinemann

The Economist Intelligence Unit (1993). *Managing Cultural Differences for Competitive Advantage*.

G. Hofstede (1991). *Cultures and Organizations: Software of the Mind*. McGraw-Hill.

D. Quinn Mills (1985). *The New Competitors*. John Wiley & Sons.

Payne, Christopher, Clark and Peck (1995). *Relationship Marketing for Competitive Advantage*. Butterworth-Heinemann.

Tom Peters and Robert Waterman, Jr (1982). *In Search of Excellence*. Harper & Row.

Tom Peters (1988) *Thriving on Chaos*. Alfred A. Knopf.

Michael E. Porter (1980). *Competitive Strategy*. The Free Press.

Michael E. Porter (1985). *Competitive Advantage*. The Free Press.

'Philip Kotler Interview' (1994). *European Management Journal*, December.

Fons Trompenaars (1993). *Riding the Waves of Culture*. Nicholas Brealey Publishing.

Robert H. Waterman, Jr (1987). *The Renewal Factor*. Bantam Books.

2 Total quality management

We are what we repeatedly do. Excellence, then is not an act, but a habit.

Aristotle

Summary

Total quality management was one of the most pervasive aspects of management thinking of the 1980s.
* Product and service quality has been part of marketing teaching for a number of years. What is so different about total quality management?
* The influence of Juran, Deming and Crosby – the 'gurus' of the total quality.
* The seven basic tools of quality management: control charts, Pareto charts, cause and effect diagrams, bar charts, histograms, scatter diagrams and flow charts.
* Quality functional deployment (QFD) – listening to the voice of the customer.
* Quality awards: the Deming Prize, the Baldrige Award and the European Quality Award.
* The eligibility and criteria of assessment.
* ISO 9000 – reasons for obtaining certifications, expectations and benefits.
* TQM sucess stories: Rank Xerox, ICL and Miliken Industrials.
* Reasons for companies failing in spite of going through quality initiatives. How not to fail.
* Quality soundbites of the 1990s.
* Find out if your organization is quality-driven.
* How to make your organization a quality master.

Total quality management (TQM) was on of the most pervasive aspects of management thinking of the 1980s. Many experts believe that those organizations who want to remain profitable and achieve competitive advantage in the 1990s have to go through the TQM journey. The cornerstone of TQM is customer satisfaction. Without focus on customers TQM becomes a futile and expensive exercise.

Products and customers

The link between a product and customer's perception is not new thinking. Philip Kotler, a well known author on marketing, defined a product as 'anything that can be offered to a market for attention, acquisition, use, or consumption that might satisfy a want or need. It includes physical objects, services, persons, places, organizations and ideas'.

In developing or designing a product, the planner has to think about the product at three levels. The first level is the 'core product' level incorporating all the benefits to the consumers. The second is the 'tangible product' level. At this level the product assumes the characteristics of quality, features, packaging, styling and brand name. Finally the product planner has to enhance benefits and make up an 'augmented product'. At this stage the benefits are enhanced to meet customer needs and aspirations in relation to that product. Kotler argued that 'consumers perceive the product as a complex bundle of benefits that satisfy needs ...'

Another marketing guru, Theodore Levitt, was also an advocate of looking beyond the physical attributes of a product and focusing attention on adding value to the product to meet customer needs. In the 1970s and early 1980s the cry was to listen to the voice of the marketplace and of adding value to a product.

While in marketing terms 'value added' became the buzz word of the 1980s, especially after Michael Porter reinforced the concept of the value chain in the 1980s, total quality was taking over some of the boardrooms of the US companies. The enthusiasm for quality came about because many businesses were finding it hard to compete with Japanese products. In the 1950s and 1960s, Japan acquired the reputation of copycat country and shoddy mimicry. In the 1970s and

1980s it acquired a reputation of producing goods that delighted customers. Soon Japanese goods penetrated Western home markets in the form of cars and electronic consumer goods. Hand in hand while marketing gurus were redefining the concept of a product to be more responsive to customer needs, US businesses decided to embark upon the TQM initiative in order to remain competitive.

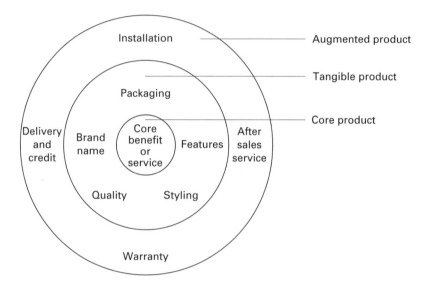

Figure 2.1   Attributes of a product. Source: Kotler, Philip, *Principles of Marketing* (6th edn), © 1994, p. 277. Reprinted by permission of Prentice Hall, Upper Saddle River, New Jersey

What is TQM?

TQM is concerned with continuous improvement in performance aimed at delighting customers. These are some of the definitions put forward:

'Achieving total quality through gaining everyone's commitment and involvement.'

'Improvement of the quality of the organization's products and services for the customers.'

'Customer-oriented, continuous improvement process.'

'Quality is conformance to requirements.'

'Fitness for use.'

Whichever definition we examine the two things that stand out are **customer and continuous improvement**. The word 'total' is designed to send the message that all processes, systems, all levels of management and all employees must be concerned with quality: 'Quality is everyone's business'.

Who are the gurus of total quality?

There are numerous gurus dealing with different aspects of quality management. But we will deal with three of them, namely, Juran, Deming and Crosby.

Joseph M. Juran
Juran was born in December 1904 in Braita, Romania, and emigrated to the USA in 1912. For almost fifty years he has remained a leading proponent of quality. From the 1950s he advised Japanese senior and supervisory management on a broad range of management issues as well as writing several seminal books on quality.

His significant contribution was his formulation of methods for creating a customer-oriented organization. Achieving quality, he emphasized throughout his career, is about communication, management commitment and people.

Juran was influenced by Margaret Mead's writing on cultural anthropology and he adopted her ideas when writing about resistance to change.

Juran offers the following implementation framework to any organization setting out to establish total quality:

Juran's ten steps to quality improvement

1. Build awareness of the need for quality and an opportunity for improvement.
2. Set goals for improvement.
3. Organize to achieve goals.
4. Provide training.

5. Carry out projects to solve problems.
6. Report progress.
7. Give recognition.
8. Communicate results.
9. Keep score.
10. Maintain momentum.

Source: Various writings of Juran. Also Course B889, the Open University Business School.

In his ten steps, Juran highlights the need to plan, set targets for improvement, organize for implementation and then highlights the training, communications and recognition aspects of quality project. To put such a system into practice requires 'total' commitment and understanding from top management to all levels of management and operations.

Juran received several awards including Japan's Order of the Sacred Treasure conferred in 1981 by Emperor Hirohito. It took the USA a very long time to appreciate Juran's message on quality. Why was this the case?

• Most senior managers in the USA were almost entirely focused on finance and short-term financial performance.
• International competition in the early stages was not posing any threats to the US businesses. US businesses after the Second World War were working in a 'comfortable' climate. As Tom Peters would say, 'even if they had tried they could not have done wrong'.
• Quality was delegated to functional departments. It was a 'nitty-gritty' aspect of business whereas captains of industry only dealt with strategic issues.
• Most top management had their heads buried in the sand.

W. Edwards Deming
Deming believed that quality must be the foundation of everything businesses do. He was born in October 1900 and died in December 1993. As a graduate in mathematics and physics he worked at the Hawthorne Plant of Western Electric Co. in 1925. While there he came in contact with Walter Shewhart who pioneered statistical quality work. He later worked with

the US Department of Agriculture and the National Bureau of the Census.

In 1950 he was invited by Japanese scientists and engineers to address them. This was followed by a meeting with 21 Japanese companies including such names as Nissan, Toyota and Sony. He showed the Japanese how they could improve quality by the use of the statistical control of processes. He is considered by many to be the father of the Japanese quality revolution.

A consistent theme in Deming's work has been the reluctance of managers to accept that theirs is the key role in changing processes and driving the improvement in quality. He developed a very simple method of problem solving which is now known as the Deming cycle. The cycle (Figure 2.2) has four stages namely, plan, do, check and action. Deming also developed 14 points for successful total quality management.

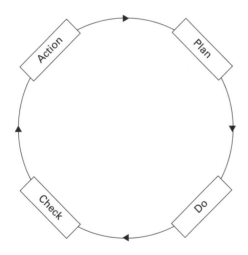

Figure 2.2   The Deming cycle

Deming's 14 points for management

1. Create constancy for the purpose for improvement of products and service. Allocate resources to provide long-term needs with a view to becoming competitive.
2. Adopt the new philosophy. We are in a new economic age. We can no longer live with mistakes and defects. Western manage-

ment must awaken to the challenge, must learn their responsibilities and take on leadership for change.

3. Eliminate dependence on mass inspection. Quality must be built into the product. Quality must be the foundation on which the organization is based.

4. Eliminate awarding business based on price alone. Instead minimize total cost. Move toward a single supplier for any one item, on a long-term relationship of loyalty and trust.

5. Improve constantly and permanently the system of production and service, to improve quality and productivity and thus constantly decreasing costs. What is good enough for today is not good enough for tomorrow.

6. Institute training on the job.

7. Institute leadership. The aim of supervision would be to help people and machines do a better job. Supervision of management is in need of overhaul, as well as supervision of production workers.

8. Drive out fear. Create a climate in which everyone may work effectively for the company.

9. Break down barriers between departments. People in research, design, sales and production must work as a team to tackle problems encountered with the product or service.

10. Eliminate slogans and exhortations and targets for the workforce asking for zero defects and new levels of productivity. Such exhortations only create adversarial relationships, as the bulk of the causes of low quality and low productivity belong to the system and thus lie beyond the power of the workforce.

11. Eliminate work standards (quotas). Eliminate management by numbers and numerical goals.

12. Eliminate barriers to pride of workmanship. This implies, inter alia, abolishment of the annual or merit rating and of management by objectives. The responsibility of supervisors must be changed from sheer numbers to quality.

13. Institute a vigorous programme of education and self-improvement. Workers should be educated to use tools and techniques of quality as well as develop new methods of working in teams.

14. Take action to accomplish transformation. The transformation is everybody's job.

Deming's 14 points constitute his basic principles of management philosophy which is sometimes referred to as his 'operational theory of management'. His 14 points taken together assume a holistic approach to quality management.

Philip B. Crosby

Philip Crosby gained prominence with the 'zero defects' movement in the 1960s. His quality improvement process is based on the following 'absolutes':

- Quality means conformance to requirement, not goodness.
- Quality is achieved through prevention not appraisal.
- The performance standard is 'zero defects'.
- The only performance measurement is the price of non-conformance.

Like Deming, Crosby also formulated the following 14 steps to quality.

Crosby's 14 steps to quality

1. Make it clear that management is committed to quality.
2. Form quality improvement teams with senior representatives from each department.
3. Determine where current and potential quality problems lie.
4. Evaluate the cost of quality and explain its use as a management tool
5. Raise the quality awareness and personal concern of all employees.
6. Take actions to correct problems identified through previous steps.
7. Establish a committee for the zero defects programme.
8. Train supervisors to carry out their part of the quality improvement programme.
9. Hold a 'zero defects day' to let all employees realize there has been a change.
10. Encourage individuals to establish improvement goals for themselves and their groups.
11. Encourage employees to communicate to management the obstacles they face in attaining their improvement goals.
12. Recognize and appreciate those who participate.
13. Establish quality councils to communicate on a regular basis.

14. Do it all over again to emphasize that the quality improvement programme never ends.

Source: P. Crosby Quality Without Tears (1984). McGraw-Hill, New York. Reproduced with permission of McGraw-Hill Inc.

Like Juran and Deming, Crosby places the greatest responsibility for quality on management and he emphasizes the fact that all levels in the organization should receive appropriate quality education.

Crosby is an exponent of the 'zero defects' principle. Juran was a fierce critic of this principle because he believed that a significant proportion of imperfections are due to poorly designed manufacturing systems that workers cannot change. However, Crosby's 'zero defects' principle has been misunderstood and for a number of years he was at pains to explain it. In his book *Let's Talk Quality* (1989) published by McGraw-Hill, he wrote, 'I learned that whenever I come up with what seems like a good idea, it is an even better idea not to spread it around until I know how best to explain it to people'. Zero-defects has become a symbolic way of saying 'do it right the first time'.

Apart from the three gurus mentioned there were other influential individuals. Armand V. Feigenbaum wrote a book entitled *Total Quality Control* (1961) which is considered by some quality engineers as a bible. Professor Ishikawa was the originator of the Ishikawa or 'fishbone' cause and effect diagram and proponent of the seven basic tools of quality management. Genichi Taguchi, a Japanese engineering specialist advocated the method of analysing quality known as 'total loss function'.

Quality circles

One of the most publicized aspects of the Japanese approach to quality has been quality circles. When Deming went to Japan in 1946 to offer advice on reindustrialization he advocated that it was not necessary to have 'specialists' in order to have quality control. The idea gave birth to quality circles in 1962, an invention of Professor Ishikawa. The main objective of the quality circles was to encourage volunteer workers to find ways to improve processes. The onus of improving quality and coming up with the suggestions for improvements was put on workers.

In many Western organizations who saw quality circles as a quick fix, such circles mushroomed. The growth rate of quality circles during the 1980s was phenomenal. The quality circles consisted of a group of volunteers, between five and twelve, who worked for the same supervisors and who met regularly in normal working time under the leadership of their supervisors to identify, analyse and solve their work-related problems. They were expected to recommend solutions to management.

Even though the quality circles were very popular in Japan, it was not until the mid 1970s that US companies became active in introducing quality circles in their organizations. The quality circles appeared in the companies like Lockheed Missiles, an aerospace company of California, Westinghouse, Harvey Davidson and General Motors. By 1980 quality circles became a world-wide movement. It is estimated that in the early 1980s there were one million quality circles and ten million members.

By the mid to late 1980s the quality circles began to lose their enthusiasm and excitement. First of all there was a lack of resources allocated to make such ventures successful. Time was the most important resource. Secondly top management expected quality circles to deliver quick results; this did not happen. Thirdly most members felt that in many cases the suggestions for improvements they were making were not being taken on board for a variety of reasons. In some cases the facilitators were not adequately trained. Some companies also began quality circle programmes without any real understanding of the nature of the concept. For some, forming quality circles was purely a window dressing exercise. As Juran and Deming always said, success of any quality initiative depend on total commitment and understanding.

Quality – basic tools of the trade

Everyone involved in quality improvement has to understand the basic tools of quality management. These basic tools are charts, graphs and diagrams that measure and document quality of products, processes and services. These tools are described very briefly as follows:

1. Control charts

The control charts show visually whether a product or activity is within normal specifications. Once a process is operating in a controlled way, random samples are taken to monitor it for a changed outputs. Once these reach a level which is significant in statistical terms, the need for adjustment is considered.

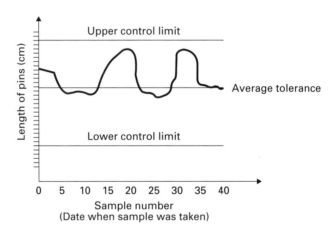

Figure 2.3   An example of a control chart

2. Pareto chart

The Pareto principle states that 80 per cent of results are caused by 20 per cent of causes (the 80:20 rule). In quality terms 80 per cent of the defects in a product fall into 20 per cent of the types of faults. Pareto charts can be used to focus on the few (20 per cent) causes that are responsible for the majority (80 per cent) of the quality problems.

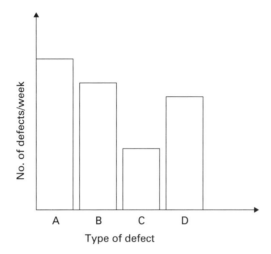

Figure 2.4   An example of a Pareto chart

3. Cause and effect diagram (or Ishikawa or fishbone diagram)

The defect is shown at the head of the arrow with branches from the backbone indicating potential causes and effects categorized into machines, techniques, materials and people. Such diagrams are widely used to understand relationships that must be attended to in order to improve any given situation.

4. Run charts

A run chart is essentially a running tally of data points over a specific time reference. It is used to find critical times or periods when various problems are prone to occur. For example, some problems may occur on Mondays or Fridays (Friday car syndrome) or at certain specific times of the day.

5. Histograms

This is a commonly used graph. On a histogram the number of products in each control category is displayed using a bar. By placing the bars next to each other, comparisons can easily be shown.

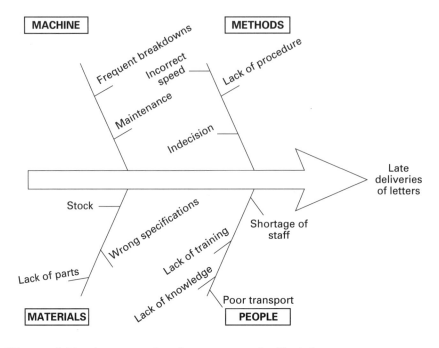

Figure 2.5   An example of a cause and effect diagram

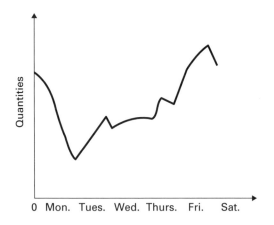

Figure 2.6   An example of a run chart

6. Scatter diagram

A scatter diagram is very useful tool to establish a potential relationship between two factors, e.g. speed of delivery and

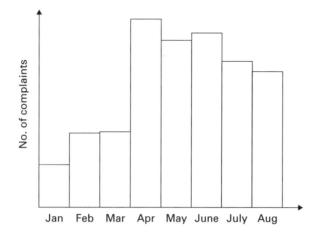

Figure 2.7 An example of a histogram

the number of complaints. Federal Express for example, prides itself for speed of delivery. It will be interesting to chart the number of complaints in order to ascertain the effectiveness of Federal Express's services and clustering of values suggests that there may be a correlation between the factors in question.

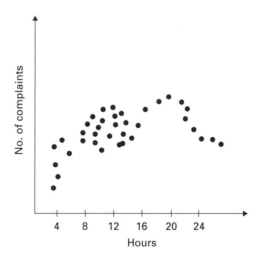

Figure 2.8 An example of a scatter diagram

7. Flow charts

A flow chart is a visual presentation of steps in a specific work activity. A flow chart is helpful in understanding how a specific process works and how it can be improved.

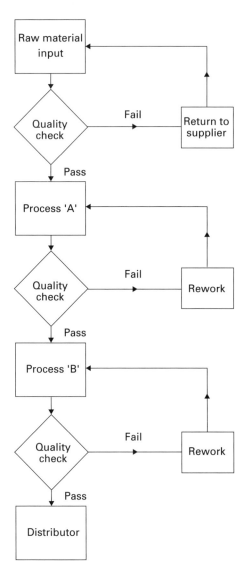

Figure 2.9   An example of a flow chart

Quality and the customers – quality functional deployment

Quality functional deployment (QFD) is a technique of getting the designers to listen to the voice of the customer. The approach, which enables designers to take into consideration consumers' needs, was pioneered by Professor Yoji Akao and Shigeru Mizuno. A matrix is used to set product characteristics and attributes against customer needs (Figure 2.10).

Product 'X' attributes

Customers' needs*	ATT 1	ATT 2	ATT 3	ATT 4	ATT 5
A	0	0	0	5	0
B	5	3	2	3	0
C	5	2	2	3	3
D	2	1	2	0	5
E	1	5	1	0	0

*Information from surveys, market research, salesforce, etc.

Scoring: Strong correlation = 5
Weak correlation = 1
No correlation = 0

Figure 2.10 How QFD works in relation to a product. There is a very strong correlation between attribute 4 of the product and customer need A, attribute 1 and customer needs B and C, attribute 2 and customer need E and attribute 5 and customer need D. In this case all five attributes of Product 'X' are important from all customers' needs

Quality awards

Deming Prize

The Deming Prize is named after W. Edwards Deming who set off Japan's post-1945 quality revolution. This award was created in 1951 and became Japan's most coveted industrial award. The Deming competition is run by the Japanese Union of Scientists and Engineers (JUSE). Total quality control became a pre-requisite for winning this award. Komatssu Ltd was the first winner and Toyota Motor Corporation was the second winner in 1965 under the revised guidelines incorporating quality control techniques.

The British Deming Association was formed in 1987 with the assistance of a number of leading UK businesses and individuals. Its principal aims are:

* To promote a greater awareness and understanding of the importance of Dr Deming's philosophy.
* To help people adopt the Deming approach.
* To provide a forum for members and facilitate exchange of information.
* To form a supportive network with links to Dr Deming's and other international authorities.

Malcolm Baldrige National Quality Award

The Baldrige Award was instituted in 1987. It is named after the US Commerce Secretary, who died in 1986. The competition is managed by the National Institute of Standards and Technology. Each year two awards are given in each of the three categories, namely, manufacturing, service and small business.

To win a Baldrige Award companies have to submit an application form describing their quality practices and performance in seven required areas which are then added together and marked out of 1000. These are:

* Leadership (90 points)
* Information and analysis (75 points)
* Strategic planning (55 points)
* Human resource development and management (140 points)
* Process management (140 points)
* Business results (250 points)
* Customer focus and satisfaction (250 points)

What are examiners looking for under each category?
1. **Leadership**: Personal involvement of senior executives;

the company's quality values and public responsibility.

2. **Information and analysis**: Scope and management of quality data and information; competitive comparisons and benchmarks and analysis of quality data and information.

3. **Strategic quality planning**: Strategic quality planning processes and quality goals and plans.

4. **Human resource utilization**: How the company's human resource efforts support quality initiatives; employee involvement; quality education and training, employee recognition and performance measurement and employee well-being and morale.

5. **Quality assurance of products and services**: Design and introduction of quality products and services; process quality control; continuous improvement of processes, quality assessment; documentation; business process; support service quality and supplier quality.

6. **Quality results**: Product and service quality results; business processes; operational and support service quality results and supplier quality results which involves comparing suppliers' quality with that of competitors' and with key benchmarks.

7. **Customer satisfaction**: Determining customer requirements and expectations; customer relationship management; customer service standards; commitment to customers; complaint resolution for quality improvement; determining customer satisfaction; customer satisfaction results and customer satisfaction comparison which involves comparisons with competitors.

Baldrige applicants are screened by examiners from industry and academia. Then the high scorers are visited by examiners who make recommendations to the panel of judges.

Early winners of the awards have included companies like Motorola, General Motors' Cadillac division, and Xerox. Robert Galvin, chairman of electronics group Motorola, calls the award 'the most important catalyst for transforming American business'. However, there are some people who feel that, for some companies, a Baldrige Award has been a kiss of death. There are examples of companies who have won a Baldrige Award and yet were delivering very poor financial results. It has been reported that General Motors' Cadillac division won the Baldrige Award at a time when surveys showed American consumers did not rate its cars very highly. Other companies' quest for quality also did not have happy business endings.

European Quality Award

The European Quality Award (EQA) was developed by the European Foundation for Quality Management. The foundation was set up originally by 14 leading Western European businesses in 1988. Its membership now exceeds 300 companies. In addition to providing a forum for quality issues, the Foundation launched the annual European Quality Award in 1992.

The model is shown in Figure 2.11. A distinction is drawn between how the results are achieved (Enablers) and the results themselves (Results). There are nine criteria which are assigned a weighting and under which the assessment has to be undertaken. These are:

Enablers
- Leadership (100)
- People management (90)
- Policy and strategy (80)
- Resources (90)
- Processes (140)

Results
- People satisfaction (90)
- Customer satisfaction (200)
- Impact on society (60)
- Business results (150)

1. **Leadership**: How the executive team and all other managers inspire and drive total quality as the company's fundamental process for continuous improvement. Evidence is required of visible involvement in leading total quality, a consistent total quality culture, timely recognition and appreciation of the efforts and successes of individuals and teams, support of total quality, involvement with the

customers and suppliers and active promotion of total quality outside the company.

2. **People management**: How the company releases the full potential of its people to improve the business continuously. Evidence is required of how human resources are planned and improved, the skills and capabilities of the people and their development, agreements of targets by individuals and teams, continuously reviewing performance, involvement of everyone in continuous improvement, empowering of people and effective top-down and bottom-up communication.

3. **Policy and strategy**: How the company incorporates the concept of total quality in the determination, communication, implementation, review and improvement of its policy and strategy. Evidence is required of how policy and strategy are formulated on the concept of total quality in relation to relevance and comprehensiveness of information, the basis of business plans, communication and regular updating and improvement.

4. **Resources**: How the company improves its business continuously, based on the concept of total quality. Evidence is required of how improvements are achieved by the management of financial, information and technological resources and by the management of suppliers, materials, buildings and equipment.

5. **Processes**: How key and support processes are identified, reviewed and, if necessary, revised to ensure continuous improvement of the company's business. Evidence is required of how processes critical to the success of business are identified, systematic management of these processes, process measurement and feedback and targets for improvements, innovation and creativity in process improvement and evaluation of benefits.

6. **People satisfaction**: What your people's feelings are about the company.

7. **Customer satisfaction**: External and internal customers' perception.

8. **Impact on society**: The community's perception of your company's performance.

9. **Business results**: What the company is achieving in relation to its planned business.

The criteria highlighted by the European Quality Award differ from the Baldrige criteria in that the European model stresses business results and focuses on businesses' impact on society.

The first European Quality Award was won by Rank Xerox in 1992. The EQA encourages organizations to take the self-assessment route and then to receive feedback from independent assessors.

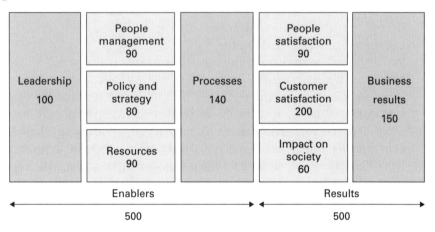

Enablers   Results

←――――――――――――――――――→ ←――――――――――――――――――→
        500   500

Figure 2.11   The European Quality Model. *Source*: European Foundation for Quality Management, EFQM Brussels Representative Office, Avenue des Pléiades 19, B-1200, Brussels, Belgium. Tel: 32 2 775 35 11. Fax: 32 2 775 35 35.

Who is eligible to apply for the European Quality Award?
Below is an extract from the application brochure produced by the European Foundation for Quality Management.

Any European company or any subsidiary or division of a company based in Europe may apply for the European Quality Award provided it fulfils the eligibility requirements set out below. Companies employing fewer than 500 people must submit their whole company for the Award. To be eligible as a whole company, your answers should be in all the shaded boxes 1 to 4. To be eligible as a part of a company, your answers should additionally be in the shaded boxes 5 and 6 or 5, 7, 8, 9, 10 and 11.

Potential applicants should check through the following questions:

1. Has your company received the European Quality Award within the last 5 years?

2. Has at least 50 per cent of the company's business activity in terms of physical assets or numbers of people employed been operational in Europe for the past 5 years? Or, was the company founded in Western Europe more than 5 years ago and management control for global activities been retained in Europe? (This does not apply to subsidiaries of non-European companies.)

3. Are the quality practices forming the content of an application inspectable in Europe?

4. Are you a government agency, non-profit organization, trade association or professional society?

Additionally companies employing more than 500 people not wishing to apply as a whole company, but wishing to submit part of their company, should check the following questions:

5. Are there more than 3 applications from separate parts of your company?

6. Does your part of the company have its own unique company name and use its own unique brands?

If the answer to 6 is 'no' then check the following further questions:

7. Is your part of the company a clearly differentiated independent business entity in corporate literature, organization structure and accounting system and are key entrepreneurial decisions taken within your part of the company?

8. Does your part of the company employ more than 500 people or at least 25 per cent of the whole company?

9. Does your part of the company supply more than half of your products and services to the remainder of the whole organization?

10. Does your part of the company perform business support functions only (e.g. sales, distribution, human resources, legal services)?

11. Is your part of the company an individual unit or partial aggregation of units of a chain organization (such as hotels, retail stores, banks or restaurant)?

Source: European Foundation for Quality Management. The European Quality Award. 1995 Application Brochure.

UK Quality Award

The UK Quality Award is managed through the British Quality Foundation and is based on the European model. The first awards were presented in November 1994 to the Rover Group and TNT Express (UK) Ltd.

ISO 9000

ISO 9000 is the international quality management systems (QMS) standard. In its present format it was introduced in 1987. It was subsequently identified by the European Commission as a vital element in the creation of the Single European Market. Many companies sought ISO 9000 registration as part of their market strategy rather than an essential part of their quality management strategy. ICL was the first company to receive group registration for ISO 9000.

According to the Lloyd's Register Quality Association and Mobil Oil research data, in 1994 the total number of European approvals was over 55 000. Significant growth was recorded in France, Italy, Germany, Austria, Norway and Portugal.

The total number of world-wide approvals at the end of 1994 was just over 70 500. Strong growth was recorded in the USA, Brazil, Japan, Taiwan, Hong Kong, South Korea, and India. Progress was also made in China and Israel.

Quality management systems focus on internal processes, by installing management controls that are written down. Total quality management is concerned with developing the total organization's philosophy in relation to dealing with its customers. The two systems complement each other.

Eight steps to ISO 9000
1. Evaluation of existing quality procedures against the refinements of the ISO standards.
2. Identification of corrective action needed to conform with ISO 9000 series.
3. Preparation of a quality assurance programme.
4. Definition, documentation and implementation of new procedures.
5. Preparation of a quality manual.
6. Pre-assessment meeting with registrar to analyse quality manual.
7. Actual assessment visit.
8. Certification

Source: Eurobusiness, January 1995. p. 71.

In 1993 Lloyd's Register Quality Assurance Ltd commissioned Research International to carry out research into reasons why organizations obtain ISO 9000 certification, what impact it has on their business and whether or not ISO 9000 has lived up to expectations. In her presentation at a quality conference organized by the Economist Conferences, Linda Campbell, general manager and director of Lloyd's Register Quality Assurance said that in 89 per cent of cases, ISO 9000 certification met or exceeded expectations. Some companies were motivated to tender for work which demanded certification. In most cases internal benefits of ISO 9000 in a form of management control, delivering better customer service and productivity gains, etc., were greater than external benefits. The benefits of ISO 9000 are greater the longer an organization has held certification.

Figures 2.12-15 highlight the key findings of the report, which states:

'Around one half of the organizations interviewed were involved in the development or implementation of total quality management systems. This proportion increased considerably in the food sector and amongst larger companies. The overwhelming majority of these organizations (97 per cent) said they were developing TQM in conjunction with, rather than instead of, BS 5750/ISO 9000.'

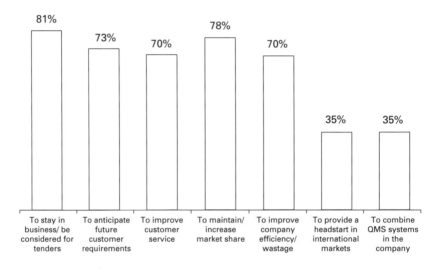

Figure 2.12   Reasons for obtaining certification. *Source*: Lloyd's Register Quality Assurance

Does quality pay: results of LRQA's survey

Another interesting survey conducted by Lloyd's Register Quality Assurance (LRQA) is the market study to measure the effect of ISO 9000 on the financial and sales performance of companies in the mechanical engineering manufacturing sector. The research shows that firms registered to ISO 9000 by LRQA significantly outperformed their competitors across all the main business ratios from profitability to return on capital employed. The research was conducted between 1990 and 1992, at the height of the UK's recession and involved 200 companies from the mechanical engineering manufacturing sector.

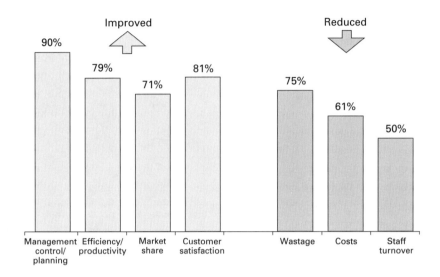

Figure 2.13 Benefits of ISO 9000. *Source*: Lloyd's Register Quality Assurance

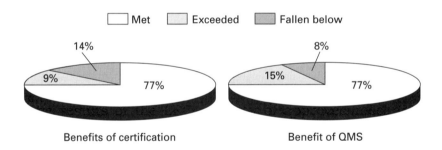

Figure 2.14 ISO 9000 expectations. *Source*: Lloyd's Register Quality Assurance

The results of the LRQA survey of approved mechanical engineering manufacturing companies were:

- Small organizations (turnover £5-10 million) have the highest profits compared to the industry average at 6.8 per cent.
- Medium organizations (turnover £20-50 million) and large organizations (turnover in excess of £50 million) both

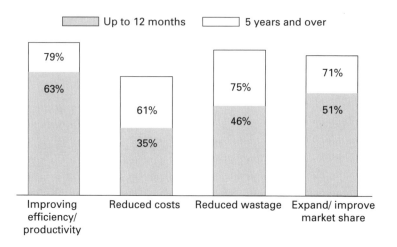

Figure 2.15   ISO 9000 benefits increase over five years. *Source*: Lloyd's Register Quality Assurance

recorded profit margins of 4 per cent, more than twice the industry average.

• Large and small companies reported return on capital employed (ROCE) figures of 16 per cent and 17 per cent respectively, more than double the industry average.

• Large organizations showed the greatest improvement with a 95 per cent increase in sales per employee over the industry average of £93 500 per employee.

• Small and medium sized companies both recorded a profit per employee figure more than double that of the industry average.

Source: Lloyd's Register Quality Assurance Ltd, Norfolk House, Wellesley Road, Croydon, CR9 2DT.

TQM success stories in a nutshell

Rank Xerox UK Ltd

Rank Xerox UK Ltd launched a world-wide programme in 1989 called 'Leadership Through Quality'. This led to winning the Deming Prize, the Malcolm Baldrige Award and the very first European Quality Award. To Rank Xerox TQM means the totality of quality management. The company achieved transformation by focusing attention on reward and compensation, training, communication, senior management behaviour and standards and measurement. The director of quality and communication at Rank Xerox categorized enablers of quality achievement as 'open honest communication', 'organizational reflection and learning' and 'process improvement'.

TQM philosophy means managers are expected to promote and use 'leadership through quality' tools personally. They hire and promote exponents of 'leadership through quality', seek and act on feedback and recognize and reward effective application of 'quality through leadership'. The emphasis throughout is on behaviour and performance. No wonder Rank Xerox is constantly cited as an organization that turned itself round and became more competitive through pursuing a company-wide quality programme.

ICL

At ICL the quality initiative began in 1986 and over the years it has gone through three stages, each one with a focus of its own. The director of quality and customer care presented the following explanations at a conference:

Stage one began in 1986 with a focus on quality conformance – Do It Right First Time. At this stage 35 group quality staff were involved and detailed reporting to the headquarters was required. There was very little ownership of the initiative at line managers' level.

At stage two the focus changed to customer care. Measures and processes were restructured to change the company culture to focus towards customers. Various senior management workshops, user groups and independent satisfaction surveys were organized to meet the objectives of delighting the customer. There was no reporting to the headquarters and the line managers experienced some ownership of the programme.

At stage three the focus changed to self-assessment using the model of the European Quality Foundation. The progress has been fast and there is total ownership of the quality programme at all levels.

Miliken Industrials

According to Clive Jeanes, managing director of Miliken Europe, quality is a moving target. At Miliken they have realized that the pursuit of excellence requires a constant reappraisal of what 'quality' actually means.

Miliken has been working on total quality management for 15 years. In 1980 Mr Roger Miliken went to Japan to study competitors. In February 1981, soon after he returned from Japan, Miliken had its first company-wide meeting of some 300 managers to examine how to introduce a quality improvement process. The initiative began with narrow focus on improving the quality of the products. Subsequently, due to the influence of Tom Peters, the definition of quality was extended to incorporate customer focus. This shifted the focus from the internal to the external perspective. Miliken initiated what is now a formal, regular survey of all major customers. Then the focus moved to statistical process control to monitor and improve process. Quality came to mean conformance to customer requirements with a minimum of variability.

Gradually over time the ideas of other gurus like Schoenberger and Ishikawa were taken on board. Now quality means 'the use of all aspects of total quality to delight our customers and thus ensure our survival and long term profitable growth'.

The quality initiatives led to dramatic improvements in reducing non-conformance costs, making the right products and delivering on time. The on-time shipment performance was 77 per cent. This in 1991 went up to 99.9 per cent. Miliken has seen breakthroughs in area after area in businesses where they thought this would not have been possible.

There are numerous other success stories of companies who have achieved significant improvements as a result of adopting total quality management. The success stories act as incentives for suppliers to embark upon the total quality journey. Miliken, for example, suggested to Ciba Geigy, the Swiss chemical giant, that the company should adopt total quality management practices. Toyota asked Philips Electronics to improve its quality in supplying headlamps. Philips, which made light bulbs for Honda, was told that its defect rate of one faulty bulb in 50 was not good enough. Philips met and even exceeded Honda's requirement. Motorola helps its suppliers wade through the Baldrige applications and it even holds coaching classes.

Why total quality management fails for some companies

Various surveys conducted by Arthur D. Little of 500 American manufacturing and service companies found that only a third felt their total quality programmes were having a 'significant impact'. A. T. Kearney's survey over 100 British firms indicated similar results

For some companies, going for quality awards has been a kiss of death. Consider the fate of Company 'A'. This company manufactures cleaning equipment. In 1993 the company decided to go through the route of total quality management in order to satisfy its customers and increase the market share.

All its 800 employees were put through the quality training programmes and the workers were divided into groups and put into work teams. Every employee was given a key ring on which was inscribed 'I am for quality'. Every two weeks a senior manager would gather all his employees and talk on different aspects of quality. The factory floor was buzzing with quality fever. All the conversations were along the line of cycle time, service excellence, on-time delivery. The company saw its operational performance improve dramatically. However the financial results and market share analysis did not prove to be consistent with operational performance improvements.

What was happening was that the company became very inward-focused. In order to go through the hoops of the quality journey this company 'forgot' its customers. Staff were so busy improving operational procedures and delivering on time that they did not find out about their customers' needs. The company was losing sales and the costs were escalating. When the company posted a big loss after making profits before taking quality initiatives it decided to get rid of 200 employees and abandoned the quality initiative.

There are many examples of other companies like Company 'A' who have gone through considerable efforts to become quality-driven companies and ended with failures.

Why well-intentioned companies do not find success in quality

These are some of the reasons which were highlighted in various studies, reports and surveys:

- Failure of management to set realistic goals or look for measurable benefits at the outset.
- Objectives set have not been sensible and there were no time limits.
- TQM was embarked upon to impress customers and suppliers but the company itself had no conviction.
- There has been no focus on customers but only on processes.
- Quality was treated as an operational issue and delegated to the quality department.
- A company set up a bureaucratic system to achieve quality goals.
- TQM was treated as a 'quick fix'.
- There was a lack of a powerful set of company values.
- Staff were not adequately trained.
- Some companies introduced TQM as an excuse for downsizing.
- TQM was not aligned to corporate strategy.
- The company lacked strong leadership.
- Employees were not empowered.
- Teams were formed without giving serious thought as to their structure and objectives.
- TQM was instituted to win awards.
- Some companies introduced TQM without monitoring costs.
- Lack of support from employees especially where morale is undermined by redundancies.
- Lack of integration with strategic objectives.
- The company had adopted wrong strategic choices.
- Many companies did not apply bottom-line discipline to quality.
- To some companies standards became more important than sales.

How not to fail

Total quality management is both a philosophy and a way of doing business in the 1990s. Organizations have to reflect about what, how and why they do what they do and they have to take appropriate actions continuously in order to listen to their customers and consequently improve their business performance.

Companies like Rank Xerox, ICL, Motorola, Miliken, Philips Electronics, Rover Group, TNT, Design to Distribution (D2D), the ICL subsidiary, have worked with TQM for a very long time in order to become 'quality companies'. Quality to these companies is not a destination but a journey. The quality programme has to be constantly monitored and changed as the competitive scenario changes.

In management a distinction is made between an efficient organization and an effective organization. Efficiency is doing the right thing whereas effectiveness is doing the right thing right. In relation to Figure 2.16 the quality company should aim to occupy the segment marked 'A'. To do 'the right thing right' in TQM means a company should avoid all those failure factors highlighted in this chapter and set a vision that will put 'fire in their employees' bellies'.

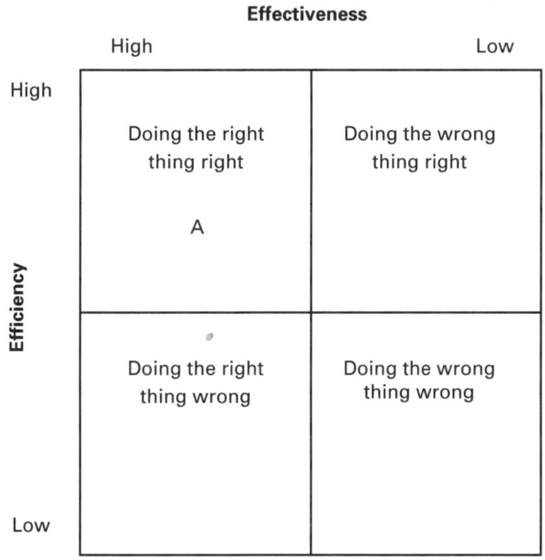

Effectiveness

	High	Low
High	Doing the right thing right A	Doing the wrong thing right
Low	Doing the right thing wrong	Doing the wrong thing wrong

(Efficiency on vertical axis, High at top, Low at bottom)

Figure 2.16 Efficiency versus effectiveness

In November 1989 Tom Peters articulated the following 'six steps to quality' in his presentation at the Economist Conferences seminar:

* Step 1: Conformance to specification.
* Step 2: Ask whose specifications.
* Step 3: Move beyond the envelope called specification and add perception.
* Step 4: Getting everybody out in front of the customers.
* Step 5: Work on a project with a customer.
* Step 6: Remove internal barriers and external borders.

He also said 'It is impossible to progress very far down the road towards true customer satisfaction in quality improvement unless the orientation of the organization is completely changed'.

The top management should make themselves personally responsible for quality and gain commitment and involvement from their staff. There should be a commitment and conviction throughout the organization. The quest for quality depends on an employee's conviction and commitment and his or her behaviour towards his colleagues and customers as driven by the organization's mission and vision (Figure 2.17.)

The author was recently speaking to two employees from a pharmaceutical company who were celebrating the end of the quality project. They said they have been working on the project for nearly three years. The project is now finished and they went on to say 'Thank God, we can get back to our proper work'. Where does the blame lie?

For total quality management to be successful the philosophy must be prevention not detection, commitment and involvement of all staff must be 100 per cent, the approach must be senior management-led, the scope must be company-wide, the scale must be everyone in the company as well as suppliers and distributors, the control must be cost, the theme must be continuous improvement, and the focus must be customer satisfaction.

Quality in the European Union

According to the EC Directorate manufacturers and distributors throughout the European Union will in the future have to make sure that their products meet the requirements of the appropriate directive and that their products conform to standards by displaying the CE Mark. Failure to comply and display the CE Mark is a legal offence and will lead to prosecution. Some directives are already in force while others are imminent.

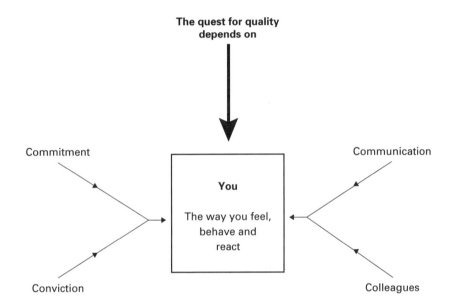

Figure 2.17 The quest for quality

Quality soundbites of the 1990s

- Good quality does not necessarily mean high quality.
- Quality means delighting the customer.
- Quality is philosophy of business.
- Quality is not a destination but a journey.
- Love to learn quality.
- Quality management is a source of profit.
- Quality is everybody's business.
- Quality differentiates companies from the competition.
- The only way you are going to retain your business is to

deliver 100 per cent quality.

- A quality company lives for its customers.
- The key to quality success is to focus total commitment outside the individual to within.
- Total quality management is implemented by many organizations out of desperation rather than inspiration.
- Customers measure quality to competition not to specifications. Ignoring quality in the 1990s is tantamount to corporate suicide.
- Total quality should be a core part of everyone's job description.
- Training for quality is not a programme – it is a process.
- Quality is like a religion: you have to have a faith in it.
- Total quality is synonymous with the strategic plan of a business.
- Quality is excellence in execution.
- Total quality unlocks people's potential.
- Total quality creates a commitment by the company to its employees. Total quality brings an end to 'either/or' thinking.
- Total quality philosophy challenges conventional Western management.
- Total quality creates high-performing organizations.
- Total quality enables organizations to out-think their competitors.
- Quality should be considered as a marathon, not a 100-metre race.
- Total quality requires sustainable commitment.
- The foremost requirement of TQM is to get people to internalize and own the initiative.

Is your organization a quality organization? Find out for yourself

Scoring: Score 1 for 'Definitely yes', 2 for 'Yes but ...' and 3 for 'No'.

1. Our company's mission statement explicitly mentions quality and customer service.

Yes/Yes but .../No

2. Our strategic plan includes a strategy for quality.
   Yes/Yes but .../No

3. Our chief executive officer himself or herself gets involved with quality.
   Yes/Yes but .../No

4. Senior managers in our company regularly visit our customers.
   Yes/Yes but .../No

5. All levels of management in our organization get training on quality and customer service.
   Yes/Yes but .../No

6. We regularly conduct customer surveys.
   Yes/Yes but .../No

7. We believe in product quality and service quality.
   Yes/Yes but .../No

8. We treat everyone outside as well as inside the organization as our customers.
   Yes/Yes but .../No

9. All departments and divisions are concerned about quality.
   Yes/Yes but .../No

10. Quality is an investment not a cost.
    Yes/Yes but .../No

11. We are allowed to make mistakes as long as we learn from them.
    Yes/Yes but .../No

12. Quality is a never ending process.
    Yes/Yes but .../No

13. Our appraisal system incorporates assessing our behaviour towards our customers and colleagues.
    Yes/Yes but .../No

14. We benchmark our competitors.
    Yes/Yes but .../No

15. We communicate freely and honestly within our company.

Yes/Yes but .../No

16. We have a flat organization.

Yes/Yes but .../No

17. We get recognition for our efforts in the company's performance.

Yes/Yes but .../No

18. Quality in our company is everybody's business.

Yes/Yes but .../No

19. We work with our suppliers and distributors as partners.

Yes/Yes but .../No

20. Employees are empowered in our company.

Yes/Yes but .../No

Score: 20.   You are definitely working in a top quality company.
21–30. Your company is almost a quality company.
31–40. Your company should make an extra effort to become a quality company.
41–50. You are heading towards extinction unless you embark upon a quality initiative.
51–60. Your company is a dinosaur. Its days are numbered.

How to make your company a quality master

The following advice appeared in the *Business Week* Special Report on quality.

Novices that try to match the techniques used by world-class performers may actually make things worse by trying to do too much too soon. So finds a three-year study of 580 companies in North America, Germany and Japan by Ernst & Young and the American Quality Foundation. Instead they suggest making gradual progress toward excellence.

Start by measuring your existing performance. Two key measures are return on assets which is simply after-tax income divided by total assets, and value added per employee (VAE). Value added is sales minus the costs of materials, supplies, and work done by outside contractors. Labour and administrative costs are not subtracted from sales to arrive at value added.

The chart of path to quality is divided into novice, journeyman and master and the guidance is given under 'techniques and 'measures'. The $ sign shows activities that should reap the highest paybacks.

Novice – getting started	
Profitability	Less than 2 per cent return on assets (ROA).
Productivity	Less than $47 000 value added per employee (VAE).
Employee involvement	$ Train heavily. Promote teamwork, but forget self-managed teams, which take heavy preparation. Limit employee empowerment to resolving customer complaints.
Benchmarking	Emulate competitors, not world-class companies.
New products	Rely mainly on customer input for ideas.
Supply management	Choose suppliers mainly for price and reliability.
New technology	Focus on its cost-reduction potential. Don't develop it – buy it.
Manager and employee	Reward front-line workers for teamwork and quality evaluation
Quality process	$ Concentrate on fundamentals. Identify processes that add value, simplify them, and move faster in response to customer and market demands. Don't bother using formal gauges of progress – gains will be apparent.

Journeyman – honing new skills

Profitabiliy	2 per cent to 6.9 per cent ROA.
Productivity	$47 000 to $73 999 VAE.
Employee involvement	$ Encourage employees of every level to find ways to do their jobs better – and to simplify core operations. Set up a separate quality-assurance department.
Benchmarking	Imitate market leaders and selected world-class companies.
New products	Use customer input, formal market research and internal ideas.
Supply management	Select suppliers by quality certification, then price.
New technology	Find ways to use facilities more flexibly to turn out a wider variety of products or services.
Manager and employee evaluation	Base compensation for both workers and middle managers on contributions to teamwork and quality.
Quality progress	$ Meticulously document gains and further refine practices to improve value added per employee, time to market and customer satisfaction.

Master – staying on top

Profitability	ROA of 7 per cent and higher.
Productivity	VAE of $74,000 and up.
Employee involvement	$ Use self-managed, multiskilled teams that focus on horizontal processes such as logistics and product development. Limit training, mainly to new employees.
Benchmarking	$ Gauge product development, distribution and customer service against the world's best.
New products	Base around customer input, benchmarking and internal R&D.
Supply management	Choose suppliers mainly for their technology and quality.
New technology	Use strategic partnerships to diversify manufacturing.

| Manager and employee evaluation | Include senior managers in compensation schemes pegged to teamwork and quality. |
| Quality progress | Keep documenting gains and further refine practices to improve value added per employee, time to market and customer satisfaction. |

Source: Business Week, December 1992.

The quest for quality

The quest for quality depends on the inner feelings of employees. How employees feel about their job, about their organization and about their bosses' influence, their behaviour in delivering total quality. Organizations which have won quality awards have to sustain their standards over a very long period and the sustainability depends on employees' conviction in what they do, and their commitment. They have to trust their organizations in recognizing their efforts and it is the trust within the organizations that motivates them and that drives them to achieve business excellence. Without such trust organizations can spend millions of dollars on consultancies and on grand quality projects and win awards but very soon they will lose out.

Selected reading

Business Week (1991). The Quality Imperative. December 2.
Business Week (1994). Making Quality Pay. August 8.
W. Edwards Deming (1986). *Out of Crisis*. Massachusetts Institute of Technology Center for Advanced Educational Services.
Philip B. Crosby (1984). *Quality Without Tears*. McGraw-Hill.
Philip B. Crosby (1989). *Let's Talk Quality*. McGraw-Hill.
John Macdonald and John Piggot (1990). *Global Quality*. Mercury.
The Open University Business School, Course B889, Unit 7.
The Economist Intelligence Unit (1992). *Making Quality Work*.

3 Benchmarking

Mirror, mirror on the wall who is the prettiest of them all?

Summary

- To compete companies now copy other companies' best practice. This practice is called benchmarking.
- Benchmarking is a method used to improve business performance in order to adopt best practice.
- Xerox is recognized as an originator of benchmarking practice. Benchmarking is practised by many companies including Rank Xerox, AT&T, Motorola, Miliken, Ford and Federal Express.
- Benchmarking is now used across all functions.
- The practice has become the cornerstone of total quality management, business process re-engineering and time-based management.
- Step by step guidelines are provided in conducting benchmarking.
- How to use quality models as a framework for benchmarking.
- How to incorporate 'the voice of the customer' by benchmarking.
- Benchmarking the use of 'self assessment' in quality initiatives. Case studies: ICL.
- How benchmarking has been conducted in practice. Case studies: Royal Mail, Rank Xerox, Thomson Travel Group and Rover.
- Troubleshooting guidelines.
- Sources of information.
- Benchmarking as a means to an end.

Copycat era

Over the past few years benchmarking has become very popular in many organizations. Achieving sustainable levels of growth and profitability have become increasingly difficult for many organizations as competitive pressures are intensifying. To improve organizational performance and effectiveness businesses over the past few years have embarked upon benchmarking in the areas of manufacturing operations, marketing, and customer service. Recently the practice has been extended to other functions such as finance and people management.

What is benchmarking?

Benchmarking is a method of improving business performance by learning from other companies how to do things better in order to be the 'best in the class'. Rank Xerox defines benchmarking as:

A continuous systematic process of evaluating companies recognized as industry leaders, to determine business and work processes that represent 'best practice' and establish rational performance goals.

Other organizations define the practice as:

The ongoing and objective measurement ... of relative performance ... against relevant organizations ... in key process areas.

A change programme which enables the achievement of the 'best practice'.

At IBM benchmarking is 'the continuous process of analysing the best practice in the world for the process goals and objectives leading to world class levels of achievement'.

It does not matter which definition we look at; all of them emphasize the fact that the benchmarking practice should be **continuous**, **systematic** and that it should involve **evaluation** and **measurement** with a view to achieving excellence and becoming the 'best in the class'. Benchmarking is the cornerstone of total quality management.

To quote John McClelland, European director of manufacturing and product development, IBM UK Ltd, the main objectives of benchmarking at IBM are:

* 'To ensure that our business process goals are set to exceed the best qualitative results achieved by world class leaders.
* To incorporate best practice throughout IBM business processes.
* To reach a level of maturity where benchmarking is an on-going part of the management system in all areas of the business.'

Benchmarking originated in the USA approximately a decade ago. Now 95 per cent of US companies say they are practising it. In the late 1970s, Xerox, who are recognized as being the originator of benchmarking, found that the retail price of Canon photocopiers was lower than Xerox's manufacturing costs. They a sent a benchmarking team to Japan to compare their performance in a wide range of areas with their Japanese counterparts and returned to undertake the 'step change' needed to catch up. Benchmarking thus developed in Xerox in 1979 and it became a company-wide effort in 1981.

Benchmarking in Europe

As far as Europe is concerned, benchmarking seems to be well established. Coopers & Lybrand undertook a survey in 1994 covering *The Times* 1000 companies or their equivalent across five European countries: the United Kingdom, the Netherlands, Switzerland, Spain and France. The survey defined benchmarking as 'the process of comparing business practices and performance levels between companies (or divisions within companies) in order to gain new insights and to identify opportunities for making improvements'.

The survey showed that over two-thirds of companies in the United Kingdom, the Netherlands and Switzerland, over half of French companies and a third of Spanish companies are using benchmarking techniques. Benchmarking is used across all of the principal business functions.

Figure 3.1 shows the percentage of companies using benchmarking across Europe. Figure 3.2 shows the use of benchmarking across all principal business functions. Figure 3.3 shows the use of benchmarking to measure competitive position and Figure 3.4 shows companies using benchmarking to measure performance against direct competitors or within their industry.

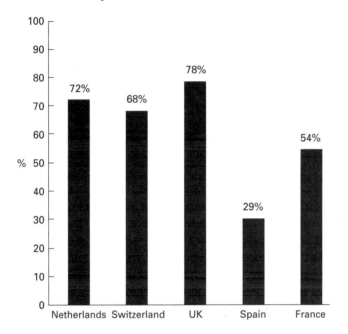

Figure 3.1 Percentage of companies using benchmarking across Europe. *Source*: © Coopers & Lybrand survey 1994

In Japan benchmarking has been practised for a long time. Although the term benchmarking was not used, Japanese firms were conducting benchmarking exercises in the leading companies.

Early experience of benchmarking was in the manufacturing sector because manufacturing output is tangible and measured (what gets measured gets done). Gradually the techniques came to be applied to processes, logistics, financial performance, research and development and so on.

Rank Xerox, in its quest to become an excellent company, benchmarked against different companies in various operational areas (see Table 3.1). This is a classic example of benchmarking outside the direct competitor set.

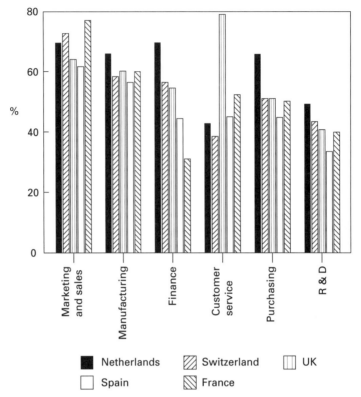

Figure 3.2   Use of benchmarking across all principal business functions. *Source*: © Coopers & Lybrand survey 1994

Table 3.1   Benchmarking by Rank Xerox

Companies benchmarked against	Areas benchmarked against
Miliken	Employee suggestions
Toyota, Fuji, Xerox	Total quality management
AT&T, Hewlett Packard	R&D
Proctor & Gamble	Product marketing
LL Bean, Hershey Foods	Logistics
American Hospital Supply	Inventory control
American Express	Billing and collection

A benchmarking analysis can be conducted for any type of organization covering a wide range of functional areas. They can be commercial or not-for-profit organizations. Functional areas include manufacturing, finance, marketing, health and safety, personnel and so on.

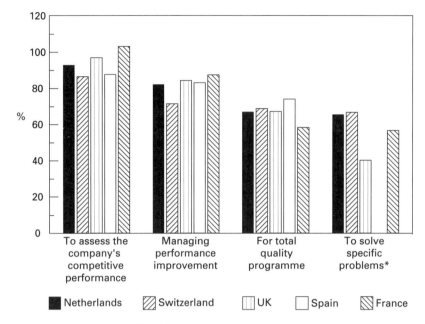

Figure 3.3 Use of benchmarking to measure competitive position. *Source*: © Coopers & Lybrand survey 1994

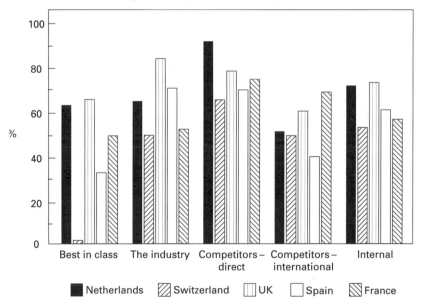

Figure 3.4 Benchmarking used against direct competition in national markets. *Source*: © Coopers & Lybrand survey 1994

These days various organizations are forming strategic alliances and partnerships which give them an opportunity to benchmark with their partners. In the early 1990s, the Rover Group started a benchmarking programme. They bench-marked against Honda, with whom they had a collaborative relationship. Rover Body and Pressings was chosen to pilot the benchmarking process within the Rover Group.

In some cases, benchmarking developed from conducting competitor analysis. This was the case for Royal Doulton who took its first steps towards benchmarking in 1987. Royal Doulton undertook competitor analysis with Wedgwood in the UK, Rosenthal, Hutschenreuther and Villeroy & Boch in Germany, Noritake in Japan and Lenox in the USA. The benchmarking exercise that was undertaken subsequently led to technical and process best practice.

Benchmarking is embedded into various approaches to organizational development and improvement. It is the cor-nerstone of the total quality management, business process re-engineering and time-based management.

What are the advantages of benchmarking?

First of all, benchmarking can only happen in a culture in which people are prepared to have their thinking challenged and are prepared to learn from one another.

The practice offers the following advantages:

* Provides direction and impetus for improvement.
* Indicates early warning of competitive disadvantage.
* Promotes competitive awareness.
* Becomes the stepping stone to 'breakthrough' thinking.
* Identifies the 'best practice'.
* Provides an objective attainment standard for key areas of business operations.
* Links operational tactics to corporate vision and strategy.
* Exposes performance gaps.
* Triggers major step changes in business performance.
* Helps companies redefine their objectives.
* Challenges the 'status quo'.
* Allows realistic stretch goals.

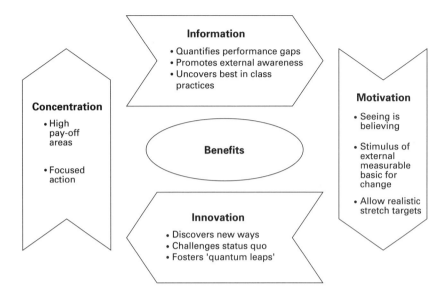

Figure 3.5   The different benefits of benchmarking

Benchmarking at work

The following is an example of benchmarking at work which appeared in *Business Week*, 7 December 1992.

Benchmarking at work: improving procurement		
	Typical company	World-class company
Cost factors		
Suppliers per purchasing agent	34	5
Agents per $100m of purchase	5.4	2.2
Purchasing costs as a % of purchase made	3.3%	0.8%
Time factors		
Supplier evaluations (weeks)	3	0.4
Supplier lead times (weeks)	150	8
Time spent placing an order (weeks)	6	0.001

	Typical company	World-class company
Quality of deliveries		
Late	33%	2%
Rejected	1.5%	0.0001%
Materials shortage (no. of		
instances per year)	400	4
Data: McKinsey & Co.		

How to benchmark

Rank Xerox proposes 10 steps to benchmarking under the categories of Planning, Analysis and Integration.

Planning
Step 1   Identify subject to benchmark.
Step 2   Identify the best practice.
Step 3   Collect data.

Analysis
Step 4   Analyse determine current competitive gaps.
Step 5   Project future performance.

Integration
Step 6   Communicate results and analysis.
Step 7   Establish goals.
Step 8   Develop action plan.
Step 9   Implement plan and monitor results.
Step 10   Recalibrate the benchmark.

Source: The Economist Conferences. 'Benchmarking' conference

Step 1
Assume that organization 'A' is intending to benchmark. First of all 'A' should identify the subject to benchmark. It could be corporate vision, or specific function or a specific process or a specific product attributes. Let us assume that 'A' has identified customer service as the subject for benchmarking.

Customer service can be defined in the operating terms of

quality and delivery performance. A customer-driven operating system impacts the measurement of workflow from department to department.

Step 2
Identify the best practice in customer service area. What constitutes best practice in this area and how would one measure it?

One could look at customer ratings from surveys, number of complaints received, revenue per customer, retention rate, repeat business, lapse rate, on-time delivery, delivery of defect-free products etc. The best practice in customer service is identified, let us say, in Company 'B'. Company 'A' will choose company 'B' as its benchmarking candidate.

Step 3
This stage involves gathering data on various criteria chosen. For example, if company 'B' is a parcel delivery service then Step 3 would involve collecting information on parcel deliver services.

Step 4
This step involves analysing data collected and comparing the level and quality of service to that provided by Company 'A'. This stage would determine performance or competitive gaps in providing customer service (Figure 3.6).

Different companies use combinations of methods to find out the level of customer service they provide. IBM, for example, during the design of the AS/400 mini-computer solicited users' opinions on the product and brought software companies into the planning process.

Other ways of 'staying close to your customers' involve visiting customers, conducting surveys, and instituting quality functional development as done by Hewlett-Packard and the Ford Motor Company. As has already been explained, quality function deployment is a system of designing a product or service which integrates marketing, design and manufacturing functions. This method involves all 'specialists' right from the beginning when the product is conceived.

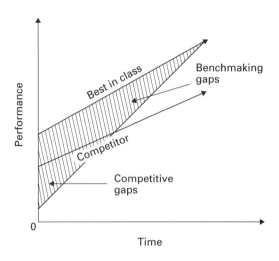

Figure 3.6 Competitive gaps

Step 5
This level would demand formulation of the project to close the competitive gaps and to set benchmarks towards achieving best practice.

Step 6
This stage involves communicating the objectives of the project to all those involved in effecting improvements. Communication at this stage is crucial to set the direction of the project. The subsequent steps lead to formulating strategy (what you want to do), setting time scale (when you want to finish the project), preparing an action plan and setting benchmarks for implementation. Finally the best practice project is implemented and regularly monitored. The Deming cycle (plan, do, act, review) mentioned in Chapter 2 should come into play.

Benchmarking can also be done with reference to value chain. A comparison can be made for each stage of the value chain. Benchmarking can be undertaken in relation to inbound logistics, outbound logistics, and so on, see Figure 3.7.

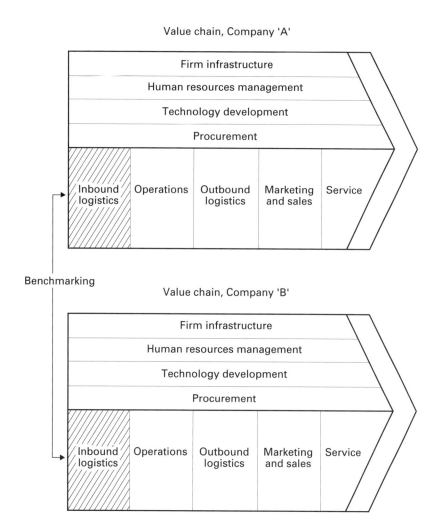

Figure 3.7 Benchmarking a competitor's value chain

What aspects of business to benchmark?

In general all aspects of business operations can be benchmarked. In achieving organizational transformation all aspects of business should be benchmarked. However in order to prioritize it is recommended that considerations be given to the shareholders' as well customers' values (see Figure 3.8). The

High-High box should be the first candidate for benchmarking where it is not possible to undertake benchmarking for all aspects of business.

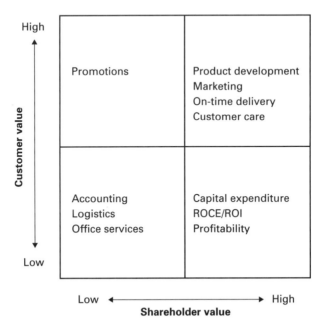

Figure 3.8   Aspects of business to benchmark

The European Quality Model and benchmarking

The European Quality Model can be used to provide a structure to benchmarking. If we take 'Enablers' then each part can be taken to benchmark against 'partners'.

Enablers

- **Leadership**: In this aspect benchmarking can be done to find the involvement of top management in any change project; if employees get due recognition for their efforts and, if so, what type of recognition. What type of leadership is practised in partner's organization; is top management involved with customers, suppliers and distributors directly?

- **Policy and strategy**: How is corporate strategy formulated; the content of the mission statement; the inclusion of employees' and customers' needs in the mission statement; the way objectives are formulated and communicated across the organization; the use of control cycle and regular review.
- **People management**: Formation of self-performing teams; extent of empowerment; development of competences and training; employees' needs analysis; employees' development and advancement; employees' appraisal and the subsequent actions.
- **Resources**: How are people enabled to perform their tasks; availability of appropriate financial and non-financial resources; use, type and level of technology.
- **Processes: Identifying key processes**; activities connected with key processes; how are key processes monitored and reviewed; how is creativity and innovation encouraged; methods of process improvement.

Types of benchmarking

There are different types of benchmarking depending whether the benchmarking is conducted with external organizations or within the organization. Then there are benchmarking practicies which relate to product, processes, people and different functions.

Competitive benchmarking

When Xerox sent a team of manufacturing people to Japan to study processes, products and materials, the objective was to gain a benchmark that could be used by Xerox to measure against Canon, their competitor. This is an example of competitive benchmarking.

The best example of competitive benchmarking that was used to achieve a quantum leap is given by Michael Hammer in his book *Re-engineering the Corporation* in which he gives an example of the Ford Motor Company's efforts to improve its account payable operations. Ford benchmarked against Mazda and ended up removing its non-value added activities and thus achieved a reduction in headcount from 500 people to 5 people. This story is told by everyone at every benchmarking and process re-engineering conference.

Strategic benchmarking

PIMS (the profit impact of marketing strategy) defines strategic benchmarking as the development of measures for a business unit which quantifies its key strengths and weaknesses, to give some external reference to the strategic planning process. In an article entitled Strategic benchmarking at ICI Fibres, Clayton and Luchs cite the example of how ICI Fibres, when faced with crisis in 1980, undertook an extensive competitive analysis of the European market. The strategic problem facing ICI Fibres was in the area of quality and productivity in its polyester division. The strengths and weaknesses of ICI's competitors were recorded in each fibre area. The factors influencing the long-term profitability were reviewed and ICI came to the conclusion that its share positions in most of the nylon businesses were still strong and its quality in textile fibres was good enough to justify a price promotion. Evaluation of sustainable earning power from strategic benchmark comparisons showed a clearer picture of the future earning potential. Strategic benchmarking, therefore, aims at strategic changes and prioritized resource allocation.

Process benchmarking

Organizations can compare internal processes between countries or companies or divisions within the same group. They can compare their own processes with industry-leading service providers.

Sears plc benchmarked the retail supply chain, focusing attention on core delivery processes which develop, select and deliver product to the customer. They looked at range, design, source, price, distribution, display and sales, all these constituting components of supply chain management. Externally they benchmarked against Xerox, Wallmart, Nestlé, ICL, Marks & Spencer and British Airways.

Florida Power and Lights (FPL) in pursuit of a Deming Award benchmarked with Kansai Electric of Japan. They benchmarked the process of repairing boiler tube leaks.

Product benchmarking

In the 1970s IBM issued instructions that all new products must have a superior performance to both their IBM precursor and the best of their competitors' products from the moment of the very first customer shipment. Thus, product benchmarking was born throughout the corporation. Products were benchmarked on the basis of functionality, reliability and availability.

Product benchmarking is the most widespread form of benchmarking in Japan. This is due to the 'me too' mentality of Japanese firms.

Benchmarking customer service

Customer service is a complex supply chain of service to customers. Benchmarking in this field will identify where performance is below expectation and where there is room for improvement compared with competitors.

Some organizations like ICL, started benchmarking customer service first by defining customer needs and then by using customer satisfaction surveys to identify the level of service being provided. The next stage was to compare the service level with the customer requirement. By matching customer needs with the level of service delivered and by using service delivery costs from the benchmarking surveys, the appropriate action was taken to implement change and deliver excellence.

Internal benchmarking

Some organizations undertake internal benchmarking in order to improve existing performance and also as a first step towards external benchmarking.

Taking Sears plc as an example again, the company is a grouping of autonomous businesses with varied backgrounds and culture. These businesses are represented by

Selfridges, Saxone, Freeman Hardy and Willis, Olympus, Adams and others. They have focused their attention on operations, sourcing, in-store presentation, supply chain and service in order to deliver retail brand and image.

Pitney Bowes has carried out a number of internal benchmarking exercises over two years, focusing attention on new product introduction, order fulfilment, customer satisfaction and purchasing.

Internal benchmarking is undertaken to compare similar operations or functions across the company or a group. For example, if you were to take the Economist Group, the internal benchmaking would be conducted between the Economist Newspaper Ltd and the Economist Intelligence Unit in relation to a specific service or process, e.g. order fulfilment.

Some authors recommend doing internal benchmarking for the following reasons:

* To establish an internal base line.
* To identify performance gaps in various activities.
* To identify areas that need improving.
* To establish common practice and procedures.
* To bring about effective communication processes within the organization.
* To promote an understanding of the nature of benchmarking.
* To instil confidence in undertaking external benchmarking.

The gap between internal and external practice has provided change champions with powerful evidence with which to overcome internal resistance to change.

Benchmarking, quality and the voice of the customers

Benchmarking is the integral part of the total quality management initiative. Let us assume that an ice cream company called 'Delight' wants to compare its product in relation to its competitor, another ice cream company called 'Haven'. 'Delight' can use the quality deployment function to match the attributes of its product and its competitor's product in relation to customers' needs (Figure 3.9).

'Delight can then benchmark its product's attributes against the attributes of its competitor's product (Figure 3.10). Based on the findings 'Delight' can make the best ice cream and gain competitive advantage over 'Haven'.

Product attributes

Consumer needs	Taste	Colour	Texture	Flavour	Hard/ soft
Taste	8				
Colour		8			
Texture			7		
Flavour				4	
Hard					1 Soft

Figure 3.9 Quality function deployment – ice cream

Product attributes	'Delight'	'Haven'
Taste	✓	
Colour		✓
Texture		✓
Flavour		✓
Hard/ Soft	✓	

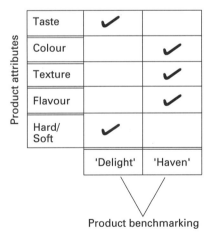

Product benchmarking

Figure 3.10 Benchmarking – 'Delight' versus 'Haven'

Benchmarking the use of self assessment

Initially Trevor Mills of ICL discussed the possibilities of forming a group of companies who would share their experiences in the area of self assessment. Self assessment is becoming a valuable way in which companies improve the quality of their organizations, their products and their service to customers. I am grateful to ICL and the European Foundation for Quality Management for allowing me to quote their experience as appeared in the feedback report, Benchmarking the use of Self Assessment.

Background to the company

ICL plc is one of Europe's leading computer systems and services companies, and the most consistently successful European IT company. Operating in more than 70 countries, it has some 25 000 employees, of whom over half are now outside the UK.

In 1986 ICL embarked upon its quality programme by putting a continuous improvement process into practice across the whole company – a process not limited to the manufacturing function. During 1990 ICL became the first IT company to achieve company-wide registration in the UK to the ISO 9000 systems standard and in 1991 they began the process of achieving similar registration for all their operations outside the UK.

Also in 1991 the company introduced customer care. This is part of the ongoing quality process emphasizing understanding customers' requirements and it has been developed with the objective of making ICL a household name for quality and customer satisfaction.

In 1993 ICL's manufacturing division won a European Quality Award.

Why self assessment?

ICL operates in a very competitive and fully open market. The industry trends towards 'open systems' have reduced the barriers to new entrants and reduced the switching costs when a new customer wants greater freedom of supplier choice.

As part of ICL's response to this, a company-wide quality improvement process was initiated in 1986. This Crosby-based approach has been adapted over the years and branded as 'Quality the ICL Way'.

Adaptations have included emphasis on customer care and internal and external benchmarking. The use of self assessment against the new EQA model has been a recent (1992) addition to 'Quality the ICL Way'. Simply stated, if this is the current best practice self assessment business model, then ICL wants to use it to benchmark themselves to see what they can learn and how they can further improve their business results.

They do not yet have statistical proof that points mean profits but they can see internally a direct relationship between a high self assessment score and above average business performance. They also have somewhat less evidence to show the opposite is true.

What is our approach?

ICL has a variety of approaches that can be chosen by individual business units. Basically, a unit which does not yet have ISO 9000 registration should concentrate on that for marketplace reasons and then move ahead on self assessment. The option used for self assessment was the use of a computer-aided model with a facilitator. A single management team can give perceptions of their own organization's position against the guidelines in the model. This form of group decision support system allows, in a long half day, an initial score based on perceptions and 10 key actions to improve upon.

To date, ICL have trained more than 200 assessors. These trained assessors go back to their own units and implement plans for self assessing each of the criteria in the model. Working within their own management teams, they carry out in-depth interviews and evidence gathering to allow a full written internal assessment.

ICL have encouraged and helped four of their business divisions to make a full entry for the European Quality Award, that is two divisions for each of the years the award has run. This involved a full report of up to 75 pages based on their own self assessment. Each year they have had a division shortlisted for a prize and benefited from a site visit from external assessors. In addition to giving areas for improvement, this method helps share internal best practice via the documents, and enables them to 'calibrate' their internal assessment methods.

What lesson have we learnt?

In-depth self assessment by either internal or external assessors helps the business divisions go way ahead of what an ISO 9000 audit would produce. They operate a different level of performance with more emphasis on evidence of real improvements over several years.

Self assessment has helped create a more balanced score card for managers. ICL have always had strong financial management and the EQA model reminds them that customer and people satisfaction are crucial for long-term company health.

The divisions that have made full entries to the Eupean Foundation of Quality Management (EFQM) have benefited from the feedback report from the external assessors. In some cases this has been passed on to other divisions.

Additionally, they have improved their own process of self assessment. Within the company, they now have the ability to form a team of both internal and external 'experts' to carry out an in-depth assessment at site visits by invitation of the managing director.

No matter what approach is used they all seem to identify key business improvements.

What have been the benefits?

'Quality the ICL Way' is only one of several long-term strategic commitments that have helped to make the company strong. They are able to see how the use of self assessment has given an extra impetus for continuous improvement. They can show how the key areas of customer and people satisfaction together with financial and non-financial business results are being measured, and in many cases improved. The model has forced them to find out who is better than them at what they do, and how they do it. This push for benchmarking is a real basis for a never-ending drive for business improvement.

What are our future plans?

ICL have plans to form networks of activists to champion improvements in each of the criteria. The main board directors of the company will champion each criteria and the first set of pilot meetings to establish the networks has taken place with some success. They intend to use these to assist across-company learning and the sharing of practices to benefit the business.

Since this article was written Design to Distribution (D2D) has won the 1994 European Quality Award. D2D is a contract electronics manufacturing company and it uses benchmarking to measure its processes internally against ICL's corporate strategic model. D2D is a wholly owned subsidiary of ICL and has a turnover well in excess of £300 million.

Benchmarking without emotions

Avon Products Inc. is the world's leading seller and marketer of beauty related goods. The annual turnover in 1994 was in excess of $3.5 billion and it markets its products in more than 100 countries through 1.5 million independent representatives. Avon is also the world's largest manufacturer of fashion jewellery. The trigger point for them was to review their business with the customers. They used a service quality survey method called 'servqual' which measured customer expectations and perceptions from which they identified performance gaps.

They grouped together into regional teams in order to identify 'best practice'. The benchmarking was done against the 'ideal service unit' which enabled everyone to work towards a goal without the emotions of feeling unfairly compared.

Benchmarking methods can now be viewed as falling into three broad categories depending on whether the focus is on metrics, processes or strategy, or the structures and culture of the organization. Within each category, a different type of benchmarking can be used to diagnose a problem or assess a performance gap, or help redesign a process or strategy to help implement a new change programme. The categories are illustrated in Figure 3.11.

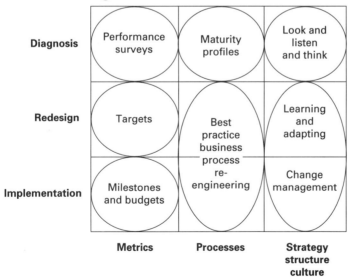

Figure 3.11   Categories of benchmarking. *Source*: Coopers & Lybrand.

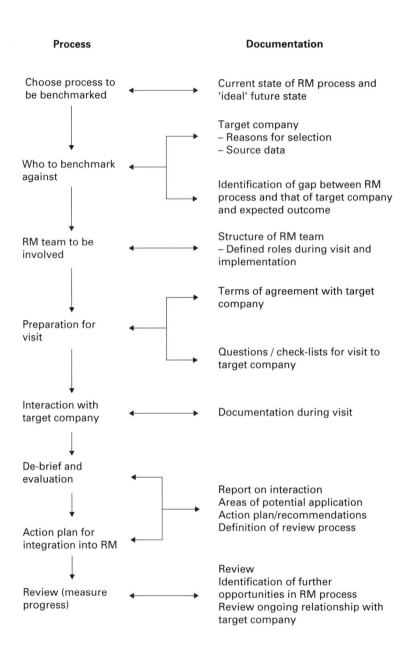

Figure 3.12   Benchmarking – strategic approach. © Royal Mail 1990

Benchmarking case studies

Case study 1: Royal Mail

Royal Mail sees best practice benchmarking (BPB) as a valuable tool in achieving its declared mission to be recognized as the world's best distributor of text and packages.

The quality department developed materials to help benchmark teams, based on the flowchart in Figure 3.12. The same process can be followed for any benchmarking activity.

This clarity in defining how the benchmarking process works has helped communicate the value of it and involve all staff in implementing it. An example of how the awareness of benchmarking has cascaded throughout the culture can be seen in a benchmarking exercise recently started within the marketing department. Brought together at a departmental conference, a team of benchmarking volunteers is working through the process defined by the flowchart. The team, which is given special training, is made up of a mixture of functions within the marketing department, giving a variety of perspectives.

The team decided to focus on aspects of product development, including the management of consultants and internal communications. It found that the best practice in product development transfers easily between industries, opening up the opportunity for a wide spread of benchmarking partners. One over-riding criterion it imposed in selecting partners was that they should share a total quality focus.

Case study 2: Rank Xerox

Best practice benchmarking (BPB) has become an everyday activity for every department in Xerox and Rank Xerox. The guiding principle is 'Anything anyone else can do better, we should aim to do at least equally well'. It is closely tied into the company's quality management programme because BPB is one of the most important ways of identifying where quality improvements are needed. Not only has Xerox improved its financial position world-wide and stabilized its market share, but it has increased customer satisfaction by 40 per cent in the past four years.

Typical of the way Rank Xerox uses BPB is a recent study of distribution, as explained by John Welch, quality manager.

We compared our distribution against 3M in Dusseldorf, Ford in

Cologne, Sainsbury's regional depot in Hertfordshire, Volvo's parts distribution warehouse in Gothenburg and IBM's international warehouse and French warehouse.

We found, for example, by comparing with the best that:

- We had an extra stocking echelon, which could be removed (i.e. we had international, national, regional; they had only international and regional).
- We took one extra day in information flow between the field and the centre, so we need to update our systems.
- They had transport logistics as a board function.
- Warehouses became efficient not through a high level of automation but through efficient manual routines.
- 'First pick' availability of parts averaged 90 per cent in the best warehouses; we made only 83 per cent.
- Now we are putting those lessons to work, in upgrading our operations to be at least as good."

Source for Case studies 1 and 2: 'Best Practice Benchmarking'. Management and Technology Services Divison, Department of Trade and Industry. Copies are available free of charge through the DTI's mailing house.

Case study 3: Thomson Travel Group

Thomson have been a market leader in tour operations for over 20 years. In his presentation at the Human Resources Benchmarking conference organized by the Economist Conferences, Martin Brackenbury of Thomson Travel Group said, 'We continuously track our competitors on a number of indicators. In our competitor comparisons, we track more than 30 key indicators and maintain our leadership in more than 95 per cent of them.

'But it is not sufficient for us to benchmark within our industry. As well as considering our competitors' performance, we need to look world-wide to identify who, anywhere, in any service industry is doing anything exceptionally well, and to identify what we can learn from them to add to our own competitiveness.

We arranged a benchmark tour to the USA and within a week we visited ten organizations, from different industry sectors with one thing in common: a reputation for excellence in customer service. The companies visited were:

Hampton Inn	Low cost hotels
Stew Leonard's	Supermarket

Paul Rever	Disability insurance
Fidelity	Financial services
Ritz-Carlton	De luxe hotels
Polaroid	Cameras and film
Nordstrom	Department stores
Southwest	No frills airline
TGI Friday	Theme restaurants
Sewell Village Cadillac	Car dealer and maintenance
Home Depot	DIY warehouse stores
Super Shuttle	Airport transfers

What did we learn?
* 'You have to focus on key aspects of organizations only.
* We discovered, when comparing ourselves with the very best that we have a lot to learn. While we may be better than our competitors we are a lot less good than the best.
* Benchmarking is exhilarating. Despite the fact that as our tour progressed we discovered that, measure for measure, we had more to learn than to teach, we were exhilarated by what we had seen because we knew that there was much that we could apply.
* It was confirmed that customers set their expectations of service from your industry in relation to their experience of excellent service from other industries.
* Measuring a range of different companies changes your outlook and understanding of what is excellent.
* Excellence is achieved through people at all levels with the right attitudes, knowledge and skills, and all distinctive performing companies have distinctive HR practices.
* We learnt more about:
– the mechanics of empowerment
– hiring the right people
– fun and recognition
– communication
– selection
– incentivization...'

Case study 4: Rover Group's experience – learning from Honda

The following is an extract from the case-study which appeared in UK Quality, March 1995. Mr John Towers is a group chief executive.

Learning from Honda

Rover took a long time to recognize why Japanese cars were more successful, but a visit by senior staff to Honda's North American plant in Ohio precipitated an attitudinal breakthrough. Though executives had visited Japan earlier, the US visit enabled them to see Japanese best practice in a Western context. The realization, as Mr Towers puts it, that 'we couldn't just copy Japanese techniques but we had to observe the benefit of what was being done and why, then determine ways in which we could apply it to our business' led to the Rover 'Working with Pride' initiative and the start in 1987 of the total quality improvement (TQI) programme.

Rover's breakthrough came when it recognized that culture plays only a small part in Japanese business success. 'In fact, the Japanese philosophy for success is extremely straightforward', Mr. Towers says. 'Get the design of the products and processes right to the smallest detail, empower your employees to run and continually improve those processes, and profits will naturally flow.'

From Honda, Rover learned the 'new model centre' concept. 'This was an example of our new diligence, using a people-centred philosophy', Mr Towers says. First used on the Rover 200 series, the objective is to produce a world class fit and finish through continuous process validation. A small flexible core planning team works on the product from concept through the various stages of design and development. When pilot cars are built for product engineering (using parts provided by their ultimate suppliers) a launch team is formed that includes manufacturing and engineering staff who eventually take production management positions to ensure continuity. Supply centres are set up to support the launch team, buy components and take responsibility for controlling quality.

Benchmarking – troubleshooting

As in any process, problems do arise in practice. Table 3.2 helps troubleshooting in the benchmarking process.

Table 3.2

Problem	Likely causes	Solution
Benchmarking the wrong measure.	Inadequate knowledge of own organization and operation.	Further research to find significant measure.

Problem	Likely causes	Solution
Benchmarking the organization.	Inadequate desk research.	More detailed initial research.
Benchmarking not leading to action.	Senior management not involved.	Ensure that management is seen to be in support.
Failure to sell idea to senior management	Lack of information, poor presentation.	Tie benchmarking firmly to the existing business plan; show how other companies have bene-fited.
Lack of resources for benchmarking.	Lack of management support; exclusive ownership by the benchmarking team.	Lobby and promote benchmarking as a company-wide approach.
Data not meaningful.	Too much/too little data; data not comparable.	Tighter focus to measure and test the assumption about your process that generated the measures.
Inaccurate/false data.	Over-reliance on public or competitor sources.	Double-check sources through personal checks.
Failure to sell idea to target organizations.	Scepticism and protective instincts.	Make clear the benefit of shared information, reassess criteria for selection of partners.
Over-reliance on superficial similarity.	Lack of rigorous criteria for assessing partners.	Re-define search to find closer fits.
Benchmark partner unwilling to share useful data.	Benchmark partner too alike.	Define search by process not industry.
Benchmark too many measures.	Unclear priorities.	Relate benchmarking to business plan.

Source: Best Practice Benchmarking. Management and Technology Services Division, Department of Trade and Industry.

Buying into benchmarking

Benchmarking is rapidly becoming acknowledged as one of the most powerful business improvement techniques in the competitive armoury. Benchmarking centres and clubs have been formed and are being formed to enable organizations to find out how one should organize and manage benchmarking practices and how to choose benchmarking 'partners'. Just as quality caught the corporate imagination during the 1970s and 1980s, benchmarking 'clubs' are proving to be an international success in a variety of industrial sectors.

Sources of information

Information about other companies and organizations can be obtained from various sources. Highlighted below are some of the sources of information:

- Annual reports.
- Press material.
- Analysts' reports.
- Market research reports.
- Trade associations.
- Academic case studies.
- Books.
- Competitor advertising.
- Benchmarking clubs.
- Benchmarking partners.
- Joint-venture partners.
- Government reports.
- Site visits.
- Conferences.
- Consumer surveys.
- Trade surveys.
- Media surveys.
- Retail audits.
- Salesmen.
- Product comparisons.
- Distributors and suppliers.

The Coopers & Lybrand survey (1994) shows that companies prefer to receive data from competitors, internal departments, customers and use published external data (Figure 3.13).

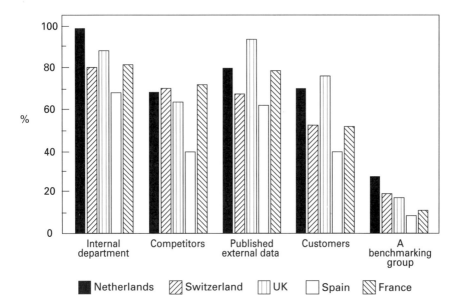

Figure 3.13   Preferred sources of data. *Source*: © Coopers & Lybrand survey 1994

The bottom line of benchmarking

Although any operation or process is open to analysis and improvement through benchmarking, without strategic direction, the approach may not have a significant impact on the organization's overall competitive position and profitability.

Identifying industry's 'best practice' is a powerful focus for change. The gap between internal and external practice can provide a starting point to overcoming resistance to change.

Research has shown that satisfied customers will tell an average of five others about their experience, but dissatisfied customers will tell an average of ten others. It is also said that quality of service is never an accident, it is the result of intelligent efforts! Benchmarking helps identify the nature of the effort made to bring about customer satisfaction or even delight.

Benchmarking as a means to an end

Most change programmes have not 'delivered the goods' so to speak because they are treated as ends in themselves. Change initiatives such as total quality management, benchmarking, process or business re-engineering are means to ends. These initiatives are not 'solutions' but are means of improving the organization's capabilities and overall performance. Benchmarking, therefore, should be undertaken with specific goals in mind rather than just bringing about any change. **It is what organizations do after benchmarking that matters**.

Selected reading

Business Week (1992). Beg, Borrow – And Benchmark. December 7.

Coopers & Lybrand, London (1994). *Survey of Benchmarking in Europe*.

Department of Trade and Industry. *Best Practice Benchmarking*.

European Foundation for Quality Management. A Feedback Report on Benchmarking the Use of Self Assessment by Seven Member Companies.

Management Review (1995). Benchmarking: People Make the Process. *The American Management Association Magazine*, June.

The Economist Intelligence Unit Report. *Best Practices: Management*.

Various papers presented by IBM, ICL, Rank Xerox and Miliken at the Benchmarking conference organized by the Economist Conferences.

4 Delivering service excellence

The kind of world one carries in oneself is the important thing, and the world outside takes all the graces, colour and value from that.

James Russell Lowell

Summary

- Customer service became the focus and the slogan for many organizations in the 1980s and 1990s.
- It is not what is produced that matters but how it is delivered.
- What customers perceive, they must receive.
- In the 1980s, organizations like ABB and Avis made customer satisfaction part of their corporate strategy.
- What Peter Drucker and Tom Peters have to say on customer satisfaction.
- Many researchers show that the key drivers of corporate strategic directions are customer satisfaction, quality leadership and innovation.
- Listening to the customer or getting close to the customer involves forming customer focus group, visits to customers, conducting surveys and researches and providing training on customer care.
- Customer satisfaction is one of the core components of various quality models.
- Customer service at DHL: a case study.
- How ICL learned to serve customers.
- Why some companies fail to deliver service excellence.
- Winning the hearts and minds of employees.
- Use of transactional analysis in providing service excellence.

Focus on customers

In the 1980s many organizations found it very hard to compete in spite of the fact that they invested heavily in numerous quality systems and projects. And the many quality projects which were to be their saviours did not help. We have already highlighted several reasons why for some companies quality management did not deliver what it promised to deliver. One of the key reasons for failure was lack of attention and consideration for customers.

Customers became the focus in the late 1980s and 1990s. Those organizations who paid attention to customers succeeded. The slogan was not just to satisfy the customers but to delight them. Many books, articles and research reports took on board the theme of delivering service excellence.

Forum Corporation research uncovered that almost 70 per cent of the identifiable reasons why customers left typical companies had nothing to do with the product. In 1988 it surveyed the customers of the 14 major companies in both manufacturing and service industries serving both business-to-business markets and relationship-oriented consumer markets such as banking. It was found that:

- Only 15 per cent of the customers switched their business to a competitor because they found a better product.
- Only 15 per cent switched because they found a cheaper product.
- 20 per cent switched because they had experienced too little contact and individual attention.
- 49 per cent said they had switched because the attention they received was of poor quality.

The customers were sending the following message from their behaviour, 'It is not just what you produce that matters but how you deliver it matters very much to us'. Many organizations started taking initiatives to listen to the voice of the customers. At the conference in October 1994, a speaker from Canon Europe NV highlighted various customer satisfaction surveys used in the European services operations. These included end-user customer satisfaction surveys and distribution satisfaction surveys. At the same conference a spokesman from Asea Brown Boveri AG (ABB) explained how his organization focuses attention on customers.

ABB's core businesses are power generation, power transmission and distribution, industrial automation and transportation. The strength of the group lies in the flexibility of the local units, compared with the benefits of belonging to a big organization.

Customer focus initiative started at ABB group level in 1990. Every business area had to create an overall approach which was to be introduced in all units world-wide. The three key elements of the approach were:

1. Continuous improvement of performance and process based on an interaction between time-based management, total quality management and supply management.
2. The results shall exceed the expectations of the customer and support ABB goals.
3. The approach shall be a substantial part of the strategy and completely integrated in all issues.

Regional and business areas work closely together. Figures 4.1 and 4.2 represent the customer focus model and the customer focus matrix of ABB.

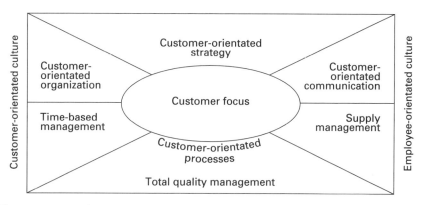

Figure 4.1   The ABB customer focus model

There are a number of other examples of companies in the late 1980s and 1990s which have adopted 'focus on the customers' as a key aspect of their corporate strategy. SAS Airways is one such company.

Avis, the car hire firm, used to measure and monitor service by looking at the volume of complaints. They subsequently developed a tool to find out how many customers are being lost; the tool was the 'customer service balance sheet'. It is based on periodic mail surveys of complaining and non-complaining customers. Avis's employees are told how well they are delivering service through the 'customer care income statement'.

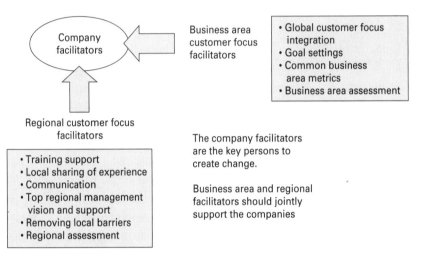

Figure 4.2   The ABB customer focus matrix

The 'customer care balance sheet' tells the organization how much business they are losing both from customers who do not complain but who experience problems and from customers who do complain but are not satisfied with the way their complaints are handled. Data from the 'customer care balance sheet' is then converted into annual lost sales or renewal.

Customer care balance sheet

| Sales lost from customers who experienced a problem and did complain | + | Sales lost from customers who experienced a problem but did not complain | − | Sales lost if customers had no problem | Total = sales lost |

Total sales lost / Years of loyalty   =   Annual sales lost

Poor customer service can cost organizations millions of pounds. It is said that 90 per cent of unhappy customers do not complain but they do tell at least 10 people about their bad experience or inadequate service. Based on this fact one can work out very simply the cost of losing one customer.

If I spend £50 per week at my supermarket on groceries but I decide not to shop anymore at that supermarket because of the poor service the supermarket will lose £2600 per year from me. At this stage this loss is insignificant! If I tell ten other customers not to shop there because of poor service and assuming they spend £50 a week as well then the total loss of business will be £28 600. This loss of business occurs when one person is sharing his or her poor experience with others. If there are numbers of customers who start sharing their bad experience the loss would be significant. In addition the supermarket has to advertise and invest in order to win other customers. Outflow of customers may exceed inflow of new customers and the supermarket would eventually go out of business (Figure 4.3).

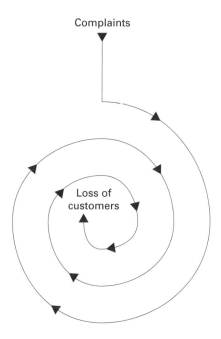

Figure 4.3   Loss of customers/business spiral

The focus on customer satisfaction has also been high-lighted by numerous management writers. According to Rosabeth Moss Kanter satisfied customers are the single best source of new business. According to Ohmae, in formulating business strategy it is important to pay painstaking attention to the needs of the customer. In this section we will examine some of the views on customers expressed in the writing of two very influential management gurus of our time, Peter Drucker and Tom Peters.

Peter Drucker

Peter Drucker in his book *Innovation and Entrepreneurship*, published in 1985 as *Creating Customer Utility*, tells the story of Ronald Hill's invention.

> Hill created utility. He asked: What do the customers need for a postal service to be truly a service to them? This is always the first question in the entrepreneurial strategy of changing utility, values and economic char-acteristics. In fact the reduction in the cost of mailing a letter, although 80 per cent or more, was secondary. The main effect was to make using the mails convenient for everybody and available to everybody. Letters no longer had to be controlled to 'epistles'. The tailor could now use the mail to send a bill. The resulting explosion in vol-ume which doubled in the first four years and quadru-pled again in the next ten, then brought the cost down to where mailing a letter cost practically nothing for long years.

He then goes on to give other examples of the companies who succeeded by listening to the customers:

> Price in itself is not 'pricing' and it is not 'value'. It was this insight that gave King Gillette a virtual monopoly on the shaving market for almost forty years, it also enabled the tiny Haloid Company to become the multi billion-dollar Xerox Company in ten years, and it gave

General Electric world leadership in steam turbines. In every single case, these companies became exceedingly profitable. But they earned their profitability. They were paid for giving their customers satisfaction, for giving their customers what the customers wanted to buy, in other words, for giving their customers their money's worth.

In his book *The Practice of Management* Peter Drucker wrote:

If we want to know what a business is we must start with its purpose ... There is only one valid definition of business purpose: to create a customer. What business thinks it produces is not of first importance – especially not to the future of the business or to its success. What the customer thinks he is buying, what he considers 'value' is decisive – it determines what a business is, what it produces, and whether it will prosper.

This passage was written 40 years ago! We are still struggling to grasp the importance of listening to customers in order to survive and succeed in business. *In Innovation and Entrepreneurship* Drucker writes:

'But this is nothing but elementary marketing,' most readers will protest, and they are right. It is nothing but elementary marketing. To start out with customer's utility, with what the customer buys, with what realities of the customer are and what the customer's values are – this is what marketing is all about. But why, after forty years of preaching marketing, teaching marketing, professing marketing, so few suppliers are willing to follow, I cannot explain. The fact remains that so far, anyone who is willing to use marketing as the basis for strategy is likely to acquire leadership in an industry or a market fast and almost without risk.

Tom Peters

Tom Peters is co-author of *In Search of Excellence* and *A Passion for Excellence*, the first and second management books ever to rank number one on the *New York Times* national bookseller list. His book *Thriving on Chaos: Handbook for a Management Revolution* was published in 1987 and ranked on the *New York Times* list for over sixty weeks. His fourth book, *Liberation Management, Necessary Disorganization for the Nanosecond Nineties* was published in 1992. His latest book, *The Pursuit of Wow*, leaped straight into the business best-seller lists with phenomenal sales in the USA. It was released in Europe in 1995.

In all his books and seminars, Peters makes competition and customers his core themes. In *Thriving on Chaos* he devotes a hundred pages to writing about customers. To Peters, service excellence has become the imperative of business success in the 1990s. The story of Nordstrom which appears in his book really drives the message home as far as delighting customers is concerned.

Nordstrom provides a superlative service to its customers; the salespersons greet customers by name and with politeness. If you live in the West, says Peters, you can't talk about Nordstrom service because practically everyone has a bizarre Nordstrom story. Such stories are peppered throughout the writings of Tom Peters.

Putting focus on customers is not a new thing or a phenomena of the 1980s and 1990s. In studying marketing in the 1960s we learnt about consumer behaviour, consumer characteristics and meeting the needs of customers. Philip Kotler and Ted Levitt have been writing about the total product concept for a number of years.

As Drucker said, after almost half a century of preaching customer consideration, why is it that organizations are beginning to get excited now? The reason simply is intense competition. The business salvation in the 1990s lies in delivering product quality and service quality. It is not the question of 'either/or' but of delivering total quality. The organization consistently has to perform in the High-High box in Figure 4.4.

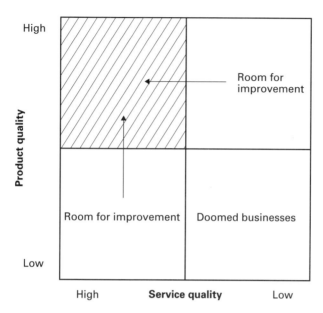

Figure 4.4 Quality matrix

John Thomson, the former chairman of CSC Index Europe, in his seminar How To Make Things Happen, organized by the Economist Conferences, gives the following advice:

Converting to a customer orientation

What is your 'value proposition' to your customers? Why do they do business with you? What is it you do better than your competition which the customer perceives as valuable? Is it:

Product innovation?
- You continuously invent new products/new versions of your product/service.
- You continually commercialize the inventions of others.
- You continuously exploit and enhance your brand image to achieve a position of dominance.

Operational excellence?
- You are ruthlessly efficient in the logistics of your supply chain.
- Your service is hassle free and error free.

Customer intimacy?
- You customize your product/service to satisfy the requirements of a customer.
- You provide a total solution for the customer wrapped around your product/service.
- You target potential customers with pin-point accuracy.

You have to be as good as your competition in all three of these value disciplines in order to survive.

Digital Equipment in association with John Humble, a management consultant, conducted a Service Survey in 1993. In this survey, one of the two key questions asked was: 'How important is each factor in influencing your customers to buy your major product or service?' Quality was at the top of the list followed by reliability, problem-solving, price (less emphasis in USA) speed of delivery, courtesy (more emphasis in Japan), after-sales service, design, guarantee and packaging.

When asked 'Where is there most room for improvement in you organization?', the response was in quality, speed of delivery, courtesy, problem-solving, reliability, after-sales service, price, design, packaging and guarantees.

The Forum Corporation undertook a research project in 1991 on the customer-focused quality company. The objectives of the research project were 'to explore and illustrate the principles and actions required to lead and implement a customer-focused quality strategy'. Among the participants were organizations who have won the Malcolm Baldrige National Quality Awards and one participant was the recipient of the 1989 Gold Award for Quality of the Canadian Awards for Business Excellence.

The findings of Forum's research project were that:

- Organizations adopt a customer-focused quality strategy to stay ahead of competition and to survive in the changing business climate.
- Organizations that adopt a customer-focused quality strategy had to undergo a fundamental change in their beliefs and values. Everyone in the organization had to understand and live by new beliefs and values.

- Leaders 'live' their beliefs, communicate them via teams and act on their beliefs by investing in people.
- Leaders become 'the voice of the customers' in their organizations.
- Leaders realized customer-focused quality strategy is no 'quick fix'.

The survey conducted by Business International (a company owned by the Economist Group) in 1990 showed that the key drivers of corporate strategic directions were customer satisfaction, quality leadership and innovation. The key objectives of global organizational structure were customer responsiveness, profit orientation and quality.

In the 1980s and early 1990s, following the focus on customer service and customers' needs, many organizations initiated various projects to bring about the 'voice of the customer' in the organizations. Among such projects were:

- **Customer focus group**: A panel of customers is interviewed about the company and their competitors; customers/prospects are invited to discuss a particular topic, for example, on-time deliveries or product design.
- **Visits to customers**: Taking cross-functional groups from the organizations.
- **Customer councils**: Groups of customers who meet regularly to advise the company.
- **Questionnaires/postal surveys/telephone surveys**.
- **Customer research**: Organizations finding out who are their major customers, what proportion of business they represent, what are their growth prospects and the degree of relationship and contacts they have with the company.
- **Customer care training**.

Most of the consultants and management experts have been advising companies to align their organizational activities to meet customers' needs. Service excellence has to be the 'core' of corporate strategy (Figure 4.5).

Self assessment

Those companies who have embarked upon self assessment quality initiatives and working along the lines of the

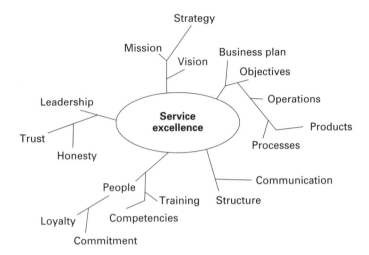

Figure 4.5   Service excellence as a core of corporate strategy and structure

European Quality Model have to demonstrate the organization's success in satisfying the needs and expectations of their customers.

The assessment is related to what the company is achieving in relation to the satisfaction of its external customers. Evidence is needed of the customers' perception of the company's products, services and customer relationships, and additional measures relating to the satisfaction of the company's customers. Twenty per cent of the total marks are assigned to meeting this result.

Evidence is required in terms of meeting product/service specifications, reliability, delivery, service performance, sales support, accessibility of key staff, responsiveness to customer needs, warranties/guarantees, value for money and fair treatment.

Additional measures relate to repeat business, lost business, complaints, defect rates, delivery performance, awards received, publicity, and so on.

External customers are defined as 'The immediate customers of the company and all other customers in the chain of distribution of its products and service through to the final customers'.

Case study: DHL International (UK) Ltd

Nick Butcher, managing director of DHL International (UK), presented a paper at a conference organized by the Economist Conferences at which he outlined how to change from providing 'lip service to true commitment'. In his view there are some very simple tactics that can be deployed to fulfil the objective of outstanding customer service. These are:

* Stay close to the customer.
* Decide close to the customer.
* Understand the customer.
* Manage the customer.
* Communicate with the customer.

He then went on to share some of DHL's experience.

DHL is the world's largest air express carrier, employing some 34 000 people in 222 countries around the world. We are in more countries than American Express – even Coca-Cola.

Customers? Oh yes, we have plenty of them – more than 1 million world-wide – and to service these customers, we have 60 of our own aircraft and 1882 stations. We also use nearly all of the commercial airlines in the world. Every 50 seconds a plane takes off carrying a DHL consignment.

In the UK, DHL is the market leader with a 67 per cent share in the international air express documents market and a 46 per cent share of those parcels that move through air express. We have over 2000 employees and satisfy 135 000 customers through 40 strategically placed stations.

As you would imagine our customer base is as diverse as commerce itself. We have clients who are one-man bands and those who are multinationals and a whole raft in between. Interestingly, 92 out of the UK's top 100 companies are clients of DHL UK.

Four or five years ago, things were not going as well as we would have liked. We felt that our service needed improving to provide a brand leader. Our people needed re-focusing and our organization, apt though it was for the 1970s and 1980s, was not right for the 1990s. So what did we do?

Let me turn to staying close to the customer. Until a few years ago DHL was a functionally driven organization where any given station or office would have someone responsible for managing the operations – the couriers, sorting and so on – and someone else responsible for managing sales. We decided to do away with this functional allocation of responsibilities and have attempted to create mini-businesses at the lowest possible level in order to take decision making closer to the customers. This resulted in the creation of station managers, who in turn report to area directors. There are three area directors in the UK and they have very clear profit and loss responsibility, driven by customer retention and acquisition, and cost control. They are responsible for managing the pick-up from and delivery cycle to customers. As you can imagine, very tight objectives are set in this area.

In effect, we have decentralized a centralized structure. In the process we have eliminated several layers of management, moving from a structure where the managing director was seven levels away from the courier to one today where he is four levels away. We have organized our business so that a small business group has responsibility for customers and service in their areas.

All this is fine, but for any organization like this to work, decisions need to be made as close to the customer as possible. This means that in our case a functionally managed organization had to devolve the power 'to decide' down the hierarchical chain to the lowest level possible. This was not easy and we still have some way to go in truly empowering our staff.

We all know of examples where companies start with a product and because of customer intimacy grow from nothing to be successful – pushed on by the entrepreneur. But then along comes the corporate acquirer – constraints grow and the business flattens. Organizations are changed to save costs – to provide shareholder returns – and that customer intimacy is replaced by a drive towards operational excellence. The cost, however, can be enormous, since this also involves a major culture change in the business. It generally takes decision-making into the centre and up to the highest level possible. Whilst this may be necessary for long-term survival, customer service suffers in the short term.

I have come into organizations where numbers and procedures clearly count for more than anything else and I have seen first hand the negative impact this has on an organization. As a result, I am wholeheartedly committed to empowerment. But let's be clear about this, empowerment carries a large element of risk with it. Most of us are used to working in environments where there are clear rules but if tomorrow all of those rules disappeared, there would be chaos and we would probably end up demotivated and confused. Moving to a fully empowered organization is not easy; to make it to work there needs to be people at the top who believe in and care passionately about the successful integration of empowerment into the organization so that it becomes an enduring and natural way of operating.

The recent problems of IBM have meant that the company is nowadays often cited as an example of how not to do things. However, going back to the 'good old days', Thomas Watson, CEO of IBM, understood that decentralized organizations cultivated closer relationships with clients. He also fully appreciated the importance of empowerment and individual initiative; a one-word motto – 'think' – summed up how he expected his salesforce support and service teams to conduct themselves when interacting with customers – a motto I am sure many of the companies represented in his room this morning – mine included – may consider taking up.

Understanding customers: listen and learn are the watchwords here. As with all market leaders, we study the marketplace very thoroughly, and invest heavily in research – both quantitative and qualitative – to gain a full understanding of the image and awareness of DHL in the marketplace but also of customers' satisfaction and needs.

Simple logic tells us that to serve customers well their needs should be thoroughly understood. Returning to the work of Treacy and Wiersema, their view is that it is vital to have an obsession with the process of solution development. Again fairly logical. The approach we have taken at DHL to gain a more in-depth understanding of our customers' wants is to use market research to build up a hierarchy of the needs of our customer base.

Hierarchy of needs and wants – summary

1. **Fundamental factors**
   - Service reliability
   - On-time delivery
   - Security/handling
   - Worldwide delivery.

2. **Efficacy factors**
   - Pricing/tariff
   - Tracking and tracing
   - Documentation
   - Pick-up/application

3. **Added value factors**
   - Personnel relationships
   - Business partner

Now if I had asked you beforehand to write down what you expect from the DHLs of this world – you would probably come up with the same issues – but their order here may surprise you.

You can see that there are fundamental factors to do with performance, reliability, value for money, but not price. Customers are prepared to pay a higher price for service reliability and on-time delivery. The next stage of needs is concerned with factors which streamline their interface with DHL. Finally there is a range of factors that add value to the service in an intangible way. These are to do with personal and partnership relationships.

Having established this hierarchy of needs, it is important to research how well a business is doing against them, and to change where necessary. Here is what our research tells us.

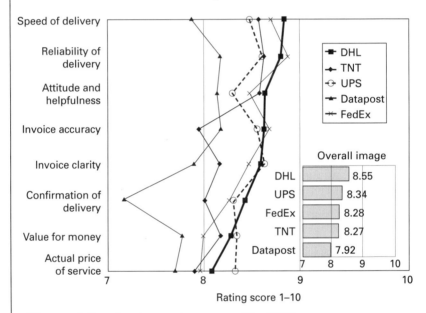

Customer image profile: total sample

DHL versus main competitors: October 1994

Figure 4.6   Customer image profile: DHL

Part of our research programme allows us to split out the various aspects of the business. As you can see this highlights the DHL courier. I think you will agree that, without a shadow of a doubt, this reiterates that people are a company's most important asset. But more of this later. Using this information we are then able to make changes to the way we conduct our business.

A word of caution. In striving to make your customer king, beware of the knowledge you have turning to ignorance. It is all too easy to do the research, get the fix on the current needs of your customers and then stand still. It is only continuous research that will ensure you are still understanding your customer needs, and that positive progress is being made.

At this stage I would like to say a few words about quality. These days a consistently high quality of product or service is a pre-requisite to entering every market. Without it, a company does not get to the first post. Customers – large and small alike – rightfully expect the highest standards not just the first time they buy a product or use a service, but each and every time.

The whole process of quality is about continually satisfying agreed customer requirements – internal as well external. By definition alone it keeps you on the path of customer service excellence. Any companies considering going down the quality route should bear in mind that universally recognized standards are extremely useful to achieve – they are goals to strive towards – but the hard work really starts once the standard has been achieved and the procedures have to be maintained!

Managing customers is another important ingredient, since during the lifespan of an account there is inevitably a shift in the demands a customer places on its suppliers. At DHL we call this our 'cradle to grave' philosophy.

Cradle to grave is an approach to communication planning which is responsive to the current requirements and potential of a customer as their relationship grows with a supplier.

As in any relationship – personal or business – there are various different phases. What 'cradle to grave' enables you to do is establish exactly where in the customer lifecycle you are currently sitting and to tailor your communications precisely to address that position.

For example, at the beginning of a new business relationship, you don't want to be talking about the benefits of long-term strategic partnerships, but introducing your company and its various different product ranges to meet the customer's needs. Taking on the 'cradle to grave' concept will ensure that new accounts will not be bombarded with communications aimed at longer-standing customers. It also ensures that existing clients do not receive a plethora of communications saying who you are and what business you are in!

You may think there is nothing radical to this process and you would be right. The difficult bit is not understanding the philosophy, but rather in marketing departments around the country being able to identify the current stage in the customer lifecycle of every customer they have and the personal business to be gained from each and every customer.

Sales people have always held this information. But to date direct marketing executives based back at head office have not been privy to these details as more often than not it is all filed away in the minds of the salesforce. With the need for this in-depth customer knowledge now identified, it is vital that good analysis tools are used to map the purchasing trends of customers over time to get a fix on the overall potential of a particular client. Then it is back to the marketing execs to trigger the next most appropriate stage of contact.

Lastly, we need to communicate with customers. This is obvious, but what and how and when are the more difficult questions to answer. The marketing slogans of the 1990s are 'database marketing' and 'relationship marketing'. Will these disappear? I don't think so, because I believe that whilst most companies will claim to employ these techniques, most only scratch the surface. Database marketing is really quite simple. It's using the information held about your customers, analysing it every which way to determine what they do with your product, why they do it, when they use it and so on. And who uses it. It does sound very simple but it isn't, yet harnessed to new technology, a very powerful market segmentation can be performed, similar groups looked for and specific marketing campaigns devised.

As an example, the salesman visiting his customer will look at his laptop just before the meeting and will see that yesterday's problem has been resolved. As a result his meetings can be sympathetic to all circumstances and anticipate and respect the agenda of the customer. The greater the depth of database management, the greater the potential sophistication for segmentation.

Then we have relationship marketing. Quite simply this is spreading the word to an individual or groups of people in a way that is personal to their needs. But the crucial difference between relationship marketing and mailshots to a named individual is that relationship marketing results in a two-way, continuing dialogue. You build an important continuous relationship.

Research shows that customers respond to a relationship – even when they say that they won't. And in these relationships the right messages have to be passed.

Brann, the direct marketing company, and the Henley Centre have done some interesting work here. This is not specific to our industry but it shows that customers want to be in control of the information they receive. Force information down their throats and the opposite effect will be achieved – dissatisfaction. And customers prefer contact in one of the three modes:

• phone
• mail
• in person

So customers welcome contact – but the right type of contact.

Of course all this takes place in a world of PCs, multimedia and CD-ROMs. We cannot ignore the role technology is playing and if today's impact is frightening, just think about tomorrow. The technological developments that are taking place in the world today defy belief. More technological advancements have been made in the last fifteen years or so than in the preceding history of the whole world. Think about it. There was the Ice Age, the Bronze Age and Iron Age, then not much else really until the Industrial Revolution. Louis Thomas said the greatest accomplishment of eighteenth century science was the discovery of human ignorance. This can equally be applied to the twentieth century.

Many cynics were citing the advent of certain technologies – the fax and EDI in particular – as the demise of our particular business at DHL. The ironic thing is that this couldn't be further from the truth. As we know, faxes abound in every office, theoretically negating the need for the hard copy document. But, as a quick DHL plug, I am delighted to say our document business is growing on an average 12 per cent year on year.

Providing customer service through technology will be a key feature of the new generation. Compare what we as ordinary consumers can do today but couldn't twenty years ago. Telephone banking and insurance are examples, with First Direct and Direct Line as the early innovators. Ring up and your details are on a computer screen in seconds. Pick the phone up in an hotel to book a morning call, or order room service – and they refer to you by name. All technology driven.

Then there are call centres dealing with incoming calls. We at DHL are by no means the largest in this area but we handle more than three million calls a year and the management of this, the supporting technology and the messages we give and take are a very important element of our business. Automatic call distribution equipment so vital for today's call centres will combine with call line identification which allows the incoming caller to be identified and allocated to a particular group or individual, thus providing a very personal touch to the regular caller since they can be put through to their regular contact. Work we have done shows that customers want to be treated as individuals – that personal touch. It's that building of relationships again. Beyond 2000 vision and voice combined will be quite a normal event.

Look at American Express. You ring them in Italy or Germany or France and you get through to customer services in – wait for it – Brighton. You speak to nationals and American Express make it their business to ensure that employees have up-to-date local knowledge – by providing the daily paper, magazines and up-to-the-minute news topics. This is using the power of technology to help keep costs down but with no adverse impact on service – just the opposite in fact.

We in DHL have sophisticated customer automation systems but they are costly and for the smaller users probably unnecessarily comprehensive. We now have a piece of Windows-based software that we will be offering customers who send an average of twenty shipments a month. The software not only enables the customer to book a collection, it prints all the documentation and provides track and trace facilities, all of which was unthinkable ten years ago.

So getting to the customer and harnessing technology are two very important imperatives for the customer service successes of the future. One has to assume that the product itself is capable of sustaining a leading market position. If it can, then there is of course one crucial element in any business that harnesses these imperatives and makes the difference.

I refer of course to people.

Let me move on to employees. How many annual reports have you seen – or even written, that contain the following messages:

- Our employees are our most valuable asset
- Their commitment and loyalty are essential to a company's well-being, and
- Thank you, to our employees, our result would not have been possible without you etc?

But does this message have any impact on employees when their belief is that life is somewhat different?

- You're expendable
- We must cut costs if we are to maintain our leading position.
- Good bye.

That is the reality for most companies today, I am afraid.

Yet customer satisfaction starts with employee satisfaction.

I would say, virtually without exception, companies that produce customer service at the top of their agenda have a particular company culture. I know that is true of my company. Since joining last year and having travelled extensively throughout the DHL network, wherever I go, there is a certain buzz amongst the staff – something intrinsically DHL.

In customer driven companies you won't see automatons – returning to Watson's motto – you see thinking people, multi-skilled, flexible and motivated employees. In a service industry, such as ours, complaints are inevitable. What always surprises me however, is the number of satisfied customers that feel they need to write and congratulate us on the level of service – a particular courier or a customer service agent. That's when it makes it all worth while.

The management of your people is always crucial. If you want the best people out there to be working for your company, it means being involved in the recruiting and interviewing process. And not always going for the logical high-flyer! For example, Sony sends its recruiters out to the engineering schools and universities looking for technical talent. They do not got directly to the doors of the straight 'A' students but look for creativity and adaptability. The general all-rounders able to work under any situation.

I believe there are major challenges facing today's managers. Somehow they have to manage and develop a highly motivated workforce capable of developing and maintaining customer service excellence – but in an environment where there is more uncertainty about their future than ever before. I would not care to be a manager setting out to make my mark in today's commercial world. But I do expect to recruit managers that can cut it in the 1990s and whose ambition and dynamism will take them forward as key players in the success of DHL in the new millennium.

Another word of warning. Organizations are not just about organograms and structures, they are about understanding the needs of employees – which are changing constantly – and responding to those needs in a sensitive manner. There are individually feminine and masculine characteristics of these needs and I for one, believe there are few managers out there who are equipped to handle both issues.

Understanding, however, is definitely a two-way street. Yes, every organization has a duty to understand the needs of its staff, but in return employees have to understand what is expected of them and where they fit in to the overall objective of achieving the company's projected results.

Introducing a level of healthy rivalry into the company culture also helps increase performance levels and standards. At DHL this healthy competition comes into play through our 'station of the year' programme. A mandatory league which encourages team work and sets out a series of key performance indicators against which every station has to perform.

Employee satisfaction is also derived from having an informed staff – keeping them abreast of developments on a regular and timely basis. At DHL we go to great efforts to communicate with all members of staff. We produce six internal communications videos a year all involving staff, a monthly magazine for employees, radio cassette tapes, regular briefings, management by running around, a national conference (where 1800 people out of a possible 2200 gave up their Sunday voluntarily this year to attend in Birmingham) and an employee survey. I don't think many companies would beat our pro-gramme. And what do our employees tell us? They tell us we don't communicate enough.

I think there are two problems here. And I expect they are both common ones. Firstly, the grapevine works faster than official communications. And secondly, the more you tell people, the more they want to know. We live in an intensive media world that has an insatiable appetite to uncover more. This sets the scene for employee communication. Everyone wants to know more – including the gossip!

Spreading the word to employees will be vitally important in the years ahead.

And where will our employees be as we pound our message? Technology – again those personal computers, modems, down the line, up the line, remote monitoring – means that homeworking is part of today's environment. It will definitely continue to grow providing more of a challenge to us in the future – but then we'll plop our videos onto the Internet and our magazine and what the hell – our conference too – and let BT do the rest. Slightly eerie – but it's coming.

As we look beyond the year 2000 business will be seeking at the very least to maintain profitability – and in most cases to grow it both in quantum and quality. I believe that a key element of any business strategy must be to achieve that state of mind amongst customers and employees – of loyalty. Customer service policies will be one of the key tactics that will help in achieving this state. Think about it now because there are many already surfing the wave. Get up on your boards and go!

And finally service comes from people. All people make a difference – some positive some negative. Informed and involved people make a positive difference.

The presentation on DHL highlights the importance of technology, empowerment and trust on delivering customer service in an age of intensifying competition.

The following article appeared in European Quality, Vol. 1, No. 5. It is a story of how ICL learned to serve customers in order to survive business crisis.

Case study: ICL

ICL's quality drive started from a crisis precipitated by IBM, but largely of the company's own making. Its heritage was that of a technically inventive company whose customer base was the mainly captive market of the UK government, defence, state-run health and public utility sectors. Its core product range, the 2900 series of multi-frames, was arguably technically as good as that of IBM or any other international competitor. But in common with others, ICL products used proprietary operating systems and programming languages. Proprietary embrace requires total confidence in the supplier and confidence that his solution is the best: there is no alternative once the commitment has been made. The old ICL lost that confidence.

In 1980, customer satisfaction, already low, was decimated by the company's introduction of an expensive mainframe range which rendered older software obsolete. A price war started in the industry when IBM effectively dropped its price by 75 per cent on the range of 4300 series mainframes in response to clone products from Fujitsu and Amdahl. These moves, plus the Thatcher Government's instructions to the public sector to introduce open tendering, forced even the most loyal ICL customers to look around. When they did, they were exposed to cheaper, better products with a wider customer base and more software possibilities.

In 1981, when ICL's losses reached £130 million, the company was forced to go to the UK Government for loan guarantees to stay in business. All this meant that a change of management, change of product range and most importantly, a change of attitude from product focus to customer focus was essential.

Robb Wilmot, who took over as managing director in 1981, transformed the company ethos to a market- and customer-led business: 'Technical people tend to think it is the product that sells the product' he said. 'It's not. Organizations sell products'. Out of necessity, costs were ripped out of the company. Layers of bureaucracy vanished along with layers of middle management.

Focus on the possible

The reborn ICL took an early crucial decision to outsource the manufacture of its mainframe processors to Fujitsu. This early partnering exercise helped technical exchange, benchmarking and internal and external focus on strength. Crisis forced managers to look at the price of non-conformance, outsource where logistics and economies of scale dictated, and examine all processes for ways to do things better, cheaper, faster.

These disciplines helped ICL ride out the waves that threatened to overwhelm other European flag carriers such as Bull of France, Germany's Nixdorf and Olivetti of Italy, for whom the crunch came later. Mr Wilmot's legacy was a slimmer business, focused on profitability. It was under the leadership of his successor, Peter Bonfield, that ICL grew the quality culture which Roger Wood, a former director and now group vice-president of Northern Telecom Europe, describes as 'like a stick of rock running right through that organization'.

Building a change culture

Quality control and quality assurance were not a problem at ICL. In fact, ICL's overblown research facilities were, for once, a distinct advantage. When American microchip makers were rubbishing the quality claims of the Japanese and accusing them of 'dumping' on the world market, ICL had the internal resources to test both sides' claims. It found the Japanese were producing cheaper chips with fewer defects per million through quality manufacturing techniques.

However, in a company which was described by Mr Wilmot as 'more like a postgraduate university of computing than a business', Mr Bonfield was faced with endemic resistance to change. He deployed organization-wide initiatives to wake up every employee to the need for proactive thinking. 'In this industry, which is so changeable, if you aren't changing so fast that it really feels painful and is just about on the edge of being do-able, then you are not changing fast enough', he observed.

Change was rapid and fundamental after ICL ceded the manufacture of its mainframe processors to Fujitsu, and the partnership exercise culminated in the Japanese company acquiring 80 per cent of ICL's equity in 1990. Despite predictions that ICL would become a 'screwdriver plant' for Fujitsu mainframes, the Japanese company continues to manufacture processors to ICL specifications. Nor was quality at ICL imported from Japan.

Deliver what you promise

The fundamental change was that of attitude. The company changed in focus from products to customers as its business emphasis shifted from manufacturing and supplying mainframes, minis, personal computers and software to systems integration. Though the company still makes and supplies its own products – indeed manufacturing divisions such as ICL's D2D serve other computer companies – the emphasis is on IT solutions. Systems integration requires a totally different mindset.

ICL aims to supply the best mixture of hardware and software on an open platform, 'to provide our customers with access to a wide and innovative range of software and hardware product, using our links to Fujitsu and our alliances with other companies'. In the brave new world of open systems, where effective monopolies are a thing of the past and IT providers are judged on merit, quality is a key measure of competitiveness. Service excellence and exceeding customer expectations are vital.

Beyond conformance to self-assessment

Quality was used as a key driver for change from the mid-1980s, but took off in 1987 when Jo Goasdoue, formerly of British Airways, was hired as quality director, the first board level appointment of an outside quality expert by a major computer manufacturer. He quickly established a number of objectives, including BS 5750 certification by all divisions. ICL was the first UK company to achieve company-wide BS 5750 certification. Ninety quality improvement teams were established to transmit the quality message across its entire workforce. 'Continuous improvement on a company-wide basis wasn't easy and still is not easy,' says Mr Goasdoue. 'When I joined the company, ICL was exceptionally good at solving problems when they arose, but continuous improvement requires something more.'

From 1987 to 1990, product reliability and on-time delivery improved dramatically. ICL saved $6 million per year in administration costs. There was an 80 per cent reduction in unresolved software faults. Planning cycles were reduced to thirteen days from forty. Inventory fell to $240 million from $385 million and productivity rose by 30 per cent. But focus on non-conformance was not enough. 'A corrective action system fits in very nicely with the requirements of the ISO 9000 standard. Recognition, systems awareness, education and other components will maintain or sustain it, but by themselves these don't actually change anything,' says Estelle Clark, an ICL business quality consultant. 'A corrective action system is reactive, not very customer focused and tries to correct mistakes because they cost money. Our old system could only measure quality in terms of non-conformance. Of course money matters for ICL but conformance is clearly not the most important measure.'

To achieve the goal of continuous improvement and avoid the common trap of allowing conformance to become a goal in itself, the ICL quality team turned to self-assessment and the European Quality Model to drive the next stage of its development. 'Customer satisfaction is conformance quality plus customer care,' states the company in Quality the ICL Way, an internal manual.

The strategic quality model

ICL describes its strategic quality model as 'the framework for harnessing best practice, for encouraging teamwork, sharing knowledge and for making ICL the successful company of which our staff want to be part.' Self-assessment is seen as powerful empowerment tool. 'The strategic quality model has helped a lot of managers understand the importance of processes in terms of business results,' says Mr Goasdoue.

Self-assessment is easier to sell to management teams than ISO 9000 because it helps them to see the link between certification and business results, according to Mrs Clark. 'The first time we introduced the strategic quality model to a group, we were not concerned with detail. Our objective is to get across its usefulness, identify the strengths of a process, discover key opportunities and explore missed opportunities for improvement. As managers became more experienced with the model, we help them find more vigorous, sys- tematic, provable ways of finding out how they can assess processes. But to start with, we make it fun, interesting, quick and light.'

Quality transport

ICL quality initiatives are driven top-down, but the company has iden- tified different levels on which quality deployment works, requiring dif- ferent approaches. Using the transport analogy, quality deployment is split into four distinct areas. At the top are board and strategy reviews – the 'corporate jumbo jet' – an expensive, scheduled mode of trans- port which moves many people but flies infrequently, whose pilots need a lot of training and which requires strict adherence to a lot of rules to keep in the air.

Business groups, which drive the strategic quality model and implement business process redesign, are visualized as a fleet of coaches. The characteristic of this mode of transport is frequent ser- vice, but to fixed schedule, with trained drivers but relatively expen- sive in cost terms.

Quality circles and strategic quality model networks are likened to a fleet of company cars. There are lots of them; they run on demand; are relatively easy to drive; but can only hold a few people. Lastly come bicycles, transport for all. These signify individuals empowered with basic quality tools. There are thousands of these, going any- where at any time. They need few rules and require minimal mainte- nance.

'Setting the strategic objectives at board level is a relatively easy procedure and mistakes can be catastrophic. Driving the strategic quality model at manager level is less costly, but is still relatively inflexible,' Mrs Clark told senior managers at a forum in Madrid earlier in 1995. 'At smaller group level there is more room for manoeuvre, and at the basic level, enthusiasm and self-propelling drive counts for everything. ICL is different from many organizations in that it recognizes the importance of cascading the same directives but sees the task of implementing them as different in each case.'

Applied quality

Business process re-design is not seen as distinct from quality, but is treated as a proactive element of strategic quality model. The approach taken is to 'challenge the why and the how'. Teams ask: Who is the customer? What value is added from a given process? Is the process necessary and when was it last reviewed? From there they look at how the process is measured, determine against whom they are benchmarking and how others might be doing it better. The process is systematic rather than intuitive. 'I see fundamentally no difference between applied quality in a consumer service company and business-to-business organization,' Mr Goasdoue says, 'if, in the final analysis we are talking about organizations which are emotionally committed to customers and thereby obsessed with customer satisfaction.'

Mrs Clark points out that the Deming plan-do-check-act cycle has been used to implement 'systematic process improvement' throughout the organization (see Figure 2.2). Standard quality tools are used here, but alongside the formal process the company has introduced some novel IT-led methods. ICL has a computerized feedback system called dELTA, an electronic suggestion box designed to facilitate continuous improvement. The quality team distributes computer games designed to familiarize staff with quality tools, and electronic voting is used in objective-setting meetings.

Enlightened self-interest

The revitalized company is focused on customer care. Every board member has responsibility for customers, and is available to discuss specific questions. Partnering exercises with clients such as Heineken have been established to cement relationships but also to explore quality improvement from a basis of mutual self-interest.

ICL appears to have pulled off the trick of creating a competitive internal market for its own products and services by virtue of allowing its departments freedom to supply on the outside market. D2D, an ICL manufacturing division, works closely as a supplier with companies such as workstation manufacturer Sun Microsystems, and with other third party equipment manufacturers and vendors.

There are few examples outside the USA of a company revival so comprehensively rooted in quality techniques. ICL shows that recession and the roller-coaster economies in the information technology field can be weathered by a steadfast adherence to quality principles. The business results section of the European Quality Model holds no fears for a company totally focused on customer needs, and committed to self-assessment and a rigorously planned cycle of continuous improvement.

Why some companies find it difficult to deliver service excellence

* Some companies only like to pay 'lip service' to customer satisfaction.
* Some company policies are formulated for companies' convenience. (How often do we still hear 'I am sorry but it is not our company policy...?')
* Many managers are remote from customers.
* Some companies believe that because they have a customer service department or a customer service manager they automatically become customer-driven companies.
* Many employees are not 'empowered' to satisfy customers.
* Many companies do not trust their staff to make decisions or resolve problems.
* Many organizations do not listen to their customers.
* Some organizations do not allocate enough resources to promote excellent customer service.
* Some employees who are still working for the organizations are psychologically retired or work under threat of being made redundant any day. (One such employee told me that his main concern is to check the company's noticeboard every Friday to see if his name appears under those sacked or made redundant – what a way to live!)
* A number of organizations are excellent in appearing to care for their customers. Just because the organizations proclaim 'We are here to serve our customers' does not mean they do it.

Charles Handy, in his book *Inside Organizations* published by the BBC in 1990, relates the following story on the theme of how appearance can be deceptive.

Appearance can be deceptive

I was once asked to talk to a group of managers at the staff college of one of the large banks. It was our formal evening. Everyone was in suits, in rows, in upright chairs. They all wore their names and titles on their lapels. After I had spoken, the session was chaired, very formally, by the head of the college. I was placed for dinner at the top table between the head and his deputy. I never felt that I got close to the student managers or their problems. I mentioned this afterwards, to the head and said that, in my view, such formality did not encourage frank discussion or any real learning, it was all just a kind of ritual.

Next time I went everything was different. This lot of managers were in casual dress. We sat in a large circle of armchairs and sofas. Drinks were available. Supper was a buffet affair. It was very informal and I enjoyed it immensely. I was staggered by the change.

'Is it always like this now?' I asked one of the young managers. 'Oh, no,' he said. 'Just today. Look' and he showed me a paper pinned on the notice board headed 'Orders for the Day': 'In conformity with the wishes of our speaker tonight', it read, 'dress will be informal, the session will be held in the Reading Room, not the Lecture Theatre, where drinks and supper will also be available. First names are to be used. These orders apply to this session only.'

'You see,' he said, 'it's all for you.'

Outward and visible signs do not always mean what they say.

Source: From Inside Organizations by Charles Handy with the permission of BBC Worldwide Limited.

'Horror stories' of customer service

- A customer wanted to buy a washing machine and visited one of the well-known distributors of electrical goods based in Croydon. She decided to spend nearly £500 to get a washing machine manufactured by a well-known brand name company. After she purchased the machine she was told by a sales assistant to purchase an extended warranty because these machines break down very often and it will be cost-effective to have an extended warranty.

  Now I realize the assistant was keen to sell an extended

warranty but to make such a statements these days when all manufacturers are striving for product quality, how can manufacturers 'allow' distributors to discredit the products?

- A shoe shop in London had a framed statement saying 'We care for our customers'. A foreign lady asked the sales assistant in this shop for size six shoes. The assistant went downstairs and fetched the shoes for the customer. After trying them on the lady said, 'I think I need one size bigger'. The assistant remarked; 'Lady, I went down to get for you the size you wanted. I am not going to go up and down just because you cannot make up your mind.' What a customer service!

- A secretary in an insurance company which has recently been re-engineered told the customer she should speak to another department and explain her problem. When asked to transfer her call to the appropriate department she said 'I am sorry I do not have time to look for which department should handle your query and in any case it is not my job to keep on transferring calls to other departments. If I did so I will not be able to do my job.'

There are numerous other 'horror stories' of bad customer service provided by utilities companies, transport companies, well-known manufacturers and distributors. Reconciling such treatment to customers with alleged interest in customers by businesses is sometimes difficult.

It pays to advertise?

A tiger met a lion as they drank beside the pool.
'Tell me,' said the tiger, 'Why are you always roaring like a fool.'
'It's not so foolish,' said the lion with a twinkle in his eyes.
'They call me King of Beasts; it pays to advertise.'
A little rabbit overheard, and ran home like a streak.
He thought he'd try the lion's plan but his roar was just a squeak.
And a hungry fox that morning had his breakfast in the woods;

The moral: it does not pay to advertise unless you can deliver the goods.

Anonymous

Delighting customers

It does not matter how much emphasis is put on delivering good or excellent customer service; what matters at the end of the day is if people and especially front-line people in an organization have the feelings, will and commitment to serve the customers in a delightful way. One can set the procedures and produce award winning manuals but if the employees are treated badly or have the bad feelings about the organizations they work for or if they have the feeling 'I only work here' then all the efforts to deliver service excellence are going to be frustrated.

Commitment is a two-sided coin (Figure 4.7). On one side employees should give their full commitment to the organization they work for and subscribe to the organization's mission and on the other side the organization has to give its commitment of employability, fair consideration and treatment to employees. This is the nature of the 'psychological contract' that exists between employees and employers nowadays. Without such a contract there will be neither people satisfaction nor customer satisfaction.

'Hearts and minds' of employees

Winning the hearts and minds of employees should be one of the strategic objectives of any organization. Many implementation strategies in practice miss this very vital fact. People-related issues are categorized as 'soft' issues and very often very little attention is paid to this aspect. If you research on the main reasons for failures of total quality management or business process re-engineering it will boil down to people rather than structure or processes. Without leadership, commitment, competencies and trust failures are guaranteed. Yet why is it that very little attention is paid to the people aspect

Figure 4.7   Two-sided commitment

in numerous books written on benchmarking, empowerment and business process re-engineering?

One of the key success factors on the people side should be the 'I'm OK. You're OK' factor. The 'I'm OK. You're OK' syndrome should relate to the feeling of employees towards their organizations and towards customers, internally and externally.

Eric Berne developed transactional analysis (TA) as a psychoanalytical approach to therapy. However, the ideas and techniques that it offers for looking at how we interact with others (colleagues, bosses, customers) are easily applied to everyday situations.

Interacting with others is a skill. Like any other skill it has to be understood, acquired and practised. Transactional analysis has some explanations on the nature of our behaviour and inter-personal transactions. According to transactional analysis theory three states exist within people. They are 'the child (C)', 'the adult (A)' and 'the parent (P)'.

The parent state consists of all the rules and the policies recorded from authority figures during the childhood. (Think of something you do now which is just like something one of your parents used to do.) These messages are played back in different situations. Some of these messages assume caring mode (I'm OK) and others critical mode (I'm not OK). Quite often when we follow rules, procedures and the policies of the company and make sure our staff follow these as well we are in 'parent ego state'.

The adult state is logical, reasonable and rational. It differentiates between the 'felt concept' of life in the childhood state and 'taught concept' of life in the parent state. Behaviour in this state is characterized by problem-solving and rational decision-making. When employees are empowered and resolve problems on their own initiatives they are in 'adult ego state'.

The child state is related to 'feeling'. People's behaviour in this state is driven by their feelings ('I only work here' or 'My company does not care for me').

All people behave from these three ego states at different times. The boundaries between these states are fragile and indistinct. There are three types of transactions, namely, complementary, crossed and ulterior. A complementary transaction is one in which the response comes from the ego state that was addressed.

A crossed transaction is one in which the response comes from a different ego state to that which was addressed. When a crossed transaction occurs, the interaction will not continue in the way intended by the first speaker.

An ulterior transaction includes an unspoken message in addition to the overt interaction. The recipient may respond to either although the greatest psychological impact will be through the unspoken message.

Problems arise when transactions become crossed. In this situation individuals read things between the lines. When a manager says to the subordinate 'Can you do this properly', the subordinate immediately reads into this statement imply-ing 'You normally do not do it properly.'

Whenever people are transacting, be they at home or at work, 'strokes' are being exchanged. Strokes may be positive or negative and they are 'give-stokes' (giving) and 'get-strokes' (receiving).

In general people adopt the following life positions:

'I'm OK. You're OK.'
'I'm OK. You're not OK.'
'I'm not OK. You're not OK.'

It is very useful to understand the importance of transac-tional analysis and to train employees in exchanging trans-actions and acquiring inter-personal skills. Open transac-tions facilitate effective communications but crossed trans-actions indicate the 'I'm not OK' feeling and it stops people listening to others (customers). To generate the 'I'm OK. You're OK' feeling there has to be concern for self and con-cern for others. In relation to providing service excellence the employee has to be in the 'I'm OK. You're OK' box in Figure 4.8.

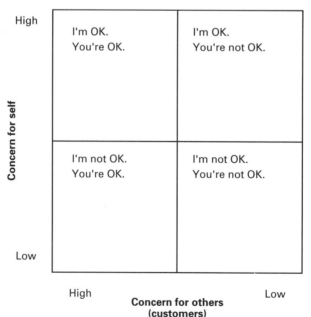

Figure 4.8   Concern for self and customers

Employees also view their situation from three perspectives. They are: What I like to do, What I have to do, and What I am able to do.

Trust is also the major driving force in injecting the 'I'm OK' feeling. It has become the most important factor in achieving effective empowerment. Trust has also become one of the key attributes of a successful leader in the 1990s. Trust comes about when there is a series of positive encounters. Such positive encounters are characterized by allowing people to make mistakes, empowering your staff to make decisions, open communication and fair treatment. In the climate of downsizing and re-engineering, leaders and captains of industry have to work hard to win trust.

One way of earning trust is to make it very explicit in the strategy that the company cares for its customers and employees. Platitudes are not enough and often they backfire on organizations. Company strategy should explicitly reflect three dimensions. One dimension should reflect structure, products and processes to deliver corporate objectives, the second dimension should reflect customer service and the need to deliver service excellence and the third dimension should show the concern for employees.

In a constantly changing environment some companies are now turning inward in search of 'soul' as a way to foster creativity and motivate leaders. An article in *Business Week* (June 1995) states that there is now a spirituality movement in the corporation and the object is to create a sense of meaning and purpose at work and connection between the company and the people.

What matters at the end of the day is not searching for 'soul' but the communion between the hearts and minds of the organizations, employees and the customers. If enough attention is paid by the companies to make sure that their employees do not burn out and that they are a valuable asset and create positive encounters and trust, then they will assume a position of 'I'm OK. You're OK' and service excellence will be delivered. Focus on personal development of employees is going to be the key differentiating factor for successful and excellent organizations in the late 1990s and the twenty-first century. As Sandra Vandermerwe, the author of *From Tin Soldiers to Russian Dolls*, wrote: 'A focus on customers is an attitude rather than a task, a state of mind as opposed to a functional responsibility.'

Relationship marketing

Once employees' frame of mind is geared to customers, organizations can start building up long-term 'win-win' relationships with their key customers. According to Kotler, in relationship marketing, transactions move from being negotiated each time to being routinized. Profitability will eventually be enhanced by building and maximizing mutually beneficial relationships.

However, relationship marketing cannot be practised by all organizations. Some experts recommend relationship marketing with customers who have long time horizons and high switching costs.

That's not my job

This is a story about four people named Everybody, Somebody, Anybody, and Nobody.

There was an important job to be done to improve customer service and Everybody was sure that Somebody would do it.

Anybody could have done it, but Nobody did it.

Somebody got angry about that, because it was Everybody's job. Everybody thought Anybody could do it.

But Nobody realized that Everybody wouldn't do it.

It ended up that Everybody blamed Somebody, when Nobody did what Anybody could have done.

Source unknown

Selected reading

Sarah Cook (1992). *Customer Care*. Kogan Page.

Gertz and Baptista (1995). *Grow to be Great*. The Free Press.

Thomas Harris (1973). *I'm OK – You're OK*. Pan Books.

Tom Peters (1992). *Liberation Management*. Macmillan, London.

Tom Peters (1995). *In Pursuit of Wow*. Vintage Books.

Sandra Vandermerwe (1993). *From Tin Soldiers to Russian Dolls*. Butterworth-Heinemann.

Richard C. Whiteley (1991). *The Customer Driven Company*. Century.

Various papers presented at 'Service Conference' 1995 organized by the Economist Conferences.

5 Business process re-engineering

There is nothing more difficult to take in hand, more perilous to conduct, or more uncertain in its success than to take the lead in the introduction of a new order of things.

Unknown

Summary

- Business process re-engineering is a fundamental rethinking and radical redesign of business processes to achieve 'quantum leap' improvements in business results.
- The practice of re-engineering has become part of management vocabulary in the 1990s.
- Hammer and Champy's view on business process re-engineering.
- Dramatic improvements associated with business re-design. Even in Asia organizations have embraced the re-engineering initiatives.
- The case studies: Taco Bell, Rank Xerox, Hall Mark.
- Key characteristics and benefits of process re-engineering.
- Critical success factors.
- Why some business process re-engineering initiatives fail. Learning from other organizations' mistakes.
- How to re-engineer: step by step guide.
- Approaches to change initiatives.
- Relationship between re-engineering and corporate strategy.
- Re-engineering and people.

Starting from scratch

Michael Hammer and Jim Champy's book *Re-engineering the Corporation* became the best-seller around the world as soon as it was published in 1995. People were buying this book to find out the nature of business process re-engineering (BPR) and what was so special about it. Some simply wanted to be assured that what they have been doing for a number of years in initiating changes in their organizations was indeed business process re-engineering.

To Hammer and Champy business process re-engineering means reinventing or starting from scratch. It means throwing away all the rule books and old procedural manuals and discarding fundamental assumptions. According to Champy and Hammer, at the heart of BPR lies the notion of 'discontinuous thinking'.

Many organizations even today are built around Adam Smith's idea of division of labour. This involves the specialization and sub-division of tasks, the minimizing and standardizing of tasks and skills. The story of the division of labour in a pin factory as told by Adam Smith in his book *The Wealth of Nations*, written in 1776, became not only popular but very influential. According to Adam Smith, division of labour brings about an increase of dexterity in every worker, it saves time and facilitates the invention of a great number of machines which enhance significantly each worker's productivity.

Initially Smith's idea was taken on board in the factories and subsequently it was extended to other businesses. Specialization led to compartmentalization of businesses into various divisions such as production, finance, marketing and sales. Many organizations even today are functionalized in this way.

The other movement which has left its mark in many organizations was the philosophy of scientific management led by Frederick W. Taylor. His book *The Principles of Scientific Management*, published in 1911, advocated the development of science of management with clearly stated rules and laws, scientific selection and training of workers and division of tasks and responsibilities between workers and management. Taylor recommended that there should be a detailed analysis of each job, using the techniques of method study and time study, in order to find the method of working that would bring about the largest average rate of production, the so called 'one best way'.

He also advocated issuing detailed written instructions, training and incentive payments in order to ensure that jobs were performed in the approved manner.

Many of the assumptions implicit in the scientific management approach still have considerable influence on the design and organization of work. Such assumptions and outmoded rules have to be discarded completely for business process re-engineering to succeed. Business process re-engineering is the fundamental rethinking and radical redesign of business processes to achieve dramatic improvements in critical, contemporary measures of performance, such as cost, quality, service and speed. Hammer and Champy stress that the change must be **fundamental** and **radical**, the focus should be on **process** and the improvements must be **dramatic**.

Short glimpses of dramatic improvements due to re-engineering

* IBM Credit Corporation slashed seven day turnaround to four hours without an increase in head count.
* Kodak re-engineered its product development process by introducing concurrent engineering. It introduced its new disposable camera in thirty-five rather than seventy weeks.
* Reuters slashed the time needed to respond to customers from weeks to days.
* The National and Provincial Building Society's chief executive officer David O'Brien created the 'process-driven organization'. He says, 'the only thing you can do in a volatile business environment is to create an organization that has the capacity to live in a permanent state of change'.
* Continental Canada Insurance embarked upon a re-engineering project which took fifteen months. Personal Automobile Insurance outperformed the industry average for profitability by 30 per cent. Twelve underwriters now do the work of 60 and 120 agents now service a more profitable base of service than 700 did previously.
* National Health Service trust in the UK has cut the cycle time from twelve weeks to less than a day. The trust wanted to reduce the time taken for an out-patient clinic to produce diagnostics to cut down administration costs and

to increase the satisfaction of patients and staff involved.

- AT&T Global Business reduced order processing ten-fold and 35 per cent reduction in headcount.
- Bell Atlantic achieved a five-fold reduction in cycle time as far as customer services are concerned and the labour costs decreased from $88 million to $6 million.
- Texas Instruments reduced process cycle time by well over 50 per cent.
- Hall Mark cards reduced the new product development cycle from between two and three years to one year.
- ABB, a Swedish-Swiss manufacturing giant, began re-engineering before the term was invented. It removed layers of management and halved the development time of its products.
- *The Economist* of 23 October 1993 reported IBM's efforts to return to profit. It embarked upon re-engineering by examining all the operational 'processes' that take products from the drawing board to the customers. The BPR became pivotal to IBM's success. The new products are now designed around modules which are interchangeable. This approach means fewer components and reaping economies of scale. Products are now updated faster and more cheaply.
- At the Thai Farmers Bank customers are served within minutes instead of having to wait half an hour or more.

There are many other success stories related to Motorola, American Express, Proctor & Gamble and so on. The most quoted example of process re-engineering is the accounts receivable operation of the Ford Motor Company. The operation once employed 500 people shuffling purchase orders and invoices amongst themselves. Now 125 people do the same job faster. The clerk at the receiving dock, using a computer to reconcile orders instantly, accepts orders on his own authority and issues payment. No more paper shuffling! IT has become the real enabler for the introduction of radical change. IT can also play a key role in the mapping and analysis of processes.

Re-engineering and organizational change – case studies

The following three cases are taken from the *European Management Journal.*

Taco Bell (1983-1992)

Context

* Negative growth (–16 per cent) in a growing industry (+6 per cent).
* Becoming smaller and less profitable.
* Assuming what was good for the customer without asking.
* Top down command and control organization, multiple-layers of management.
* Operational handbooks for everything – too much complexity (micromanaging).
* Focus on internal processes not on customer

Goals

* Turn regional Mexican-American restaurant to a 'national force'.
* Re-organization of human resources to be more innovative, customer focused.
* Dramatic redesign of operational systems.
* Reduce costs of all non-value adding activities.

Successful elements
Culture

* Created a vision – thought the (unthinkable) belief that they are a retail company not a manufacturer.
* Understood they needed to create a true paradigm shift (customer focus).
* They expected resistance and were ready to deal with it.
* Viewed re-engineering as a continuous process, new growth, new ideas, mentality that change begets change.

Process

* Turn customers into key element of TB business proposition, ask customers what they want.
* Focus on enhancing activities that bring value to the customer, change or eliminate those that do not (customer was the starting point).

Structure

* Top management commitment, hands-on visits to people involved.
* Eliminated management layers.
* Redefined nearly every job and change job titles to reflect new responsibilities and required skills, creation of market manager position.
* Empowerment, 'You are in charge now' mentality (P&L and performance measures).
* Managing by exception encourages innovation and empowerment.

Technology

* Every technological innovation had to prove that it enhanced service and reduced costs.
* Advanced IT systems.
* TACO system eliminated paperwork and administration time.

Challenges/pitfalls
Culture

* Greatest enemy was tradition-bound ideas to which many employees subscribed.

Structure

* Loss of skilled people.

Results
* Rethinking of who customer is (customer was someone who ate at TB, customer now defined as everyone who eats).
* Increased earnings by 31 per cent.
* Growing (22 per cent) in stagnant market.
* Higher customer satisfaction (tracked on a continuous basis).
* Increased peak capacity.
* Lower average pricing.

Rank Xerox, UK (1986-1991)

Context

* General recession impacting industry.
* Strategic shift forward providing integrated office system solution.
* Revenue and profits down.
* Functional organization with strong emphasis on marketing sales and service.

- Independent measurement/improvement of activities.
- Ineffective in capitalizing on technological excellence.
- No responsibility taken for overall processes.
- Obsolete information systems.

Goals

- Create integrated organization and systems to grow and offer integrated products.
- Create an orientation to business processes that cuts across functions.

Successful elements
Culture

- Clear set of corporate goals.
- Policy deployment; communication of mission, objectives of the organization and how they relate to the employees.

Process

- Focus on processes that directly touch customers (prioritization of areas to redesign; customer satisfaction, financial management, personnel management).
- Created high-level objective for each process.
- Appraisal of external environment.
- Pilot of most important processes with two dedicated full-time teams; front-end process addressed with re-engineering approach; back-end process approached with process improvement.

Structure

- Asked senior managers to act as a team; processes assigned to individual members.
- Created new cross-functional roles (assignment of director to each).
- New career system focused on facilitation skills and cross-functional management.

Technology

- Realization that IT plays an important role in fundamental changes.

Challenges/pitfalls
Culture

- Inconsistent changes with what people were used to; looked at culture as a result of system development.

Process

- Focused on streamlining existing processes instead of radical change.
- Use of tools forced level of detail and technology competence that made senior management withdraw from the effort.
- Re-engineering approach extended beyond the front end of the process making it difficult to quantify the benefits.

Structure

- Lack of broad organizational support.

Technology

- Heavy focus on system development instead of system change (not much focus on people organization).

Results

- Ensure the organization has become more process oriented.
- Some productivity benefits in building systems.
- Financial improvements (difficult to attribute to BPR only).
- Could find no evidence that the goals were achieved.
- Better understanding of how the company works.
- Billing time reduced from 112 days to 1 day 4 hours.

Hall Mark (1989-1991)

Context

- Customers want more tailored products.
- Customer segments are less homogeneous (increasing in numbers, decreasing in size).
- Small window of opportunity to get customer what he or she wants.
- Market dominance; little threat from competition.

Goals

- 'Work smarter not harder.'
- Pre-emptive competitive strike.
- Reduced time to market (get products to market in less than one year).
- Improve information flow to/from market.

- Develop products/promotional materials that consistently win over buyers and retailers.
- Improve performance at the retail level.
- Create company-wide cross-divisional teamwork (improve connection/co-operation between functions).
- Reduce costs.
- Continuous improvement to quality.

Successful elements
Culture

- Created 'the journey' concept and used as a communication tool (made people believe change is a never-ending process).
- Codified beliefs, values, strategic goals and how they relate to business priorities.
- Sense of ownership; people made to believe that they make a difference.
- Understanding that re-engineering is not a completely planned act (flexibility).
- Realism; staff don't do something because they simply said they would, they do it only if it still makes sense.

Process

- Identified and focused on leverage points (critical parts of the business).
- Clear set of objectives based on improving performance at retail level.
- Top-down driven process.
- Pilots, early wins.
- Moved from sequential product development process to integrated team approach with direct communication linkages (100 people split into nine teams.)

Structure

- Top management buy-in/open support, leading the effort (dedication and allocation of resources as required).
- Commitment of senior executives (time and energy as necessary).
- Communicated what would not change (beliefs, common values).

Technology

- Computerized code POS system.
- Decision support system.
- Involvement of technical people in the design of the system as part of the team.

Challenges/pitfalls
Culture

* Getting people to understand and accept changes, importance of people's perception (beliefs of people that they would be pushed simply to work harder).
* Thinking that more information is better than less.
* Keeping customer focus.

Technology

* Finding and implementing the right technology.

Results

* Improved flow of sales data from Hall Mark speciality stores to HQs (retail information is 'the lifeblood').
* Ability to track effectiveness of a store layout/advertising campaign to reshape how they merchandise and market.
* Integrated team products hit market eight months ahead of schedule.
* Teams review their own work, freeing managers to do other work and eliminating bottlenecks.
* Creation of organizational capability (structure /skills) that will enable Hall Mark to adapt to continuous change.

Source for three case studies: Re-engineering and Organizational Change, by Ascari, Rock and Dutta. *European Management Journal*, Vol. 13, No. 1, March 1995.

The focus of BPR is on processes. A process is defined as 'a set of linked activities that take an input and transforms it to create an output'. Processes in business are categorized into 'core' processes and 'support' processes. A core process creates value by the capabilities it gives the company from competitiveness. In practice it is alleged that there is a mismatch between business process and the voice of the customer. There are many activities incorporated in the processes that have entered into business over time which do not add value for the customers. In addition in many businesses today many barons are managing 'functional silos'.

Re-engineering in Asia

Re-engineering is not a Western business phenomenon. Many organizations in Asia have joined the management revolution. Re-engineering is being tried by banks, airlines, insurance companies, manufacturers and even some government departments.

The Thai Farmers Bank (TFB), according to *American Banker* magazine, is spending $150 million to re-engineer its operations throughout 454 branches by the end of 1996. Apart from TFB, Shinhan Bank (one of South Korea's biggest banks), Dharmala Bank (an Indonesian Bank), Thai Airways International, Yamaha Motor Co. are all embarking on re-engineering initiatives.

Re-engineering is spreading in Asian organizations for three reasons:

* Improvement of customer service.
* To gain and retain competitive advantage.
* To make effective use of resources throughout the organization.

What are the characteristics and benefits of business process re-engineering?

* Re-engineering integrates various tasks and activities into one.
* The steps in the process are performed in a natural order which is not necessarily linear.
* Work is performed where it makes most sense.
* Non-value adding activities are eliminated.
* There is no place for the 'command and control' type of management style.
* Processes are understood from the perspective of the customers.
* Full and open communication becomes important.
* It promotes 'rethinking' the nature and purpose of work.
* It restores respect for the individual.

- Work assumes multi-dimensional perspectives.
- Corporate and individual values change from being 'protective' to 'productive'.
- Smart work rather than hard work becomes the norm.
- Organizational structure becomes flat and 'functional silos' and 'functional stovepipes' disappear.
- Technology as an enabler becomes an important agent of business transformation and success.
- The organization's attention is focused on where to compete rather than how to compete.
- It promotes a provocative culture – questioning everything an organization does and seeking innovative ways of doing work.
- It aligns core processes to business strategy.
- It promotes an organization's capability to adapt.

Discontinuous thinking

Business process re-engineering is not about automation or restructuring or downsizing. It is about a radical rethinking of doing business in a changing environment. Of course 'managing change' has been a buzz word for a number of years now. In the past decade or so numerous organizations have embarked upon the journey to change. But these change initiatives are being undertaken within the given functional structures and existing assumptions. The focus of attention is still on specialization. The changes undertaken have also been incremental – evolutionary changes rather than revolutionary changes (see Figure 5.1).

Business process re-engineering creates revolutionary change. The change is 'radical' and the improvements are 'dramatic'. As far as business process re-engineering is concerned nothing is sacred. As one person put it 'a company that has successfully been re-engineered itself is like a phoenix rising from the ashes'. Business process re-engineering asks fundamental questions about processes a company is performing, the nature of the activities involved and whether significantly faster and more efficient and effective ways of achieving better results exist. Business process re-engineering is about 'quantum leap' change.

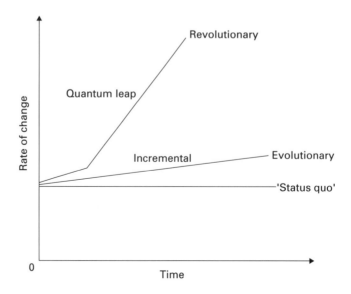

Figure 5.1   Evolutionary versus revolutionary change

In some organizations re-engineering is undertaken at one specific level, focusing on a group of processes rather than re-engineering processes across the organization. Some writers call this initiative process re-engineering in order to distinguish it from business process re-engineering. There are some writers who refer to re-engineering of the whole organization as 'corporate transformation' (see Figure 5.2).

Where a specific process or a group of processes is re-engineered and the change is radical and the improvements are dramatic at a specific level, but at organizational level the change is marginal, then the organization has been re-engineered. Where there has been a radical change throughout the organization and the improvements across the business are dramatic, then often the term used is 'corporate transformation'. This difference is important to keep in mind when readers are assessing or thinking about their situations and experiences.

Critical success factors of business process re-engineering

• There should be a desire to change the 'status quo'.

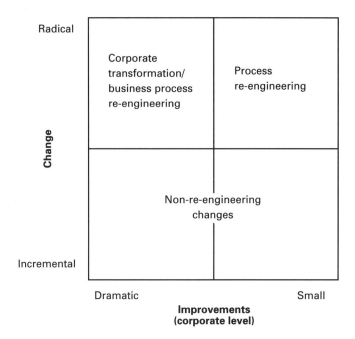

Figure 5.2 Change matrix

- There has to be trust, understanding, courage and above all patience.
- Top management must give their total involvement.
- Employees have to empowered. Some writers say 'empowered' employees have to become 'renaissance' employees.
- Organizational structure must be flexible and responsive to customer needs.
- Culture has to be supportive, 'allowing' risk-taking and not getting it right first time.
- Employees have to be trained in working in teams.
- Traditional assumptions have to be challenged.
- There should be considerable care taken in planning and implementation. Use technology as an enabler in bringing about a 'quantum leap'.

Why do some re-engineering initiatives fail?

According to the article which appeared in the *McKinsey Quarterly* 1994 (No. 2), some re-engineering initiatives have had paradoxical outcomes. There have been dramatic improvements in cycle time and process costs but still no impact on the bottom-line of the business as a whole. McKinsey examined projects in more than 100 companies. The factors which have contributed to paradoxical outcomes have found to be as follows:

- Re-design initiative did not penetrate to the company's core and did not change roles and responsibilities, measurements and incentives, organizational structure, IT, shared values and skills.
- The process to be redesigned was not broadly based on cost or customer value.
- Senior executives did not invest enough time and energy.
- Focus on processes that were too narrowly defined.
- Inadequate identification of the activities to include in the process being redesigned that were critical for value creation in the overall business unit.
- Some companies wanted to minimize disruptions.
- In some cases there was a lack of good leadership to lead the organization through the period of change.
- There was resistance from various stakeholders.
- Not enough attention was paid to processes in those areas that fell short of customer expectations and competitive performance

In addition to these factors some writers have added the following contributing to re-engineering project failures:

- Lack of resources.
- Unreasonable expectations.
- Cynicism and scepticism.
- Stress and management burn-out.
- Lack of skills and adequate training.
- Poor teamwork.
- Bureaucracy.
- Previous failures.

- Lack of strategy.

In an article in the *Harvard Business Review*, November-December 1993 entitled How To Make Re-engineering Really Work, the authors (Gene Hall, Jim Rosenthal and Judy Wade) highlight the following 'Five keys to a successful redesign' and 'Four ways to fail'.

Five keys to a successful redesign

The following five factors common to successful re-engineering efforts emerged from our study:

1. **Set an aggressive re-engineering performance target**. The target must span the entire business unit to ensure sufficient breadth. For example, aim for a $250 million pre-tax profit increase to result from a 15 per cent cost reduction and a 5 per cent revenue increase measured across the business unit as a whole.
2. **Commit 20 to 50 per cent of the chief executive's time to the project**. The time commitment may begin at 20 per cent and grow to 50 per cent during the implementation stage. For example, schedule weekly meetings that inform the top managers of the project's status.
3. **Conduct a comprehensive review of customer needs, economic leverage points, and market trends**. For example, customer interviews and visits, competitor benchmarking, analysis of best practices in other industries and economic modelling of the business.
4. **Assign an additional senior executive to be responsible for implementation**. The manager should spend at least 50 per cent of his or her time on the project during the critical implementation stage.
5. **Conduct a comprehensive pilot of the new design**. The pilot should test the design's overall impact as well as the implementation process, while at the same time building enthusiasm for full implementation.

...and four ways to fail

There are any number of ways that a re-engineering project can fail. However, our study uncovered the following four particularly damaging practices:

1. **Assign average performance**. Companies tend to enlist average

performers – most often from headquarters – for the project. Why? They reason that performance in the business unit will falter if they assign top performers to the redesign full time. For example, one company assigned a mediocre sales manager to head the project because he wouldn't be missed in the field. But because this manager lacked the credibility and skills to lead, the project ultimately failed.

2. **Measure only the plan**. Though most companies invest a lot of resources in estimating the effects of a redesign on cost, quality and time before implementation, they rarely follow through with a comprehensive measurement system that can track the new process's performance as it is actually being rolled out. Without this kind of measurement system, it is impossible to tell if and why implementation is succeeding or failing. A good tracking system should measure location-specific results and individual employee performance.

3. **Settle for the status quo**. Companies generally strive to redesign in ways that are radically new, but more often than not, they never translate their aspirations into reality. Most companies have a difficult time thinking outside their own skill level, organizational structures or system constraints. Moreover, companies that do come up with innovative approaches find them watered down by political infighting during the implementation stage. Incentive and information technology, in particular, can be politically sensitive areas.

4. **Overlook communication**. Companies always underestimate the level of communication that must occur during the implementation stage. They tend to use only one method of communication, like memos, speeches or PR videos. More often than not, they neglect the more time-consuming, but effective small group format in which employees can give feedback and air their concerns. It is essential to create a comprehensive communications program that uses a variety of methods of communication. It helps to assign a top-level manager to develop and implement an on-going communications program.

How to re-engineer

There are three stages involved in a re-engineering project. Each stage incorporates distinct activities.

Stage one

- Start with a clean sheet of paper and design all or part of the operations of a company.
- Look on the company as performing a small number of continuing processes rather than a collection of people performing specialized functions.
- Identify processes to be re-engineered.
- Define process boundaries.
- Prepare process maps.
- Identify between processes that have 'external' focus (customers, suppliers. distributors) and processes which have 'internal' focus (providing organizational capabilities).
- Distinguish between 'core' processes and 'support' processes.
- Decide on the importance and feasibility of the project.

Stage two – question time

- How are you going to do it?
- Who will be responsible?
- How should the project be managed?
- What are the baselines for measurement?
- What is the time-scale involved?
- How are you going to benchmark and with whom?
- What tools and techniques should be used?

Stage three

- Assemble a core team.
- Appoint a project manager.
- Identify board level champions.
- Start on the project.
- Keep open and full communication going all the time.

The focus of re-engineering is processes. Core processes incorporate activities enhancing customer service, logistics, new product development, cash flow and communication. A core process allows customer needs to drive the way the company should do its business.

New product development core processes involve the following:

* Generating project ideas
* Proposition development
* Test marketing
* Launch preparation
* Launch and establishment of product.

Activities involved are analysed according to the value-adding criterion and examined in terms of speed, flexibility, quality and deadlines.

Process mapping

Process mapping seeks to understand existing and possible future business processes in order to create enhanced customer satisfaction. In re-engineering the objective is to start with the boundaries of process and look at how all elements need to be reconfigured. The most important thing to do before mapping processes is to agree on definitions of what constitutes a process, agree on activities involved and agree on a mapping approach.

The key questions to ask at this stage are:

* What is it we are trying to do?
* Why do we want to do it?
* Who are we going to benchmark against?
* How are we going to do it?
* How will we know if we are on the right track?

Process mapping involves using charts to show process sequence. The simplest chart uses only operation and inspection symbols. The inspection generally is for quality. The set of symbols in common use are the ones developed by the American Society of Mechanical Engineers. A more comprehensive version known as the flow process chart incorporates additional symbols. Figure 5.3 shows the symbols normally used.

Activity	Symbol
Operation	○
Inspection	□
Transport	➡
Storage	▽
Delay	D

Figure 5.3   Activity symbols

There are many other techniques used to analyse processes, depending on the nature and complexity of the business in question.

Some approaches to change initiatives

Some writers recommend a systems approach to tackle re-designing business processes. The Open University Business School in their 'Planning and Managing Change' module put forward a technique of 'systems intervention strategy'. This technique has three overlapping phases:

- **Phase 1**: Diagnose the process by which you develop a way of tackling a particular set of change problems.
- **Phase 2**: Design the process which incorporates alternative methods of achieving change.
- **Phase 3**: Evaluate the options with 'change owners' and put an implementation plan in process.

The steps involved within the system intervention strategy are shown in Figure 5.4.

The phases and steps involved and the action needed are shown in the box. Iteration is needed when using this intervention strategy.

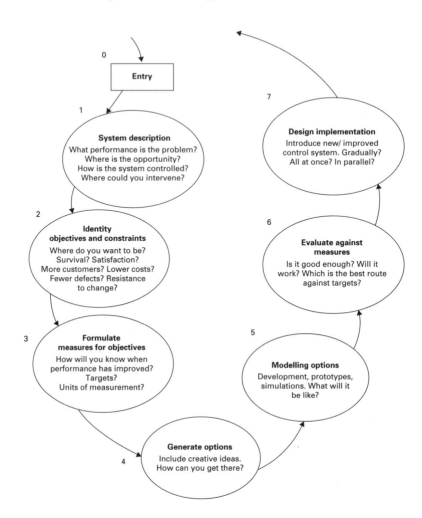

Figure 5.4   System intervention strategy. Source: The Open University Business School, Course B889

The three phases of the strategy

1. Diagnosis
Where are you now?
Where do you want to be?
How will you know when you get there?

The steps of the strategy
0. Entry.

1. Description.
2. Identify objectives and constraints.
3. Formulate measures for your objectives.

What kind of actions are appropriate to each step?
- Start by recognizing that change is a complete process.
- Structure and understand the change in systems terms.
- Get other points of view on the change problem or opportunity.
- Set up some objectives for the systems which you are examining.
- Think of the objectives of the change itself.
- Decide on the ways of measuring whether an objective is achieved.

2. Design

How can you get there?
What will it be like?

The steps of the strategy
4. Generate a range of options.
5. Model options selectively.

What kind of actions are appropriate to each step?
- Develop any ideas for change as full options.
- Look at a wide range of possibilities.
- Your objectives may suggest new options.
- Describe the most promising options in some detail.
- Ask for each option: **What** is involved? **Who** is involved? **How** will it work?

3. Implementation
- Will you like it?
- How can you carry it through?

The steps of the strategy
6. Evaluate options against measures.
7. Design implementation strategies.
8. Carry through the planned changes.

What kind of actions are appropriate to each step?
- Test the performance of your option against an agreed set of criteria.
- Select your preferred options and plan a way of putting the changes in place.
- Bring together people and resources.

* Manage the process.
* Monitor progress.

Source: Course B889, 'Performance Measurement and Evaluation'. The Open University Business School.

Process re-engineering and the value chain

The other approach to change is to focus on the value chain. As Hammer and Champy have indicated, many organizations still operate in a traditional mode. The focus is still on the value chain, which has been popularized by Michael Porter.

The value chain categorizes a firm into its strategic relevant activities in order to understand cost behaviour and sources of differentiation. Every firm's value chain is composed of nine generic categories of activities which are linked together. The first five of these nine categories are inbound logistics, outbound logistics, marketing and sales and service. All of these constitute primary activities. The four categories of procurement, technology development, human resource management and firm's infrastructure on the other hand, constitute support activities. Organizations aim to achieve optimization of each element of the value chain. The focus is on firm's activities and how value is added at each step of the value chain.

The concept of adding value is the key element of business process re-engineering. The focus is shifted from the value chain to core processes and from product innovation to process innovation.

A firm is just a collection of activities such as order processing, sales force operations, etc., and the value chain is a way of analysing each activity in terms of the value it contributes to the business. At each level of a value chain one should analyse all the activities involved and obliterate activities which do not add value to a business in terms of enhancing profitability or customer satisfaction.

The most useful method of charting any change was described by the psychologist, Kurt Lewin. He suggested that we can view organizations as being held in balance, or equilibrium between two sets of forces. These forces are categorized as **restraining forces** and **driving forces**.

Driving forces initiate change and keep it going. Examples of driving forces would be competition, the appointment of a new chief executive office or acquisition. Restraining forces decrease the impact of driving forces. For example resistance to change from workers or even corporate culture could reduce the impact of driving forces. Equilibrium is reached when the sum of the driving forces equals the sum of the restraining forces.

Kurt Lewin also identified three critical phases in the implementation of change. These phases are labelled as 'Unfreezing', 'Changing' and 'Refreezing'.

- **Phase 1, Unfreezing**: At this stage all employees should be prepared for a change. Explain the need for a change and the benefits accruing to individuals and the organization. The main objective at this stage should be to change the attitude: 'this is the way we do things in this company'. Examine all restraining forces at this stage and consider how they should be handled. This is, therefore, a very important stage. Poor preparation and lack of communication would result in failure.
- **Phase 2, Changing**: At this stage changes should be implemented in desired areas. The change could relate to redesigning the way work is done, rationalizing processes, devising a new reward system and so on. Again communication as to what is being done and why at this stage becomes crucial at this stage.
- **Phase 3, Refreezing**: This is the monitoring stage. At this stage also the newly acquired behaviour comes to be integrated as patterned behaviour into the individual's personality. It is important to see that the new behaviour does not extinguish over time.

Whichever approach is adopted, in business process re-engineering the focus should be on business processes and their relationship with customers. Processes enhance business's operating capabilities which in turn enable them to implement new strategies and envision new strategic options. So re-engineering, apart from making the organization effective in terms of achieving strategic objectives, also opens up avenues for more strategic options (see Figure 5.5).

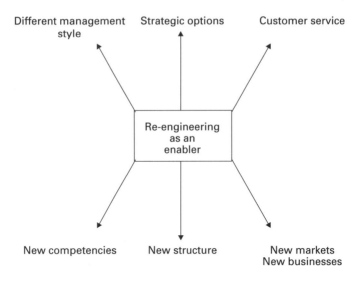

Figure 5.5   Re-engineering and strategic options

What is wrong with re-engineering?

Changes normally produce casualties and re-engineering is no exception. According to the *Wall Street Journal* it is estimated if re-engineering continues at its present pace in US industry there will be 2500 fewer managers by the end of the century. As one chief executive officer put it, 'We are going on a journey. We will carry our wounded and shoot the stragglers.' What a way to motivate. How are wounded cared for? Do stragglers not deserve better treatment?

Business process re-engineering has its critics. In his latest book, *The Pursuit of WOW*, Tom Peters writes, 'Today's re-engineering proponents match the religious zeal of yesterday's quality fanatics. And the idea is damned important. Decimating hierarchies via slash-and-burn strategies is one (big) thing. Re-engineering – linking up activities horizontally and reinventing key business processes – is quite another.' It's even revolutionary, as the re-engineering gurus claim.

But it isn't the main game – at least the way re-engineering is being played by most companies. Like most quality programmes, re-engineering is mostly internally focused busywork, i.e. streamlining. While another necessary item in today's management arsenal, it is far from the whole story.

Prahalad and Hamel feel that re-engineering has more to do with shaping up today's business than creating tomorrow's industries.

Messrs Isaacs and Jones of The Boston Consulting Group believe that re-engineering itself needs a strategy. The following is their article entitled Re-engineering Bumps into Strategy, published in *Perspectives* in 1994.

It's about to become a full-blown problem. The re-engineers are bumping into strategy, but still calling it re-engineering. They are in danger of causing their firms to miss strategic advantages as well as undermining their own methodology. Before long the reality will be clear to all – re-engineering is not strategy nor is it a strategy. Instead, re-engineering needs strategy.

Re-engineering is enormously popular, and its reach inside companies is growing. In some quarters, the word 're-engineering' is so well received. You can get almost any project approved under its banner. Re-engineering sells.

The result, however, is that re-engineering is increasingly over-extended and misused. Firms caught up with re-engineering are falling victim to two different but related errors.

* Confusing re-engineering with strategy by allowing re-engineering's focus on how to do things divert attention from what things to do.
* Letting re-engineering's familiar benchmarking and empowerment procedures mask the need for other, more analytical and inventive ways of thinking.

A telecommunications company, beset by rising costs and falling profitability, sought to re-engineer its customer acquisition and service processes. Familiar with the methodology from other successes, cross-functional teams set about to map some processes, benchmark others, and devise faster and more efficient procedures. They generated exciting ideas from improvement, but all were based on serving the market in its present condition.

In reality, the challenge included two quite different sets of needs:

* A re-engineering part: improving the speed and accuracy of order entry, billing and service functions. This is what re-engineering does best. For this they could learn from others and heed the experience of front-line employees.

- A strategic part: discovering which customer groupings are most profitable and growing, hence which to pursue most vigorously. These were new choices requiring new insights. For this, they needed strategic analysis and original data gathering. No competitor had worked the problem quite this way previously, so a real competitive advantage could be built on this new, proprietary information.

The company needed to uncover the costs, probabilities, and time-lags of attracting and retaining different types of customers. Knowing the differing cash streams among customers, they could develop differentiated marketing and picking programmes to get more of the best customers and fewer of the worst.

The original 're-engineering' programme would have missed the point – and the opportunity – by lumping both parts together under the single heading and approach.

How could such oversights arise? Arguably, it's a logical consequence of the origins and success of the re-engineering movement.

Re-engineering scales up

Re-engineering is probably the hottest current idea in European and North American business. Its aims are clear: increased competitiveness and profitability via simpler, leaner and more productive business systems and processes. Its methods are also clear: cross-functional teams, mapping, benchmarking, learning from front-line employees, customer input, throwing out old paradigms in favour of new ones. Most major firms have re-engineered at least some parts of their business – usually with dramatic impact.

At first, managers applied the re-engineering concept to the basic routines of the business. The question was mainly how to do them most effectively and productively. Greater speed and reduced head-count regularly followed. Building on success, firms then extended the re-engineering concept. What started as re-engineering of order processing became a reassessment of all customer service.

At this point, beside asking how to do it better, one must also determine what to do and for whom to do it. There are classic strategy choices, and it's vital to get them right.

Unfortunately, much of the re-engineering methodology has trouble coping with these questions. While benchmarking works well for bringing inside the best practices of others, it often amounts to strategy mimicry. It's not very good for devising an original 'best practice' that doesn't already exist. Cross-functional teams are good at pooling existing knowledge, breaking down barriers and finding new ways to work inside the existing game. But these same teams often shy away from more speculative data gathering, 'blue sky' brainstorming and going 'outside the box' to change the rules of the game itself. Few team members want to risk embarrassment and failure by going out on a limb that others may not even be able to perceive. Yet that's often what is required to create a strong and original strategy. And so it is that the re-engineers are rediscovering the need for strategy.

A business wag once asked, 'Once the trains are running on time, where should they go?' That is the question more and more firms are facing even after their re-engineering efforts are done. Finding the answer takes more than just re-engineering. It takes strategy.

Compatibility without blind spots

The same is true in reverse. Like re-engineering, strategy analysis by itself is also not enough. A strategic review can declare a business uncompetitive based on its current way of doing business, yet re-engineering can revitalize that business by changing its basic operating premises.

In one instance, a manufacturer's strategy analysis confirmed that parts of two key product lines were lagging in growth and returns. The customers described the products as top notch, highly differentiated, already highly priced, but they also complained of long and unreliable lead times, especially on custom and speciality items. Could re-engineering change this picture?

A re-engineering review showed large opportunities to improve returns by focusing on reducing time to market and streamlining the order-to-delivery process across the board. Eventually, the company made these new capabilities the centrepiece of a new 'process-oriented' strategy. The firm went from the least to the most flexible competitor in the industry with a new price schedule capturing the value of its fast customization.

The re-engineering efforts revitalized the product lines, leading to faster sales growth, even greater profitability growth, and new platforms for the future. Re-engineering triumphed where strategy alone could not.

Re-engineering needs strategy, and vice versa. Alone, each may be the blindspot of the other. Together, the two are quite different but highly compatible. Like the yin and the yang, each needs the other to be balanced and complete.

Source: The Boston Consulting Group (1994) Re-engineering Bumps into Strategies. Perspectives.

Re-engineering is means to an end. It is not a strategy. In relation to strategic intervention systems, re-engineering features in the design and implementation aspect. Of course strategy and implementation must go hand in hand. Strategy without implementation will not bring about any change and implementation without strategy will lack direction and will result in confusion.

The biggest criticism of re-engineering to date has been the point that far too much emphasis has been put on processes and very little consideration has been given to 'soft' issues of business, in particular in relation to people. In this vein a very interesting article was written by Gareth Rees, chief executive of Kinsley Lord Management Consultants, which appeared in the journal, *Focus on Change Management*, February 1994. The article is reproduced below:

The people versus re-engineering

Lawyer for the plaintiff: 'Ladies and gentleman of the jury, you are here to consider a most serious case – that a juggernaut called re-engineering (an approach to redesigning the way tasks are carried out in a firm) has inflicted psychological and social harm on my clients, the employees and staff of Cosyfirm Ltd. Our case is not that re-engineering is intrinsically bad. Indeed, my clients had hoped that in addition to improving efficiency, it would also improve the quality of their working lives. Our case is that the company has been negligent in the way in which it has applied re-engineering, and as a result has failed to achieve some of the objectives and has increased the stress and reduced the quality of the lives of its employees. Re-engineering was introduced to the company 18 months ago and is now largely complete. As our witnesses will acknowledge, it has produced real benefits for Cosyfirm and its customers. But they will also testify to the unnecessary pain and stress it has caused them as people, the damage to their self-esteem and the opportunities lost to the firm, because their skills and knowledge have not been tapped to the full. Let me call my first witness.

Witness 1: Head of engineering
'I am still called the head of engineering at Cosyfirm, though my job is a pale shadow of what it was. For me, re-engineering has been a disaster.

'As a member of the management team I went along with the decision to re-engineer. We were too set in our ways and our poor competitive performance meant that we had to do something. The consultants were plausible, though some of their jargon was difficult to understand, and the CEO seemed convinced. If we had known how much pain it was going to cause, I am sure we would have thought twice.

'I used to run a tight engineering department. All of my people knew what was expected of them; we had standards and ways of doing things. True, we had our battles with production and R&D but we knew how to sort them out. We were making progress. Rather than build carefully on this, we had a revolution, and a painful one at that.

'The new production and product department process teams are not a bad idea. But with this new organization my craftsmen are spread out among processes and it's almost impossible to maintain standards. Technical training is falling by the wayside because I can't insist they attend. Functional expertise that took us years to develop will probably be lost. There's a timebomb of falling competence here. If it continues, quality will drop and so will sales.

'We are obsessed with IT. Company-wide access to a single database sounded great, but we're bending lots of things to make it work. IT costs a fortune and is not as flexible as we hoped. Given our obsession with IT, it's no wonder we didn't think enough about the human side of re-engineering.

'I cringe when I think back. We were in panic when we realized just how many people were being shaken out – we had no severance scheme or re-training ready. They didn't know what hit them. I felt useless and incompetent for the first time in my life, morale has not recovered.'

Witness 2: Sales representative

'I have been responsible for our sales to the pharmaceutical industry for the past four years. The re-engineering exercise has brought some real benefits to my customers, mostly in reduced delivery times. I guess our costs are coming down a little, so perhaps the sales force won't have to negotiate so many unpopular price increases.

'There are some drawbacks, though. Everything is OK when we are having a good quality production run, but if a customer wants something special, or a product goes off spec., it seems to take longer to get things changed or fixed. We'll have to pull our socks up or we will let our competitors in.

'Part of the problem is that my old network of contacts has gone – they've either left or are doing different jobs. It's hard to get to the source of the problem because everything seems so fluid with all these teams. I can't even get Alice, the sales office administrator, to chase things up, she's too busy working with sales/production scheduling.

'That's another thing. A common database across the company is great in theory; the trouble is we miss the tweaking that Bert used to do. He knew what was doable and what wasn't, and kept the nonsense out. Unfortunately, Bert's intuition was re-engineered away.

'As I talk through this I'm beginning to realize why I'm feeling stressed. The firm feels more automated. There is less flexibility and less care. The new system has a hierarchy of its own – a system hierarchy, rather than the old command hierarchy. I can't seem to influence things as much now. I feel more lonely, just when I thought teamwork would make the place more human and flexible.'

Witness 3: Team leader
'I was a foreman in sub-assembly but now I'm production team leader. My job hasn't changed much in some ways – I still have to make sure we hit our production quota – but in others it's changed a lot. We make more of the finished product now and I don't know this team so well. I'm not used to maintenance people in the team and being responsible for our own QA is frightening.

'We found it difficult to understand what they wanted us to do to start with but we're getting the hang of it. They changed our production methods to reduce waiting and tool changing times, formed us into new teams, set us targets and told us to work together to improve output and quality. We're not getting on badly now, but management made a pig's ear of introducing the new system. First, no one told us what was happening, we got no warning. Then they turned up with a bunch of consultants who generally ignored us, kept appearing and disappearing and held endless mysterious meetings with management. They brought in these new production methods, which didn't work until we sorted them ourselves. Why didn't they ask us in the first place?

'It was bedlam for months. We lost a lot of output, not only because the new production process didn't work but because the blokes were too tee-ed off to bother. I don't think they'd heard of motivation, the lot of them. If the blokes were really switched on we'd move into another gear, find ways of sorting out problems quicker and add at least 15 per cent to output.

'It's the production managers, what's left of them, that I feel most sorry for. They had little to say on the changes, and because we're supposed to solve our own problem, they're lost. How can you turn a sergeant major into a football coach overnight? Somebody had better show them how before all their hair falls out.'

Witness 4: Fitter
'This lot in my new process team are space-cadets. I don't know what they are talking about half the time. Mary from marketing, Alistair from new product development, Susan from sales; it's kids, holidays and playgroups. What happened to sex and football and sex? No one takes the micky and there's no-one to take the micky out of.

'This high performance team, as they call it, ain't performing much and ain't much fun. True, we did sort out the Johnson's new product prototype problem quickly, but that was more by luck. Having Ralph, the engineer, and Alistair on the same team saved the usual to-ing and fro-ing; but we hardly knew each other, had different ways of tackling a problem and seem to speak different languages. It was a bit of a miracle we hit on an answer.

'When they set up the team we got no help from the managers, who seemed as confused as we were. We were just told that we were a new team whose job it is to streamline and speed up new product introduction, and left to get on with it. No training, no game plan, no organization. If I ran the Angling Club like that way we wouldn't catch a sprat, and I'd have a mutiny on my hands.

'We can't fiddle the overtime like we used to, but I still spend half the shift waiting for parts or waiting for Fred to wire up a plug. I could have finished it and gone home hours ago. I miss my mates, but not Harry, the foreman. At least I don't have him checking up on my every nut and bolt.'

Witness 5: Process development owner
'Getting involved in the re-engineering exercise at the outset, especially as 'process owner', was great for me. I'm doing an MBA part-time, specializing in corporate change, so it's given me first hand experience. I've come to a number of conclusions about BPR as we applied it.

'One of the most obvious differences from the theory of change is that we missed the 'unfreezing' phase – helping people to understand the reason for change and the benefits that would flow from it, and giving them time to get used to the idea and prepare for it. Once the management made a decision to go ahead we formed process teams, looking across the business to the customers rather than reporting vertically to the boss, and got started. People couldn't understand why 'if it ain't broke' we were fixing it. We failed to make the case for change and gather enough support. It was an uphill task as a result.

'From the outset, I struggled to get my managerial colleagues to commit enough resources to the job. They seemed to think it could be added onto the week's work and that substitutes would do. It created a lot of friction and unhappiness. As a result we didn't involve properly the people who really do the nitty-gritty, so we didn't benefit from their ideas; it was a constant struggle between the process teams and the functional line people – and still is.

'We've got it going now, but it's a curate's egg. The main manufacturing process works best. It seems to lend itself to this sort of approach – a straightforward flow of material operations through the factory, easy to measure progress and variances. I don't think though, that we have really improved quality of life. Somehow, we've reinvented the worst aspects of Taylorism in designing repetitive, non-thinking jobs. The textbooks say that we should re-design operations to take account of social and technical factors. I think the technical bias caused us to miss important people aspects.

'I have tried to rectify that in the product development process, but we've had trouble redesigning the way we work. I called the consultants back, they followed us around the iterative loops that product development inevitably takes and have now announced that it is very difficult. Apparently, current re-engineering techniques don't work well on 'non-linear' processes. Great ammunition for my MBA dissertation, but useless in sorting me out.'

Summing up

'Ladies and gentlemen of the jury, the evidence is clear. Through lack of thoughtfulness, indeed negligence given that thought is management's prime duty, Cosyfirm's employees have been seriously hurt. They have suffered needless pain, stress and even hardship. The firm has failed to reap the maximum benefit from what is a very valuable concept, largely as a result of mishandling people issues. The witnesses have given you first-hand accounts of the damage inflicted. The failures were:

- in not fully understanding the implications of the re-engineering exercise; could they not have explored the implications thoroughly before committing themselves?
- in not communicating the case for change and enlisting the support of people; could they not have demonstrated the likely impact of future competitive pressure? Didn't they think that staff would see it?
- in being seduced by the possibilities offered by IT and being blind to the importance and needs of people; why did they not pilot test the solution?
- in not preparing adequately for severance and retraining; the damage to morale is directly hurting the firm itself through reduced

levels of initiative;
- in not working out how to maintain functional competence when re-organizing along process lines; can you hear the time-bomb ticking?
- in not being sensitive and responsive to mistakes; by not building in simple problem solving routines which ensure learning from past experience;
- in designing a new order which does not make the best use of the knowledge and skills of staff; they dumped problems on staff rather than developing them as empowered teams, and expected high performance.

'Management has driven re-engineering like a juggernaut through the firm, unnecessarily hurting its people and not achieving the full benefits. Ladies and gentlemen, I ask you to find the defendants guilty and award substantial damages to my client.'

Source: Gareth Rees, CEO, Kinsley Lord. First published by Armstrong Publications Ltd in Focus on Change Management © 1994.

The article very clearly demonstrates the point that in any change initiative, be it total quality management, re-engineering business processes or working in teams, the most important way to gain understanding, involvement and commitment is to pay attention to employees in terms of training them, trusting them and being honest in open communication. **Success ultimately depends on people**.

Selected reading

Gerard Burke and Joe Peppard (eds) (1995). *Examining Business Process Re-engineering*. Kogan Page.
Michael Hammer and James Champy (1995). *Re-engineering the Corporation*. Nicholas Brealey.
Henry J. Johansson, Mchugh, Pendlebury, Wheeler III (1993). *Business Process Re-engineering*. John Wiley.
Richard K. Lochridge (1994). *After Re-engineering: Organizing for Growth*. Chilmark Press.
Management Review (1995). Re-engineering: Tales from the

Front. January.

Management Review (1995). Why Re-engineering Fails. July.

The Economist Intelligence Unit/Anderson Consulting Report (1995). Business Re-engineering in Asia.

6 Performance measurement

To become what we are capable of becoming is the only end in life.

Robert Louis Stevenson

Summary

- Performance measures are necessary for organizations because they show if organizations are achieving their targets set at strategic and operational levels.

- Business results have to be measured and monitored regularly.

- Performance can be focused on products, processes and people (employees and customers).

- Performance measures have quantitative and qualitative dimensions.

- Financial performance measures/sources of financial information: balance sheet, profit and loss account, applications and sources of funds.

- Financial ratios in a nutshell.

- Organizational performance: economy, efficiency and effectiveness.

- Measuring customer service.

- Balanced scorecard approach.

- Staff appraisal and associated problems.

- Designing performance appraisal.

- Three-hundred-and-sixty degree feedback: key success factors.

- Strategy and performance measures: British Airways case study.

- Self appraisal and time management: improving your personal and professional performance.

- How do you rate as an employee? Your SWOT analysis.

Measuring performance

All organizations formulate strategies to determine the direction of their businesses. At a strategic level the fundamental questions asked are What business do we want to be in? How are we going to achieve our mission? What kind of competencies and structure do we need to meet our objectives? and finally, What is the time scale of achievement? Strategic decisions determine the direction of business and tactical decisions decide the nature and the type of operations

Having set up the direction and the operations the next stage is to formulate performance measures to assess the progress. In some situations being on the right track is not good enough. Businesses have to move faster in order to remain competitive. It is very important to measure progress against the objectives set. There is a need for regular monitoring and review. If there are any adjustments to be made we have to make quick decisions to get back on track. Control, therefore, is an integral part of business management (see Figure 6.1).

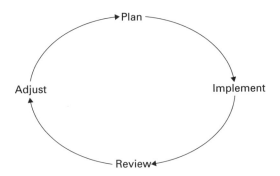

Figure 6.1   Control loop

Performance management is about setting standards of performance and tracking performance to monitor business results consistent with business objectives. Performance can be focused on processes, products and people (customers, employees); see Figure 6.2. Unfortunately in practice many organizations focus on the financial performance of the organizations and pay very little attention to processes and people. Financial performance is one of the dimensions of performance measurement.

Figure 6.2   Dimensions of performance

Measuring financial performance

'What gets measured gets done.'
'When conflicts arise, financial considerations win out.'

Organizations at the end of the day have to make profits and remain solvent. This is the expected outcome by all the stakeholders of the organization.

There are three sources of financial information as far as organizations in the private sector are concerned. These sources are the balance sheet, profit and loss account and sources and application of funds.

Balance sheet
The balance sheet is a financial situation showing what a company owes (its liabilities) and what the company owns (its assets) at a given point of time. It is a financial snapshot of a

company. It gives information on capital (share and loan capital), current liabilities (creditors, taxation, dividends, overdraft), fixed assets (plant, buildings, machinery, equipment) and current assets (stock, debtors and cash).

Current assets minus current liabilities gives information on the working capital. The management of working capital is the lifeblood of a business. Figure 6.3 shows the working capital cycle.

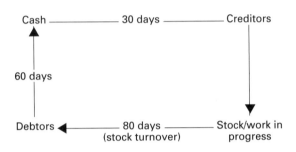

Figure 6.3   Working capital cycle

In the above illustration, cash is locked in for 110 days (80 days + 60 days – 30 days). The size of the net figure for working capital has a direct effect on the liquidity of a company. The return on capital employed is also affected by the level of working capital; the higher the investment in working capital, the lower will be the return on capital employed.

From the balance sheet one can measure stock days, debtor days, creditor days, asset turn, short- and long-term liquidity ratios, gearing ratio and the return on capital employed.

Stock days (Debtors/Cost of sales × 365): This gives an indication of the number of days' sales for which payment is outstanding.
Debtor days (Debtors/Sales × 365): This gives an indication of the number of days' purchases for which payment is still

due. The credit taken from suppliers is a source of short term finance.

Asset turn (Sales/Capital employed): This ratio tells us how many £ of sales is generated each year for every £ of capital employed.

The acid ratio (Debtors + cash/Current liabilities): This shows the company's ability to finance immediate liabilities.

The current ratio (Current assets/Current liabilities): This shows what resources are available to meet the liabilities.

The gearing ratio (Total debt/Shareholders' funds × 100): This gives an indication of the ability of the company to finance its operations in the long term.

Return on capital employed (ROCE) (Operating profit (or profit before interest and tax)/Capital employed (fixed and current assets): This tells us how management has used the total funds available to the business; it measures its earning power. Value is only added to the business if it earns a higher ROCE than the rate of interest it pays or would pay on borrowings. If ROCE is less than the cost of borrowing then the money would be better invested elsewhere.

There are also other measures such as return on equity (Profit after tax/Ordinary shareholders' funds) and return on net assets (Profit before interest and tax/Net assets). These are both return on investment (ROI) measures.

Profit and loss account
The second source of financial information is the profit and loss account. It shows how the company has traded in the year it is reporting. From the information given one can measure sales growth, gross margin (gross profit/sales × 100), operating margin, sales per employee, and operating profit per employee.

Sources and application of funds
The final source of information is sources and application of funds. This tells us where the money in the business has come from (sources) and how it has been spent (application).

Financial performance measures highlighted so far fall under the categories of profitability, solvency and financial structure. These are shown in Table 6.1.

Table 6.1　Financial performance measures

Profitability	Solvency	Financial structure
ROCE	Acid ratio	Gearing ratio
Return on asset	Current ratio	
Return on investment		
Profit margin		
Profit per employee		

Finally as far as financial measures are concerned there are measures from stock market perspectives such as earnings per share (Profit after tax/Number of ordinary shares issued), and price/earning ratio (Market price per share/Earning per share).

Performance is not simply measured by financial targets though many businesses obsessively measure short-term financial performance in their budgeting and forecasting cycles. Many executives are constantly involved in such corporate financial 'rituals'.

There are other forms of performance measures depending on what is being assessed. For example, the sales department might measure volume of sales by value, product, customer (key accounts), invoice, country, distributor or region.

Traditionally performance measures grew from financial reporting systems. Financial performance measures still dominate and pre-occupy many organizations. According to the Economist Intelligence Unit's research conducted in association with KPMG (1994), most companies still track profits, earnings per share and growth in sales as key performance indicators of their businesses. The same report concludes that more than 70 per cent of the respondents feel dissatisfied with the company's performance measure system.

Obsession with financial performance – counting rather than measuring

Case study – Company A

Company A is a book publishing company based in London and New York. Its annual turnover is £50m. The company is divided into four product divisions namely, Science, Social Science, Business and Arts. It also has a small training division providing public seminars on taxation issues.

In December each year all divisions are asked to think about their business goals for the following year and start putting together total revenue figures and propose gross margins. This process continues throughout December until mid-January. The managing director then issues revenue and total cost figures for all divisions to achieve during the year. These figures are extrapolated from past performance without analysing the causes behind the performance. This is 'performance management by extrapolation'.

From mid-January until the end of February, divisional managers have to come up with detailed information on how the revenues and the costs figures prescribed by the managing director are going to be achieved and in consultation with the IT department volumes of spreadsheets are produced.

In March each division has budget reviews and significant pressures are put on divisional managers to propose prescribed revenues and costs. When this is done all the divisional budgets are submitted to the management committee. The budget submissions are then fine-tuned and finally submitted to the management board in April.

In July each divisional manager is asked to forecast their financial performance for the period May-June-July – the first quarter of the financial year – and provide commentaries on forecasted performance. All the forecasts are then discussed by the management committee. At this stage again considerable pressures are put on the divisional managers who are forecasted to under-perform financially. The first quarter financial forecasting finishes in July.

In October, January and April, second, third and fourth quarter forecasting begins. Meanwhile from January the following year's budget process begins and all the managers go through the same 'corporate rituals'.

In between these periods, so that the people aspect of performance is not forgotten, all business managers are asked to conduct appraisals for their staff. Managers view such practice as an intrusion into their work and, therefore, they try 'to get over' staff appraisals as soon as possible.

No performance appraisal is done on any qualitative dimension nor is serious attention paid to the reasons behind the financial performance. Financial results tell you the 'what' but not the 'why' of performance.

There are other dimensions of performance that this company should pay attention to. Unfortunately, because Company A is doing very well financially the management think they have got it right. It is unfortunate because the people development aspect is ignored and there is lack of enthusiasm and motivation for managers to over-perform under this culture.

In the long run Company A will suffer financially and it will be too late to save it!

Dimensions of organizational performance

Organizations can measure performance from the point of view of **economy**, **efficiency** and **effectiveness**. Economy focuses attention on the cost of inputs used. Efficiency focuses on the relationship between input and output (productivity), whereas effectiveness relates to achieving results consistent with corporate objectives.

- Economy means 'doing it cheap'.
- Efficiency means 'doing it right'.
- Effectiveness means 'doing the right thing right'.

Organizations have to formulate measure of effectiveness which involve measuring and monitoring corporate objectives and how these objectives are being implemented and monitored.

Performance measures in relation to quality

Chapter 2 dealt with criteria as applied to the Malcolm Baldrige National Quality Award. To win this award requires measuring seven areas, namely, leadership, information and analysis, strategic quality planning, human resource utilization, quality assurance of products and services, quality results and customer satisfaction. Different points are allocated for each category and measures are performed to determine the level of achievement.

In relation to the European Quality Award, nine areas are designated for assessment. They are leadership, people management, policy and strategy, resources, processes, people satisfaction, customer satisfaction, impact on society and business results. Again points are allocated against categories of 'enablers' and 'results' and assessment is made as to the level and degree of achievement.

Measuring customer service

In delivering service excellence, organizations measure repeat business, lost business, number of complaints, defect rates, delivery time, and so on. Measures of customer needs and satisfaction are facilitated by visiting customers and finding out their needs, forming customer focus group, issuing questionnaires, conducting customer research, and so on. In Chapter 4 we have seen how Rank Xerox, DHL and ICL measure customer service in order to improve the performance of their businesses.

Balanced scorecard approach

The balance scorecard approach was proposed by Robert Kaplan, professor of accounting at Harvard Business School, and David Norton, president of Renaissance Strategy Group, a consulting firm. The advantage of this approach is its comprehensiveness in measuring various dimensions of business and the way it translates corporate strategic objectives into a 'coherent set of performance measures'.

Measurement focuses on four dimensions of business, namely financial indicators, customer performance, internal processes and innovation and learning. By selecting a limited number of critical indicators under each perspective the scorecard helps focus the strategic vision.

The type of scorecard approach used will depend on the nature of the organization and the business it is in. Manufacturing businesses would adopt a different approach, for example from service industries. According to Michael Morrow, a consultant at KPMG, the balanced business scorecard is now widely used as a framework for the whole business. The first significant application in Europe was by Aer Lingus and the largest to date is NatWest. The balance business scorecard approach aims to provide performance measures at strategic level, business unit level, process level and individual level.

From a financial perspective a business can measure its growth, liquidity, shareholder value, cash flow, return on capital employed and other significant indicators. From an internal business perspective the measures could focus on cycle time, unit cost, defect rate, safety rate and other operational variables. From an organizational learning perspective, one would assess technological capability, time to market, new product introduction, rate of improvement, employee attitude, etc. And from a customer perspective the measures would relate to assessing market share, customer satisfaction, supplier relationship/partnership, key accounts and so on (see Figure 6.4.)

Building a balanced scorecard

Robert Kaplan and David P. Norton in their article Putting a Balanced Scorecard to Work, published in the *Harvard Business* Review, September-October 1993, give the following advice on building a balanced scorecard.

Each organization is unique and so follows its own path for building a scorecard. At Apple and AMD, for instance, a senior finance or business development executive, intimately familiar with the strategic thinking of the top management group, constructed the initial scorecard without extensive deliberations. At Rockwater, however, senior management had yet to define sharply the organization's strategy, much less the key performance levers that drive and measure the strategy's success.

Companies like Rockwater can follow a systematic development plan to create the balanced scorecard and encourage commitment to the scorecard among senior and mid-level managers. What follows is a typical project profile:

1. Preparation
The organization must first define the business unit for which a top-level scorecard is appropriate. In general, a scorecard is appropriate for a business unit that has its own customers, distribution channels, production facilities and financial performance measures.

2. Incentive first round
Each senior manager in the business unit – typically between six and twelve executives – receives background material on the balanced scorecard as well as internal documents that describe the company's vision, mission and strategy.

The balanced scorecard facilitator – either an outside consultant or the company executive who organizes the effort – conducts interviews of approximately 90 minutes each with the senior managers to obtain their input on the company's strategic objectives and tentative proposals for balanced scorecard measures. The facilitator may also interview some principal shareholders to learn about their expectations for the business unit's financial performance, as well as some key customers to learn about their performance expectations for top-ranked suppliers.

3. Executive workshop: first round
The top management team is brought together with the facilitator to undergo the process of developing the scorecard. During the workshop the group debates the proposed mission and strategy statements until a consensus is reached. The group then moves from the mission and strategy statement to answer the question, 'If I succeed with my vision and strategy, how will my performance differ for shareholders; for customers; for internal business processes; for my ability to innovate, grow and improve?'

Videotapes of interviews with shareholder and customer representatives can be shown to provide an internal perspective to the deliberations. After defining the key success factors, the group formulates a preliminary balanced scorecard containing operational measures for the strategic objectives. Frequently, the group proposes far more than four or five measures for each perspective. At this time, narrowing the choices is not critical, through straw votes can be taken to see whether or not some of the proposed measures are viewed as low priority by the group.

4. Interviews: second round

The facilitator reviews, consolidates and documents the output from the executive workshop and interviews each senior executive about the tentative balanced scorecard. The facilitator also seeks opinions about issues involved in implementing the scorecard.

5. Executive workshop: second round

A second workshop involving the senior management team, their direct subordinates, and a larger number of middle managers, debates the organization's vision, strategy statements and the tentative scorecard. The participants, working in groups, comment on the proposed measures, link the various change programs under way to the measures, and start to develop an implementation plan. At the end of the workshop, participants are asked to formulate stretch objectives for each of the proposed measures, including targeted rates of improvement.

6. Executive workshop: third round

The senior executive team meets to come to a final consensus on the vision, objectives and measurement developed in the first two workshops; to develop stretch targets for each measure on the scorecard; and to identify preliminary action programs to achieve the targets. The team must agree on the implementation program, including communicating the scorecard to employees, integrating the scorecard into a management philosophy and developing an information system to support the scorecard.

7. Implementation

A newly formed team develops an implementation plan for the scorecard, including linking the measures to databases and information systems, communicating the balanced scorecard throughout the organization, and encouraging and facilitating the development of second-level metrics for decentralized units. As a result of this process, for instance, an entirely new executive information system that links top-level business unit metrics down through shop floor and site-specific operational measures could be developed.

8. Practical reviews

Each quarter or month, a blue book of information on the balanced scorecard measures is prepared for both top management review and discussions with managers of decentralized divisions and departments. The balanced scorecard metrics are revisited annually as part of the strategic planning, goal setting and resource allocation process.

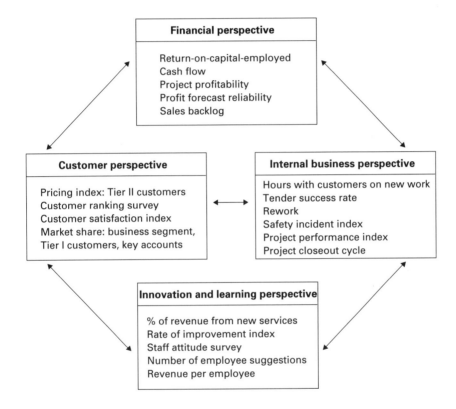

Figure 6.4   An example of the balanced scorecard

Measuring staff performance

Staff appraisals are conducted in many organizations. The objective of such appraisals should be to motivate behaviour leading to continuous improvement. Speaking to many business executives, they feel in most cases staff appraisals are ineffective because they are not done properly. Some staff find them very intimidating 'corporate rituals' they have to go through annually.

There are four categories of problems associated with performance appraisals. These are the measurement problem, the judgement problem, the organizational problem and the communication problem.

The measurement problem

Some organizations find it very difficult to decide what to appraise due to the lack of understanding of the roles and responsibilities involved or due to ambiguity of roles involved. In some cases measures formulated are inadequate because not enough thought has gone into designing them.

In some cases there is confusion between a behaviour-based performance indicator and competency-based performance.

The judgement problem

Many managers do not like to act as a judge. There are numerous examples in practice to show disagreement on ratings, different interpretations put on different indicators by appraisee and appraiser. Biases also creep in when judgements are made on the behaviour-based indicators and some find it very uncomfortable to assess their subordinates, especially when they have to criticize them.

The organizational problem

In many organizations staff appraisals are not taken seriously. They are used as a window dressing exercise and to provide comfort to top management in feeling 'we also do it'. Some managers see staff appraisals falling outside their function and some consider them to be 'distractions'. Appraisals are often cut short because of crises or lack of time.

The communication problem

There is a lack of communication as to the purpose and the

objectives of staff appraisals. For example, in one company I came across one manager who was using staff appraisals to determine annual salary increases and merit rewards whereas in the same organization another manager was using appraisals to develop his staff. There is inconsistency of purpose because of the lack of communication. There is also the problem that those who have to act as appraisers in many instances have not been trained to appraise.

The key problems associated with staff appraisals are:

- Take longer than expected to implement.
- Inconsistency of objectives.
- Inadequate communication.
- Management is distracted.
- Managers do not see it as their part of their job.
- Inadequate training.
- Mistrust.
- Inadequate interviewing technique.
- Lack of 'rapport' between parties involved.
- Ambiguous indicators.
- Change of management/personnel.
- Uncertainty.
- Too much emphasis on financial variances.
- Used to 'punish' rather than 'motivate'.
- Often not aligned to corporate objectives.
- Culture of not paying attention to 'soft' issues.

How to design performance appraisal – the people dimension

Staff should establish performance goals for themselves. Ask them to think about their job and categorize their work under about six key result areas (KRAs). These KRAs could be categorized as financial, operational, behaviour, quality-related and customer satisfaction perspective and others added according to the nature of organization and the job involved. Managers should act as facilitator and coach and give as much support as is needed at a preliminary stage.

It is always useful to ask the staff to do SWOT (strengths, weaknesses, opportunities and threats or challenges) analyses of themselves in relation to the job they are doing and the department or teams they work in. The strengths would include information on their competencies, skills, experience, adaptability, inter-personal skill, etc. Weaknesses could relate to skills, experience, speed of adaptation, lack of commitment, etc. Opportunities would encompass becoming process leader or team leader, change 'champion', facilitator, etc., and the threats would involve considering the possibility of de-skilling, moving into different areas, working with different colleagues, etc.

The approach is to sit with an a subordinate and do a job map. This would involve identifying activities, tasks, functions and responsibilities of a subordinate. The procedure would be to follow the framework set out below:

I have responsibility for achieving:

....

....

....

....

My function is (to lead, to produce) to:

....

....

....

I have to perform the following tasks to meet my objectives:

....

....

....

....

....

These tasks involve the following activities:

....

....

....

....

....

....

....

The next stage is to sit with each member of staff to go over the objectives set for him or her. At this stage it should be clear what is expected of them and by when. The objectives set should be sensible, measurable, attainable, realistic and have a time scale (SMART).

After the objectives have been explained and finalized a manager should communicate expectations (outcomes desired). Before the formal appraisal is done a manager should monitor progress according to what has been agreed and provide coaching and counselling.

At an appraisal interview it is very important that a manager has done his or her 'homework' on the appraisee and has all the information ready. The focus at the appraisal should be on analysis in order to enable an appraisee to become an active participant in the process. It is important that the right basis is established for constructive climate and action. Communication should be open and honest.

The feedback given should address the following questions on behalf of the appraisee:

- What is expected of me?
- How am I doing?
- How can I improve?
- What is my reward?
- Where do I go from here?

Finally the appraisal should be written up, recommending development action to be taken and most importantly how, when and by whom the action should be implemented.

The appraisal cycle should be iterative (Figure 6.5).

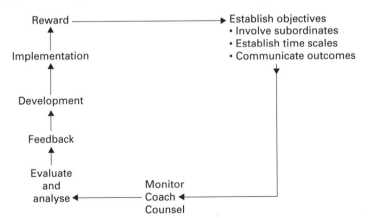

Figure 6.5 Performance appraisal cycle

Three-hundred-and-sixty degree feedback method: are you ready for it?

Quite a lot nowadays is talked about the 360 degree feedback method. Essentially this method of feedback focuses on receiving appraisal from colleagues, a manager, and the people one comes in contact with in a normal business. Performance appraisal becomes the result of feedback received from various sources (Figure 6.6). The information is usually collected through questionnaires. The feedback is given anonymously.

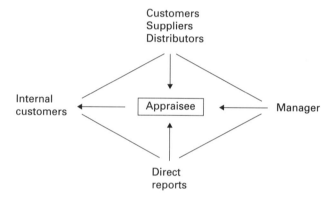

Figure 6.6   Three-hundred-and-sixty degree feedback

Usefulness of the method

- The feedback is comprehensive.
- It enables the individual to enhance his/her SWOT analysis.
- It is balanced feedback taking all the stakeholders into consideration.
- It could be used at any level.
- It appears fair.
- It describes behaviour rather than judgement.
- It is a good way of assessing how you see yourself and how others see you.
- It is meaningful.

Critical success factors of 360 degree feedback

- It must be thought out very carefully before it is implemented.
- Some organizations introduce such methods as a window dressing exercise.
- The philosophy and objectives of the system need to be understood throughout the organization.
- Those conducting appraisals have to be trained in interpreting behaviour indicators and communicating such indicators.
- There has to be a culture of trust in the organization.
- The system should focus not only on task performance but also on 'relationship' indicators.
- There should be a consensus on core values and an alignment of individual and corporate values.
- Action plans should focus on improvements and enhancement of core competencies.

Strategy and performance measures

The following paper entitled Delivering the Strategy Through Business Processes and Performance Measures was delivered by Roger Davies, manager of operational performance, British Airways, plc, at a conference organized by the Economist Conferences in 1994.

Translating strategy into action: British Airways plc case study

For strategy to be meaningful throughout the organization, there must be vision. All employees need to share that vision and it requires a human context. The pyramid builders created a monument to the Pharaoh and his passport to the next life. Similarly, our vision should link our traditions with the future. As we put in place more participative structures, our staff have to be able to answer the question 'what does the strategy mean to me?' This is particularly the case when management buzz words such as 'globalization' are involved. We all must be clear how the delivery of the strategic result will affect individuals.

This is more than a planning issue. The tactical objectives which will deliver results on our strategic progress towards the vision must be elaborated. Using globalization as an example, what will the relations between partners in such an alliance be? How will sales activities be affected? What will customers expect? And particularly, what will be the effect on jobs? These effects cannot easily be predicted a long way into the future, but we have to make an effort. We therefore seek to establish a linkage between the strategic goals and operational targets. In the case of globalization, this means that schedules need to be co-ordinated, frequent flyer schemes integrated, and joint service training initiated at the interfaces between alliance partners.

These implications of the strategic direction provide us with team tasks to be cascaded through the organization. Many functions contribute to each goal. How are their contributions to be co-ordinated? As the team tasks are driven down through the organization they come to represent individual accountabilities. Although financial objectives can be cascaded in straightforward ways, objectives in quality or service terms do not seem so easy to transfer. The teams' tasks are dynamic. They represent current priorities for improvement across the organization and we measure progress against them. As an example, the improvement of baggage performance is driving investment decisions to construct new facilities, re-organization to sharpen accountabilities, training in service recovery and information technology development.

The focus we apply to the goals also affects the future. The leadership shown by our managers will not only alter the way our service is delivered to customers, but it should also change the ethos. The interaction of culture, processes and organization merits the most careful planning to ensure that the action which is required does result. Incentives play a part. Alignment of incentives should mean that front-line decisions are taken in accordance with the company philosophy, not by instruction but by shared values, not by routines but by shared beliefs. It is only when many of the dials on our 'enterprise flight deck' are pointing the same way that alignment is starting to work.

Aligning incentives

- Setting priorities:
  - establishing what is wanted
  - rewarding group behaviour
  - encouraging core competencies
- Establishing support technology:
  - information ownership/executive sponsors
  - clear cause and effect relationship
  - 'hard' and 'soft' information

- Integrating with other systems:
  - budgets versus targets
  - individual versus corporate needs
  - monetary versus non-monetary incentives

Balancing short- and long-term indicators

For the goals to make sense, they must have concrete meaning. Progress against them must be measurable. I monitor the waymarks which indicate when significant steps towards achieving the goal have been made. Think of it as a road map, the journey to a distant town may require rivers and hills to be crossed which stand in the way (and there is not always the shortcut of a motorway). BA's Global Leader Goal required alliances to be contracted; complex and drawn out negotiations have resulted in every case. These are still continuing. These large steps can be tracked to measure progress in the long term. But what of the shorter term?

We have constructed a framework to measure shorter term progress against annual and monthly accountabilities for achieving financial efficiency and service quality performance. These accountabilities are clearly understood. They are reflected in the team tasks. Their consistency with the longer term goals is ensured by the business plan, in which targets are set and agreed.

An important ingredient in the balancing of short- and long-term objectives is the service-profit chain. In essence, this reflects the argument that you gain bigger benefits by keeping customers loyal than by having constantly to gain new ones. We are driven by the need to provide service excellence to our customers. We argue that long-term profitability comes only through well-motivated employees and quality processes. Our investment in training and process improvement should therefore be justified by the business results.

The development of organizational capabilities provides a link between the short and the long term. Much training and development will be required to direct our current skills into the altered forms we expect future service excellence to take. Our staff have people skills: warmth, friendliness, empathy. Measures of the organization's cultural development include the rate at which skills such as languages are being acquired, the provision of seamless service to each individual customer and the effect on customer retention.

Measuring business process performance

All business can be complex. We have analysed our airline's activities into nine business processes. These range from general functions like managing human resources to specific airline activities like hosting the customer. Part of hosting the customer is delivering baggage, and I want to use this baggage process as an example of how we measure business process performance.

I believe there are three ways in which we can measure achievement. Firstly, you can assess whether or not you implemented the specific policies you set. For baggage, we decided to set up a computer system for tracking the physical movement of baggage. The second area of measurement is performance indicators within the process. Such measures are how fast bags are returned to customers, if there was any damage and whether the correct labelling had been used. The third category is the customer perception of the results. Did the passengers feel that the baggage delivery was satisfactory? Measures of these three dimensions – policies, performance and perception – give a broad perspective of achievement.

Setting up a measuring system for every process in the company consumes much effort. The measures need to be appropriate to the activities involved, for example our process map of the transfer baggage system at Heathrow involves 125 activities but only six of the measures merit reporting outside the process itself.

Benchmarking for setting stretch targets

Which processes drive business success? We have used a number of approaches to assess the priorities for process improvement. Fit with strategy is the key. An example is the expansion of our Frequent Flyer Executive Club in various countries to support the Global Leader Goal. A second consideration is the scale of the gap between the results of the processes and customer needs. This can be examined from market research and direct customer feedback through complaints or customer forums. The third approach is to compare results with benchmarks. We have introduced an annual cycle of goal setting, performance planning, performance monitoring and benchmark audits for the main functions and areas of company activity. The audits comprise detailed comparison with competitors or functional comparators out in the field. We undertake these with teams drawn from the line.

Our performance planning involves setting goals and troubleshooting. To do that we have set up a range of key performance indicators starting with the most obvious – punctuality, professional service on the ground, attentive inflight service – and extending these to other areas, 'upstream' of service delivery such as the success of advertising or impact of service enhancements on customer retention. We do this for each of the functions of the company.

The aim of BA's corporate performance management system is to ensure that department and team targets are monitored and that sufficient 'stretch' is introduced to achieve our customer satisfaction objectives. Each year, we review the range of service quality targets. Continuous improvement is introduced by resetting these through benchmark audits, and making sure that this is done in conjunction with the budget process. The system is not yet perfect in application, but the clarity of a visible process has brought business focus to accepting targets which would otherwise have been thought impossible.

I believe that our model can be represented by a pyramid having vision at its top and its roots in operational framework. Direction is developed from the vision and cascaded through standards and team tasks. Feedback, of both performance and cultural reaction, is critical in influencing how the strategy is developed. This strategic perspective should weld together long-term goals with more immediate commercial priorities. This is my model for translating strategy into action.

Self appraisal – personal SWOT analysis

I often marvel that while each man loves himself more than anyone else, he sets less value on his own estimate than on the opinions of others.

Unknown

Many organizations are embarking upon self-assessment to drive continuous improvement. It is considered to be a very effective way for organizations like ICL, Kodak, Miliken, TSB and others to get a clear picture of their organization's performance. Similarly I believe self-assessment for individuals should also be undertaken to drive continuous improvement at a personal level.

Employees work under considerable pressures and in a constantly changing business and work environment. Apart from assessing their strengths and weaknesses formally they also have to assess how they are managing their time and stress at work. Time mismanagement is a key contributor factor to personal inefficiency and stress. How often do we hear 'If only I had time' or 'I wish there were more than 24 hours in a day'? If there were it would still not make any difference if you are not conducting self assessment.

The next section deals with **managing time** at a personal and professional level.

Managing your time

Time management is usually discussed within the context of work. The main objective is to manage time in order to be effective. It is said that we spend more of our life 'doing things right rather than doing the right things'.

People should manage time not only within the work situation but also manage their time to enhance their personal and family life and materialize their aspirations and personal goals.

Time management is a situational factor, i.e. it depends on the needs of different people. The type and the degree of organization depends on the type of work done, personality, culture and so on. Different people and different situations require varying degrees of organization. The techniques of managing time are easily understood but it is applying them that needs commitment, determination and self-control.

Every person is faced with numerous choices every day. One has to be many things to many people and all these people make demands on your time. In one day you have to be a team leader or a project leader, a colleague, a subordinate, a parent, a friend and so on. One therefore constantly has to make decisions to allocate time to meet various demands of the job, workplace and home. Every decision made involves an opportunity cost.

An opportunity cost is a sacrificed alternative. If you spend more time attending to interruptions or taking tea breaks then you have less time left for essential work, see Figure 6.7.

A series of assignments follow that will enable you to undertake self-assessment and improve your capability to manage time effectively.

Assignment 1: Indicate your time allocation (weekly or daily)

Activities	Hours	Per cent
Work		
Travel		
Personal		
Sleep		

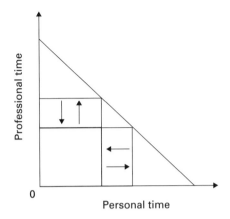

Figure 6.7   Trade-off between professional and personal time

Some people like to organize themselves while others enjoy the excitement of an unplanned day. Assuming you are one of those who believe in leading an effective life and view time as a composite but scarce resource, then going through the assignments will enable you to improve your personal and professional performance.

How one manages time at work affects not only professional benchmarks in term of one's career development but also the attainment of personal goals.

Assignment 2: List five goals you want to achieve in professional life and five goals in personal life

Professional:

1

2

3

4

5

Personal:

1

2

3

4

5

Assignment 3: Assume you have only six months to live. How would you like to spend your time?

I must do:

From Assignment 2 select three goals in your personal life and three goals related to your work and make a plan. The plan should answer the following questions:

- **What** is it you want to achieve?
- **Why** do you want to achieve them?
- **When** do you want to achieve them?
- **How** do you want to achieve them?

It is very easy to fall into the non-planning trap:

- I am too busy to plan.
- My job is too complicated to plan.
- You do not understand my job.
- I do not need to plan. I know what I have to do.
- Planning is boring.
- I have been in this job for too long.
- Planning means I admit I am inefficient.

What do I want to achieve?
Maybe you have never had an opportunity to focus your attention on what it is you would like to achieve in your life. Possibly you may have thought of your career development and career planning but not *life* planning. So start by setting one career goal and one personal goal. You may need many attempts to write down your goals but it does not matter how many attempts you have as long as you think about your goals. On this occasion getting it right first time is not important.

You need a mission for your life and for your work, just as organizations prepare mission statements of what it is they want to achieve. Distinguish between what you can be and do and what you would like to be and do. In other words the goals you set for your life and for your work should be SMART – sensible, measurable, attainable, realistic and have a time scale.

Why do I want to achieve these goals?
What is the purpose behind the objectives you have set? If your objective is to become a process leader at work then the reasons for this are:

I want to lead the team.
I want to experience working with and motivating team members.
I want to have a sense of achievement.
I want to prove I am capable.
I want to learn to manage.

When do I want to achieve my goals?
The next step in planning is to decide the time scale. I want to achieve my personal goal 'X' within the next two years. I want to achieve my work-related goal 'Y' within the next nine months.

How do I go about achieving my goals? This is a question of prioritizing.

Assignment 4: Activities analysis

List all activities you undertake from the time you arrive at work until the time you leave for home.

Daily activities

Group these activities according to your work-related goals. Some of these activities may lie outside your goals. Then categorize these activities according to:

1. Essential tasks.
2. Routine tasks.
3. Previous commitments.
4. Iterations – necessary and unnecessary.

If we take your work situation so far you have a clear picture of what goals you want to achieve, how you want to achieve them, when you want to achieve them and how do your daily activities relate to achievement of your goals.

Assignment 5 is to enable you to prioritize your activities according to the activities that are urgent and those that are important.

Urgent activities are things you must do whereas important activities contribute to your goals. Urgent jobs are unplanned, have priority over important jobs and often do not have the highest pay-off.

Assignment 5: Setting priorities

Do the activities that fall in segment A in Figure 6.8, followed by segment B and then segment C. The activities in segment D can wait.

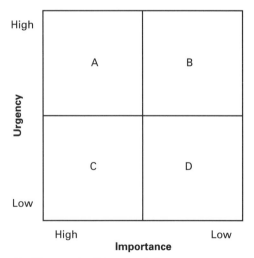

Figure 6.8   Setting priorities matrix

Managing interruptions

Look at all the daily activities which you have categorized as 'interruptions'. Examine unnecessary and unexpected interruptions and decide to avoid them. Some interruptions such as customer calls are part of your job. In handling interruptions be assertive but not aggressive, be firm but not rude. It is very important to learn to say 'no'.

On a daily basis you should analyse your activities and form a habit of going for high priority activities and eliminating time-wasters. If you are not careful, wasting time without realising it can become a way of life.

No matter how busy you are you should always take a time to plan. Time management is common sense but takes self-awareness, knowledge of procedure and commitment to turn common sense into practical sense.

Planning your time on a daily basis is like forming a new habit. Habits are behaviours that have been performed so often that they have become mechanical or automatic. Psychologist William James suggested the following approach to changing or forming habits.

Step 1: Launch the new behaviour as strongly as possible.
Step 2: Seize the first opportunity to act on the new behaviour.
Step 3: Never let an exception occur until new behaviour is firmly rooted.

Time management habits

- Keep a 'things to do' list.
- Do things in batches.
- Go after high pay-off goals.
- Distinguish between urgent and important items.
- Prioritize your activities.
- Set deadlines.
- Be realistic.
- Plan for an uncommitted time.
- Plan for 'necessary' interruptions.
- Learn to say 'no'.
- Eliminate time-wasters.
- Do not procrastinate.
- Be proactive not reactive.

- Make sure that the first hour of your day is very productive.
- Develop a personal philosophy of time.
- Become a 'being' rather than a 'doing' person.

Managing time has become one of the key aspects of modern life. With organizations de-layering, and processes getting re-engineered, business executives are constantly being asked to perfom more tasks and face more decisison-making situations.

Like organizations, executives have to review the way they do their work. Reviewing how they use their time and taking actions to improve their time utilization will minimize if not avoid stress at work. Proper time management will also improve executives' effectiveness.

Insight into stress

He who knows others is clever.
He who knows himself is wiser.

Unknown

We are the victims of our own technology and development. This does not mean that we should turn back the clock and give up modern conveniences and leave our high pressure jobs but it does mean that we should regularly take stock of ourselves, our strengths and weaknesses, our likes and dislikes and orientate our behaviour. In a changing turbulent world we are faced with so many decisions and choices to make and so much information to absorb that we frequently end up in a disoriented and confused state. Most of us manage such a state but there is always a danger of not being able to cope if we do not undertake self-assessment.

Stress is the result of our failure to cope with the pressure put upon us at domestic, social and professional levels. The classical example of the impact of change is apparent in the changing role of women. If a woman decides to pursue her career in addition to raising a family, she must be adept at balancing her career and family affairs. At work, she is expected to be 'twice as good as a man' in order to prove her competency. At home she has to work hard in order to prove that her career is not going to interfere with her traditional roles. Most women manage this state of affairs. Stress, however, affects all of us. The demands put upon us at work are increasing dramatically as businesses are adapting to the changing competitive environment.

Causes of stress can be attributed to the following:

- Unpredictable events.
- Changing lifestyle.
- Pressure of demand from home, friends and work.
- The time pressure.
- Feeling of insecurity.
- Unhappy family life.
- Unsympathetic employer.
- Lack of self confidence.
- Personal ambition.
- Expectations by others.
- Boredom at work.
- Excessive pressure at work.
- Lack of competencies.

This is not an exhaustive list. There are numerous other causes of stress.

An important distinction can be made between stress and pressure. In order to motivate ourselves and improve our performance we need some pressure. Beyond a certain point when we cannot respond to pressure and become unable to cope with situations we become stressed. Too much stress leads to a distressed state.

What are the symptoms?

Physiological:
- High blood pressure.
- Increased heart beat.
- Dryness of throat and mouth.
- Increased sweating.
- Nausea.

Psychological:
- Irritability.
- Anxiety.

212 Total Management Thinking

- Frustration.
- Fatigue.
- Migraines.
- Lack of confidence.
- Insomnia.

Behavioural:
- Addiction.
- Inability to concentrate.
- Impulsive behaviour.
- Feeling of being keyed up.

Again the lists of symptoms given are not exhaustive.

Coping with stress

- Examine what type of person you are, your strengths and your weaknesses.
- Pay attention to your weaknesses.
- Manage your time effectively.
- Review your priorities regularly.
- Identify your 'stressors' and think what you can do to manage them.
- Find time to do regular exercises.

The best person to help you when you are under stress is **you**.

How do you rate as an employee?

1. I know the mission of my organization
   Yes/No.
2. I agree with the vision statement of my organization.
   Yes/No.
3. I understand the relationship between my department's objectives and our corporate objectives.
   Yes/No.
4. I have full information on what my company wants to do.
   Yes/No.
5. I read the financial reports of my company.
   Yes/No.

6. I ask for an explanation if I do not understand the accounts.
   Yes/No.
7. I like working in teams.
   Yes/No.
8. I like sharing information with my colleagues.
   Yes/No.
9. I like assessing my own performance.
   Yes/No.
10. I can take constructive criticism.
    Yes?No.
11. I understand the nature of the project I am working on.
    Yes/No.
12. I share my feelings with my close associates.
    Yes/No.
13. I prioritize my activities.
    Yes/No.
14. I plan my daily work.
    Yes/No.
15. I do not take my work worries home.
    Yes/No.
16. I like to acquire new skills if needed.
    Yes/No.
17. I am willing to change my job within the company, if necessary.
    Yes/No.
18. I like to be involved in discussing my own targets.
    Yes/No.
19. I do say 'no' if I cannot cope.
    Yes/No.
20. I do help my colleagues if I can.
    Yes/No.
21. I do allow time for relaxation.
    Yes/No.
22. I do believe in delivering service excellence.
    Yes/No.
23. I treat my colleagues as my customers.
    Yes/No.
24. I always look for an opportunity to acquire a new skill.
    Yes/No.

Scoring: Give 1 point for 'Yes' and 2 points for each 'No'.
24 points: you are an excellent employee.
24-28 points: you are an OK employee.
29-36 points: you have to make an effort to improve.
37-48 points: you have to make a lot of effort to improve.

Selected reading

Richard Lynch and Kelvin F. Cross (1991). *Measure Up*. Basil Blackwell.

Walter Reid and D.R. Myddleton (1988). *The Meaning of Company Accounts*. Gower.

Martin Scott (1992). *Time Management*. Century.

The Economist Intelligence Unit Report (1994). The New Look of Corporate Performance Measurement.

The Open University Business School Course B889: Performance Measurement and Evaluation.

7 Empowerment

You can't light a fire with a wet match.

Texan saying

Summary

- Empowerment is another management phenomenon of the 1980s and 1990s.
- It is about getting the best out of people.
- Karl Marx and empowerment: the concept of alienation.
- Empowerment and motivation: Maslow, Herzberg and McGregor.
- Is empowerment the same as delegation?
- Delegation and how to do it: some guidelines.
- Barriers to delegation.
- Empowerment: its nature and essence.
- The empowerment plan.
- Empowerment in practice: Rover's road to excellence.
- Empowerment at Miliken.
- What organizations really do in practice: survey by Harbridge Consulting Group.
- Empowerment and organizational change: Digital Equipment Co. case study.
- Key success factors.

Power to the people

Empowerment became one of the key management buzz words in the early 1990s. Whether you talk about instituting total quality management, benchmarking, re-engineering or performance management you come across the concept of empowering people. Companies like Motorola, AT&T, Rank Xerox, ICL, BP and Miliken have all improved their business performance by empowering their people.

Empowerment is about people. In most recent times the most influential guru who has focused senior management's attention on people within the organization has been Professor Rosabeth Moss Kanter. In her book *The Change Masters – Corporate Entrepreneurs at Work*, which was published in 1983, she emphasized the need for people in organizations to work as 'corporate entrepreneurs'. The top management should learn to 'trust' their people and give them power to be innovative and bring about changes. In one of her chapters, entitled 'Empowerment', she gives examples of various situations in which people have played key roles in making organizations be adaptive to market needs.

Since then other management gurus like Tom Peters, Richard Pascale and Robert Waterman have highlighted the importance of empowering people to bring about business renewal.

The focus on people is not a new concept. It has been with us for over a century now. So how does the present focus on people in terms of empowerment differ from what has been happening in the past? Let us first look at the nature of the focus on people in the past and distinguish it from the concept of empowerment.

Focus on people – views from past gurus

For a very long time (almost 150 years), focus on workers was put on as a complement to the machine. Adam Smith in the second half of the eighteenth century had put forward his theory on division of labour and as we have seen many factories adopted his preaching on specialization.

Then came F.W. Taylor who put forward his *Principles of Scientific Management* (1911). He advocated his system to maximize 'prosperity' for employers and workers. Workers would benefit by earning higher wages and by working efficiently. He advocated the development of a true science of work, the scientific selection and progressive development of the worker, the constant co-operation of management and man.

Karl Marx was concerned about the 'modern' production methods which removed from workers control over their work to the extent they failed to be involved in it. In Marx's view technology and division of labour resulted in the alienation of workers from their work. This alienation had three aspects: powerlessness (workers have little control), meaninglessness (workers cannot relate their work to whole production) and isolation (cannot form part of production system). Alienation could result in widespread degradation and suffering.

Marx's idea was supported my many intellectuals in the 1840s. They felt the new method of working was detrimental to the workers' self-image and creativity. The theory of alienation in industry contained basic insights into the effects of socio-technical systems on human satisfaction.

It was not until the beginning of this century that the focus shifted from attention to the worker as a complement to the machine, to attention to the worker as an individual within a group.

All students of management have come across the Hawthorne investigations. Elton Mayo, professor of industrial research in the Graduate School of Business Administration at Harvard University conducted investigations at the Hawthorne Works of the Western Electric Company in Chicago during the period 1927-1932.

The investigations concluded that the favourable changes in productivity gains were attributed to increase in work satisfaction due to freedom in working environment and control over their own pace of work. The workers and supervisors developed a sense of participation and pride. These investigations led to the understanding of the 'human factor' in work situations.

In 1943 Abraham Maslow put forward a theory of motivation in the form of a hierarchy of needs. Human needs have certain priorities and each level must be satisfied to some extent before the next becomes dominant. The basic needs and their priority as established by Maslow are:

- Physiological needs.
- Safety needs.
- Social needs.
- Esteem or ego needs.
- Self-actualization needs.

According to the needs concept, management has the task of rearranging organizational conditions and structures in order to enable workers to achieve their own goals best by directing their own efforts toward the objectives of the organization.

In the late 1950s Professor Frederick Herzberg and some of his colleagues conducted research into work and motivation. The initial investigation was carried out among engineers and accountants and the results were published in the book *The Motivation to Work*. The study showed that factors which contributed to job satisfaction were different in kind from those which contributed to job dissatisfaction. Job satisfaction was due to the following factors:

* Achievement.
* Recognition.
* Attraction of work itself.
* Responsibility.
* Advancement.

Job dissatisfaction on the other hand was due to the following factors:

* Company policy.
* Supervision.
* Salary.
* Inter-personal relations.
* Working conditions.

This motivation–hygiene theory has shown the inadequacy of previous management assumptions about workers' motivation. Both Herzberg and Maslow have shown that the higher level needs cannot be met unless the characteristics of tasks are changed and workers are given opportunity for autonomy. Herzberg's theory has also led to the suggestion of 'job enrichment' – the designing of the job to incorporate aspects which provide the opportunity for the employee's psychological growth.

In 1960 Douglas McGregor published a book *The Human Side of Enterprise* in which he put forward his proposition that the traditional command and control management style implies basic assumptions about human motivation which he characterized as Theory X. These assumptions are:

* The average human being has an inherent dislike of work

and will avoid it if he can.
- Because of this they must be coerced, controlled, directed and threatened to get them to make an effort.
- The average human being prefers to be directed and wishes to avoid responsibility.

He proposed Theory Y with the following assumptions:

- Work is as natural as play or rest.
- External control is not the only means of obtaining efforts.
- The most significant reward that can be offered in order to obtain commitment is the satisfaction of the individual's self-actualization needs.
- The average human being learns, under proper conditions, not only to accept but to seek responsibility.
- Many more people are able to contribute creatively to the resolution of organizational problems than do so.
- At present the potentialities of the average person are not being fully used.

McGregor advocated making work meaningful and creating 'supportive relationships'.

McClelland in 1961 and Atkinson in 1964 emphasized the need for achievement, affiliation, power and autonomy. They believed that these needs remain 'latent' until activated by the environment, when they become 'manifest'.

In the 1960s considerable emphasis was put on delegation in order to manage the span of control. Delegation was also advocated to improve the quality of life.

Delegation

Division of labour created a hierarchy of command. Line authority relationships came into being as a result of the vertical or scalar growth of the organization. Authority in such a structure flows downward in the organization and acceptability flows upwards. Managers rely upon delegating authority to free themselves for more important activities. But managers must bear the full responsibility for their subordinates and take the blame for wrong decisions.

The Oxford Dictionary defines delegation as 'entrusting of authority to a deputy'. In management terms delegation implies: breaking down responsibility into tasks; analysing tasks to measure whether they are suitable for being carried out by specific individuals and assessing individuals to see whether they are suitable for carrying out these tasks in terms of ability, motivation and time available.

The following guidelines used to be provided for delegation:

- Consider the 'responsibility' which you wish to delegate.
- Analyse the responsibility in terms of separate tasks and write these down.
- Write down which of these tasks can be delegated and which have to be done by you.
- List those which have to be done by you and decide their order of importance and priority.
- Set a time scale for yourself for completion of your own tasks.
- List the individuals to whom you could delegate tasks.
- Rate their suitability for carrying out some or all of the tasks in terms of: (a) capability and experience, (b) availability, (c) motivation and (d) other factors which may affect them.
- Select the right candidates in terms of the above rating and urgency of tasks.
- Counsel the appropriate individual to ascertain: (a) whether he/she is capable or experienced enough, (b) whether they are available and (c) whether they are willing to do the work.

If he/she is not experienced but capable, decide whether they can be coached or trained within the time scale. If she/he is not motivated, but capable and/or experienced, then you will have to think about and initiate 'negotiation' to persuade them to accept responsibility without intimidation. If the individual is not available or restricted from doing the work, consider whether this obstacle could be overcome. If the answer is positive, the problem is avoided. If negative, move on to the most likely candidate.

Delegate work by explaining details of exercising 'active listening' to make sure that the facts are clearly understood. Set a time scale and arrange intermediary time for checking progress, if necessary.

Barriers to delegation

Barriers in the delegator:
- I like doing it.
- I can do it better myself.
- I can't explain what I want.
- I don't want to develop subordinates.
- Insecurity.
- Perfectionism. I can't tolerate mistakes.
- No time.
- Envy of subordinate ability.
- More comfortable 'doing' rather than ' managing'.
- Lack of organizational skill.
- Failure to follow up: people do what we *in*spect not what we *ex*pect.

Barriers in the delegatees:
- Lack of experience.
- Work over-load.
- Avoidance of responsibility.

Barriers in the situation:
- Boss won't tolerate mistakes.
- Decisions are too critical.
- No one to delegate to.
- Urgency.
- Under-staffing.
- Responsibility/authority position not clear.

Are you delegating properly?

- Do you leave your workplace with further tasks to do at home?
- Do you have to keep close tabs on the subordinate who is doing the job in order to exercise control?
- Do you spend more time getting the job done yourself than spending time planning and managing?
- Do subordinates bring all their problems to you instead of making decisions themselves?

If the answer to some or all of the above is 'yes' then you have to learn to delegate.

Practicality should be the guiding principle in delegation.

A manager who does not delegate has less time to interact with his colleagues. Delegation enables development of the subordinate's capability, builds his/her confidence and enriches the subordinate's work.

Delegation and the principles of delegation are very important in many organizations today. Not all organizations are ready to empower their workers and some confuse themselves between delegation and empowerment.

What is empowerment?

Empowerment is defined as an act of releasing human energy. It is about creating situations where workers share power and assume the responsibility of making decisions for the benefit of organizations and themselves.

To use the motivational perspective, it is about providing an opportunity to gain achievement, responsibility and advancement and it is also about eliminating meaninglessness, powerlessness and isolation.

It is, however, different from motivation in that empowerment happens in a different context. Success in the marketplace depends not only on the quality of top management decisions but also on their effective implementation throughout the workforce. Survival and reward go to those businesses which can develop and sustain the commitment of the whole workforce and maintain people's capacity for continuous change.

Those who advocate empowerment argue that in the de-layered organizations, where teams operate, it is important to:

- give people power to make quick decisions;
- get people's commitment and involvement;
- enable people to determine their own destiny;
- release into the organization the power that people already have to make decisions.

We have seen in total quality management, delivering service excellence and business process re-engineering, that quick responses to customers' needs are important and the only way one can manage effectively in a delayered structure is to empower employees. As Mark Brown, an independent consultant and the author of *The Dinosaur Strain*, puts it 'to empower people is to enable them to be the "customer within".'

Empowerment is different from delegation because it takes place within a different organizational structure and in a situation where work is done in teams. Delegation takes place in a hierarchical organizational structure. Secondly in delegation an aspect of the manager's responsibility is 'given' to the subordinate whereas, in empowerment there is dispersal of power throughout the organization.

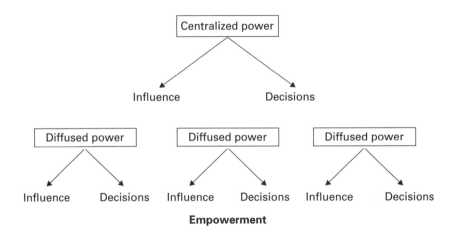

Figure 7.1   Centralized versus diffused power

Empowerment is based on the assumptions that:

- Employees want responsibility.
- They want to own a problem.
- They are all rational.
- They understand the corporate mission and goal.
- They feel that they are trusted.

Empowerment is central to the renewal of the corporation. Over the years people down the line have come up with very creative and effective solutions to help organizational renewal. Robert Waterman, in his book *The Renewal Factor*, cites stories of the *Wall Street Journal* and Delta Airlines where employee participation played a significant role in corporate renewal.

However, in empowerment trust plays a very important role. Management guru Richard Pascale believes that values and trust are pre-conditions of empowerment. These two factors encourage individuals to think, experiment and improve. Empowerment transforms commitment into contribution.

In the book *Transforming Corporate Culture* by David Drennan, the following two anecdotes illustrate the pay-off of trust. The first story relates to Marcus Sieff of Marks & Spencer.

> Sieff believed that the company was awash with duplicated paperwork, and that much of it could be eliminated by trusting employees to do a good job and to use common sense in solving day-to-day problems. He started with a team to examine the company's paperwork to see what could be cut out. They had some early successes; for example, the first experiment cut out six million pieces of paper a year. He still felt they had to do something dramatic to get the message across.
>
> At the time, stock-rooms in each store were protected by walls, and sales staff had to religiously complete stock-order forms to get stock-room staff eventually to bring down the goods they wanted to their counters. Sieff decided at a stroke that sales staff should be able to go and fetch their own stock direct from the stock-rooms. The chief accountant protested that there would be a huge increase in stealing, but Sieff went ahead anyway: he believed most people could be trusted. In the end, the level of stock was no greater than before, but in the process they eliminated some 26 million forms and documents, sold off 1000 filing cabinets they did not need any more, and 1000 stock-room assistants were able to be transferred to the sales floor. At the same time Sieff reinforced his trust in his people by getting rid of several hundred time clocks and punctuality actually improved.
>
> Do you think the message got round the company? Without doubt it did. People may hear you spouting

about simplification and trusting employees, but they are never quite sure whether you mean it, especially if they have a boss like the chief accountant.

The other story in the book relates to what Rene McPherson did at Dana Corporation in the USA. 'Almost every executive agrees that people are their most important asset, he said, 'yet almost none really lives it'.

When he took over as chairman he felt the company was far too bureaucratic and centrally controlled, effectively stifling people's initiative and ideas. When he piled the corporate policy manuals on top of one another they measured over 22 inches! He threw them all out and replaced them with a one-page policy statement. Said a vice president: 'We have no corporate procedures at Dana. We threw the books away. We eliminated reports and sign-offs. We installed trust.' That trust showed in reducing corporate staff from 600 to 100, leaving factory managers alone to mind their own 'store' and do their own buying without interference, and, as McPherson said, 'turning the company back over to people who do the work'.

Source: *Transforming Company Culture* by David Drennan (1992). McGraw-Hill.

Empowerment does not happen by issuing memos. A chief executive officer of one organization stood up at a meeting and announced to those present: 'Guys, you are now empowered. Be creative and make decisions as long as you inform your bosses and conform to the rules of the organization'. As far as new management thinking is concerned this particular chief executive officer feels he is 'with it'.

In his article entitled Navigating the Journey to Empowerment, which appeared in *Organizational Dynamics*, Spring 1995, W. Alan Randolph presents the following plan for implementing empowerment:

The empowerment plan

Share information
• Share company performance information.
• Help people understand the business.
• Build trust through sharing sensitive information.
• Create self-monitoring possibilities.

Create autonomy through structure
• Create a clear vision and clarify the little pictures.
• Clarify goals and roles collaboratively.
• Create new decision-making rules that support empowerment.
• Establish new empowering performance management processes.
• Use heavy doses of training.

Let teams become the hierarchy
• Provide direction and training for new skills.
• Provide encouragement and support for change.
• Gradually have managers let go of control.
• Work through the leadership vacuum stage.
• Acknowledge the fear factor.

Remember: Empowerment is not magic; it consists of few simple steps and a lot of persistence.

Many senior managers are afraid to empower their staff. Some of these managers have spent a number of years gaining power, so giving it away is very difficult thing to do. The problem is that power is viewed as a fixed sum. If I give you some of my power that means I have less power. There is a lack of dynamics of power. Empowering people increases the total power within the organization as most of the people already have the power to make decisions but not the opportunity. Empowerment provides that opportunity.

Richard Newton, head of human resources at BP Co. highlighted the following basic rules of empowerment at a conference on empowerment organized by the Economist Conferences:

1. Articulate clearly and openly the company's business goals.
2. Align individual aspirations with those of the company.
3. Reconcile career and personal objectives with business goals.
4. Recognize and encourage business flexibility or diversity.
5. Establish effective global linkages to achieve group synergy.

At the same conference William Guitink, vice president of management training and development at Philips Electronics BV, explained an approach to the transformation of Philips. He said vitalization at Philips is about enlisting the energies and talents of all the people to bring about lasting change. The road to successful change and sustained profitability consisted of a number of steps which he highlighted under the headings of:

- Creating a shared mindset.
- Changing behaviour.
- Building competencies/capabilities.
- Improving business performance.

Empowerment can be looked at from an organizational perspective and an individual perspective. Organizations can empower by creating an appropriate climate and good leadership to facilitate. Employees have to be convinced that top management mean business and that they have trust in their employees. However, at the end of the day it is people who have to empower themselves. They have to give commitment and involvement. This is the nature of the 'psychological contract' these days. The way businesses are going and have gone, employees feel very insecure and have less or no loyalty. If the promotional ladder has disappeared in order to get workers to be flexible and adaptive to change, then present employees expect 'modern' organizations to create a climate for them to be creative, use their heads and be treated with respect. Empowerment provides that opportunity.

At the conference mentioned above, Alastair Wright, former director of human resources at Digital Equipment Co. emphasized the fact that organizations are designed to disempower. Only the empowered can empower. People must empower themselves and that must come from within.

If organizations do not empower their people they will not be able to recruit and retain people who can help them survive in a changing profile of business world. As far back as 1970, when some organizations were having problems recruiting good graduates, a survey was conducted asking one in four male undergraduates why UK industry was not able to recruit its full share of graduates.

Among the reasons given were:

* Lack of sufficient opportunity to be creative.
* Loss of individual identities.
* Involvement in a 'rat race' within the organizations.

This was 25 years ago. In the 1990s if the employers do not make a 'new deal' with their people they will face very acute recruitment and staff turnover problems.

Recently I conducted a word association exercise with a group of business executives. The following words kept on creeping up:

* enthusiasm
* enabler
* creative
* intellectual
* human being
* energetic
* decision-making
* authority
* respect
* pride
* fulfilment
* values
* responsibility
* influence
* achievement
* confidence
* trust
* commitment
* loyalty
* employability
* initiative

These words provide us with an insight into the concept of

empowerment and should enable us to distinguish it from worker participation or delegation.

Organizational desperation or genuine desire to experiment?

In various organizations today the most amazing things are happening. Dr Steven Covey, a 62-year-old, is making his mark on many organizations. His best-selling book, *The Seven Habits of Highly Effective People,* is about moral renewal and self-help. He believes that to do good you have to be good. The focus of his 'teaching' is on individual and organizational morality.

He preaches formation of habits by doing the following:

* Individuals should take initiatives and responsibility.
* Begin any task with an end in mind.
* Put first thing first. Be in control of your feelings and moods.
* Think win/win.
* Seek first to understand then to be understood.
* Synergize the situation by thinking that wholes are greater than the sum of their parts (2 + 2 = 5).
* Take time to cultivate physical, mental, social, emotional and spiritual dimensions of yourself.

His book and his advice is addressed 'To my colleagues, empowered and empowering.'

Do businesses take him seriously? Yes. Companies like AT&T, Ford, Xerox and Dow Chemical are all serious about his advice. The organizations are beginning to search for their 'souls' with a view to maximizing the potential of their employees. Some individuals have started consultancy companies to advise organizations to search for their corporate morals.

The poet David Whyte from Yorkshire, uses poetry to help individuals and organizations to understand creativity. Organizations are now striving to change in order to make their workers feel good about working so that they become highly motivated and involved.

Empowerment in practice

The following is the abstract from the article, Rover's Road from Excess to Excellence, published in *UK Quality*, March 1995:

Empowering people

While culture, leadership and planning linked to customer focus are all important elements, world-class achievement is above all down to 'the quality and commitment of your people' Mr Towers (CEO) says. Most important is to ensure the involvement of every one of the 33 000 strong workforce.

'Continuous improvement is a formal requirement of every associate,' he says. 'Everyone is expected to participate in discussion groups, quality action teams and the company suggestion schemes.' The introduction of a 'New Deal' set of employee terms and conditions has been a key driver in this process, says David Bower, personnel director. Though Rover has shed 13 000 workers since 1989, the New Deal has instilled a sense of security and an attitude of shared destiny at all levels. Blue- and white-collar distinctions have been abolished, as have such terms as 'hourly paid' and 'salaried staff'. Rover is a 'single status' company where everyone at every level wears company overalls. The New Deal also calls for maximum devolution of authority and accountability to the people actually doing the job – 'empowering the fact holders' in Rover-speak.

Constant two-way communications are the norm, and a formal and informal code of practice is encompassed in a team-working code of practice called 'Conquer', developed on the shop floor. It upholds maxims such as 'no skulking', 'consider others' opinions', 'be truthful' and 'admit when you are wrong'. Conquer has been adopted by other groups within Rover, by choice, not by command. Productivity bonus schemes have been replaced by bonuses directly linked to the company's performance. The relationship between management and workers is formally defined as a 'partnership'.

In 1990 Rover Learning Business was formed to provide a continuous learning environment for all Rover associates. The size of its task can be seen in the results of last year's Rover Group Associate Attitude Survey. Although 85 per cent of employees 'enjoy working for Rover' and are 'happy with my job situation', many feel that the company could make better use of the talents and skills available; 80 per cent want more involvement in improving their working environment.

While 82 per cent confirmed that quality improvement became more important over the past year, and internal customer and supplier awareness moved to 69 per cent from 57 per cent in 1992, some employees still think quantity is more important than quality.

The company uses attitude surveys to identify areas where improvement is needed. The task of the TQI team is to encourage self-assessment rather than to enforce quality initiatives.

Extract published by kind permission, © 1995 European Quality Publications Ltd. Rover's Road from Excess to Excellence (March 1995).

People become the cornerstone of the success of many projects in which organizations get involved. At a conference on empowerment, Clive Jeanes, managing director, European Division of Miliken Industrials Ltd, made the following presentation on how Miliken went through the 'quality journey' and the part played by employees at Miliken.

This is the story of a large, American-owned multinational, that had the dominant share of its market around the world. They watched with amusement as a small Japanese company started to challenge them. Their amusement turned to concern when, in a few years, this upstart competitor overtook them in the Far Eastern markets; and their concern turned to alarm, when later on, the Japanese company started to grow in the USA and Europe. The two companies were, by now, the same size, and the Japanese had caught up to the extent of having the same share of the world market.

So the Western company needed to do something. They hired a consultant. 'Go and study this Japanese company,' they said. 'Find out how they have been so successful so quickly; and come back and tell us who will be the eventual winner in the contest – them or us.' So the consultant went off and studied the Japanese company for three months. When he came back, his message was short but very clear: 'They will win.' 'Why?' asked the American clients. 'What can we do to stop them?' 'Nothing,' came the reply. 'Let me put it this way. You employ about 100 000 people around the world. So, now, do they. Of your 100 000 you have about 100 looking for ways to do things better; and then telling the other 99 900 what to do. They, on the hand, have 100 000 people looking for ways to do things better. And when they find them they just go ahead and implement them.'

I will let you be the judge of whether or not that is a true story. What is certain, however, is the accuracy of this quotation from Mr Matsushita, the chairman of the company which bears the name. This quotation makes the same point as my opening anecdote; that the Japanese are convinced that they will win, because they have found out how to harness the intelligence, the experience and the skills of all their employees, towards meeting their objectives, whereas we in the West have traditionally not done so.

This is not, by the way, going to be another Japan bashing paper – I admire their management systems too much to knock them. But equally, I do not believe that it is too late for us to understand this aspect of the Japanese success, and adapt it to our needs. It is because I believe we are seeking a way to do this, that I am happy to speak at a conference on empowerment, and to share with you some of my observations, as well as some of the things we have been able to do in our company.

In Miliken, we started our quality journey in 1981; we are, therefore, now in our thirteenth year, and in that time, we can claim to have made some progress. We also found out the good news and the bad news. Let me tell you about these. The bad news is – quality is not a quick fix. You can't just hire a consultant, appoint a quality manager, tell them to 'do' quality, and expect anything to change. It won't work. The responsibility for quality cannot be delegated – it must remain with the senior management. If top management says one thing, but does another, nothing will change. It takes time, it takes effort, it takes cost and at times it can be painful. That's the bad news.

The good news is, that if you are serious about quality, and persist, it really does work. We have seen breakthroughs in area after area in our businesses and achievements, which, quite honestly, we would have thought impossible a few years ago. We have seen 90 per cent of product quality problems eliminated; we have seen lead times reduced to 25 per cent or even 20 per cent of what we used to think possible; we no longer gasp in disbelief at talk of a ten-fold improvement; we have seen all these things happen many times. So it does work; we have proved it to ourselves and we have seen other companies being similarly successful.

But on top of the good news, there is even a better news. As we have made improvements and breakthroughs we have come to understand that there is no limit to how far we can improve. Each breakthrough has led to more things being seen as possible which had not been understood before. As a very simple illustration, once you are confident that your production outfit is totally reliable then you can introduce 'just-in-time' production. But do not attempt JIT if a significant part of what you make is out of specification or needs to be worked on a regular basis – you will have chaos. It has to be done

one step at a time. So the journey is one with a very clear direction – towards total excellence – but no finite destination since the definition of excellence is continuously changing. What is seen as excellent today will be taken for granted tomorrow.

If all your competitors can deliver in 28 days and you work out how to do it in 14 you will be seen as excellent. But as soon as some of the others work out how they too can meet the 14-day promise – and they will – you are no longer excellent because customers will have come to expect a 14-day delivery as normal. So, while your competition is working out how to go from 28 to 14 days, you had better be working on how to get to seven, if you want to stay ahead.

Let me step back a while to my early working days. I am now in the thirty-fifth year of my working lifetime, and when I started in the late 1950s, what I learned about management and organization was basically a refinement of the principles which Henry Ford had used on the production line for his Model T – what the Japanese call the Taylor system. Train people to do one job, or one small series of jobs, then get them to do it faster so that you thus achieve the highest output and efficiency at the lowest cost. The cost accountant and the industrial engineer were the key people and woe betide the operator, or manager who dared to challenge their diktats.

But at the same time, on the other side of the world, in Japan, some new and different ideas were emerging. As the Japanese set about rebuilding of their industry and of their society after the Second World War, they turned among others to two American teachers, Deming and Juran. What they learned from them, and the way they developed and expanded led to a new model for an ideal business being developed. As the Japanese started to expand into overseas markets their products, which had previously been thought of in the West as cheap, junky imitations were slowly perceived to be of better quality, often at a lower price and increasingly innovative. So we started to look at the new Japanese model to try to understand what had changed to make them successful. What did we see? We saw a model where quality was an integral part of the business strategy. We saw that the model could produce better outputs – sales, volume, profits, capital equipment, inventories; we saw a faster time-to-market cycle with a far higher success rate of new products. And we saw that all the functions were aligned and focused on the key objective of meeting the requirements of their customers.

And so, with the help of people like Deming, Juran, Crosby, Peters, Schoenberger and some of the Japanese like Ishikawa, Taguchi, Mizuno and Imai, we started building our own Miliken version of the new model. I have to tell you that having operated for 20 years or more in the 'old' way, change was not easy for me, nor for the other managers of my age or more. But we stuck at it and our new model has now become pretty clear. Let me highlight what I see as some of the key differences between then and now, traditional and modern or what I have chosen to call the 'old model' and the 'new model'.

In the old model, the major objective is normally growth – growth in sales, in earnings, in return on investment or some combination of these. In the new model the major objective is normally that of customer satisfaction. In order to achieve growth the old model is based on economies of scale and long production runs, to give low cost and high efficiency. The new model is based on short runs, small lot sizes and quick changeover, to give the fastest customer response. The old model would use inventory as a buffer; the new model is based on JIT and believes inventory should be as close to zero as possible.

The old model was based on specialization of labour; the new model believes in the separation of brain power from manual labour. The assumption was that manual employees were not supposed to think about their work, so they were trained to do what they were told and not expected to suggest improvements. The new model recognizes that all workers have brains; that those actually doing the work understand it and its problems and that, if they were trained and encouraged they are the best source of problem-solving, quality and productivity investments, cost savings and other areas previously seen as the preserve of management. The old model put the system first and, in doing so, often led to sub-optimization. The new model tries to put people first and to ensure that it is the total system that is improved not just parts of it.

In the old model, there is a belief that you have to have a trade-off between quality and cost; that to pursue the highest quality level would raise costs and that quality was therefore negotiable to some acceptable level. The new model understands that the highest level of quality, with the lowest defects is the only acceptable quality level. In the old model quality means inspection, reworks, re-making, allowances and warranty costs. In the new model prevention is the aim of quality management. The old model is normally typified by a hierarchical, vertically-structured organization. I have heard this called a series of functional silos. If you were in the manufacturing 'silo', then that was where you lived and worked and fought your battles. And the enemy, as often as not, were those idiots in sales or planning or finance or design – or even perhaps customers who just did not understand or listen to your problems. The new model tries to create a culture of networking among and across functions so that teams from different disciplines can work together to solve problems and also understand that the 'enemy' is not another department or function, nor is it the customer – but that the competition are the ones who have to be beaten. Linked to this, the old model is likely to contain many layers of management, with short spans of control and have people who will very jealously guard their turf. The new model puts service, value and customer satisfaction first. Finally the old model hates change and will always pursue stability and the maintenance of the status quo, whereas the new model company is characterized by a divine discontent which will cause it to seek continuous improvement in everything it does and welcome change in the interests of better performance.

If I had to say in one phrase what is the single most important factor in changing a company's culture, I would quote Deming and say 'drive out fear'. People problems are the biggest barrier to TQM. Until the operator feels that he can speak openly with management at any level he will not be willing to contribute fully. So we at Miliken set out to create an environment which focuses on people, based on the principle that each person is part of the overall process, each has a role to play and has to be recognized as being of value. In a total quality organization the associate must be part of any decision-making which concerns their area within the overall process. The environment must support continuous improvement throughout the organization where the focus of that improvement effort is on the downstream customer and where ownership for that improvement is accepted by the process owners and the associates working in the process. But be sure this is what you want to do before you start because once you have created an environment where everyone wants the whole organization to succeed you cannot easily reverse the process. And morale is critical. Unless there is honest and visible commitment from the very top of the organization the process will be seen as just another short-term management programme which probably won't work and which will go away in a month or two.

Roger Miliken initiated and still personally leads our company's pursuit of excellence with a zeal which Tom Peters describes in a dedication in his book Thriving on Chaos, as one of two people 'whose flexibility of mind and raging impatience with inaction have inspired the most dramatic and fruitful organizational revolutions I've witnessed'.

Our quality improved because our production associates realized we really were serious. They understood that we weren't doing studies to be used in disciplinary procedures but were asking **them** to measure every part of their own process to highlight the areas where there was an opportunity for improvement. And our leaders began listening, asking open questions and listening naively to the answers. Our associates realized that they were being asked for advice and help in our pursuit of excellence. For years they had been performing like machines, conforming exactly to carefully written specifications and we were beginning to realize that we had always interpreted our customer needs as we had wanted to. We were moving ahead at a great pace and across a very bold front.

So broad and so fast in fact that communication did not always work. For example, when we introduced JIT to one of our plants there was very visible reduction in work in process inventory and in work apparently waiting to be done. So word quickly got round that we were closing the plant down. We had forgotten to communicate and to educate our associates in what JIT meant! Our vocabulary also changed. We went

From employee to associate;
From staff to support;
From management to leadership.

We started to focus on people. We moved from open-door policy to no-door policy as we changed to open plan offices.

We abolished privileged parking. The barriers come tumbling down when the MD or CEO gives up his special parking space and the only reserved places are for visitors. We all wear identical name badges; these show our names but no job titles. Any necessary safety clothing is worn by all associates in an area including leaders.

Our old system focused on things going wrong. We had been brilliant fire-fighters. Our associates could always be relied upon to put right all the wrong things we managers had told them to do. We recognized that management really was the problem. We implemented training and education. Associates became multi-skilled and started job-rotation and they were educated to realize their multi-talents. We shared problem-saving techniques and tools like statistical process control, Pareto's analysis, cause and effect diagrams, brainstorming and flow charting. And we found that production and administrative associates could be just as effective in using these as management ever had been.

We removed piecework pay from our system. We'd been paying for quantity not quality. Our production associates now work increasingly in self-managed teams as we have continuously reduced line management and redeployed these managers into process improvement roles. Through education and involvement, our production associates are becoming eager to contribute towards our company's success. They take a keen interest in our customers and suppliers. One example involved an opportunity (a problem in non-TQM language) where we were producing off-quality products due to poor raw material coming into one of our UK plants. Our production team arranged a meeting with the operators in our supplier's shop floor. No management were present. The result was an 80 per cent improvement in quality in the next delivery with further improvements ever since. In the old days our management talking to our supplier's management could have successfully kept the problem going for years!

By empowering our associates to make their own decisions and educating them in the use of diagnostic tools we feel we are giving ourselves the best possible chance to survive and prosper into the next century.

Now I want to talk about the most neglected, yet probably the most valuable tool in the whole of TQM lexicon, recognition. If people are not recognized as valuable contributors and innovators they will stop contributing and innovating. If they are recognized by their peers and leaders there are no bounds to the effort they will expend to acquire more and more recognition.

... The road to total quality is not easy one. Nor can senior management delegate its responsibility. To give yourself best chance of winning, be like the Japanese company I referred to: empower 100 per cent of your people to help you get the job done. Is that easy? No. Do you have to do it? No. But if you want to be around in the twenty-first century I do strongly advise you to work out how best to deploy empowerment in your company.

There are many stories from various organizations of how some of their employees have taken initiatives to bring about corporate renewal or new products in the market. The story of 3M and 'Post-its' is very old now but it does make the point of employees' 'freedom' to be creative. 3M always believed in 'allowing' their workers to work in their own way. Empowerment in some organizations has been practised long before it became a fashionable management thinking.

Empowerment is important now for all organizations mainly because of the intensive changes taking place in the marketplace. Yes, it has been practised in some organizations for a number of years but what is important is that it should be practised by all organizations who want to survive in business and it is also very important that the concept is understood properly. Empowerment should not be an exception in the philosophy of managing people in the 1990s or in the twenty-first century.

Empowerment – what organizations really do

Harbridge Consulting Group Ltd, which is now a part of Coopers & Lybrand, conducted a survey on empowerment and the report was published in 1994.

The following is the 'Summary and Conclusions' of the survey.

Thirty-three senior human resource and management development managers who had identified their organizations as having at least started a process of empowerment participated in an in-depth interview with a member of the Harbridge House research team. Interviews were carried out in the Autumn of 1993.

What is empowerment?

Drawing on an extensive literature review, and our own work with US clients dealing with empowerment issues, we developed the following definition of empowerment: sense of ownership and fulfilment while achieving shared organizational goals.

Survey respondents also stressed the implications of empowerment for decision-making: in particular, allowing employees freedom to make decisions relating to their own work, and allowing decisions to be made as close to the point of delivery as possible.

Reasons for empowerment initiatives

It may be that many organizations have no choice but to empower individuals as a consequence of reductions in employee numbers (78 per cent of organizations in the survey had reduced the number of employees in the last five years).

Notwithstanding this effect, 97 per cent of our sample saw empowerment as being of high importance to business success. Of the business 'drivers' affecting organizations in the current decade, customer focus emerged as the most significant, all respondents rating it as of high importance. In addition, a third of our sample specifically identified customer focus when asked to list the main benefits of empowerment. The responses to this question are summarized in Table 7.1.

Table 7.1   The benefits of empowerment (percentage of sample)

Increased motivation, commitment, energy and enthusiasm	41
Improved customer focus	34
Job enrichment, increased sense of ownership	31
Reduced staff turnover	19
Improved financial contribution	16
Increased innovation	16
Greater flexibility	16
Higher skill levels	13
Improved individual performance	9
Lower administrative costs	6
Better ability to cope with change	6

In many of the organizations we spoke to, however clear the organization may be about the ultimate benefits, the word 'empowerment' is never used, the process existing instead as a component of broader initiatives such as customer focus or business process re-engineering.

One area of concern surrounds the level of commitment of the board or senior management to empowerment. Certainly a significant number of respondents told us that their organizations' initiatives originated from one lone board member or, in three cases, from the respondent him or herself, who had to champion the process in isolation.

Initiatives supporting empowerment

A number of organizational management development interventions lend themselves to the empowerment process. Some, like continuous improvement, enjoy a symbiotic relationship with empowerment in which each requires elements of the other. Others, like basic skills training or performance management, can be used to support and contribute to empowerment initiatives.

We found that training needs analysis, skills training, performance management and continuous improvement, were the most commonly used contributors; the least common were quality circles, self-directed work teams, changes in job title and job guarantee schemes. In fact, none of the organizations we spoke to offered any kind of job guarantee scheme. This is not exactly surprising in the current tightly belted business environment, but a lack of job security provides a shaky foundation for a process which makes significant demands upon the energy and commitment of junior level staff.

The role of the team

The self-directed work team, which takes collective ownership and accountability for a discrete part of an organizational process, is still a rare sight in organizations. Nevertheless, work teams in an organization may display many of the qualities of a self-directed team without being fully autonomous. The extent to which teams within our survey displayed these qualities is shown in Table 7.2. The figures refer to the percentage of organizations in which at least one significant work team displays the quality in question.

Table 7.2   Work team practices (percentage of sample)

Plan/control/improve own process	75
Co-ordinate work with other departments	56
Collective responsibility for quality	50
Set own goals	44
Create own schedules	44
Review own performance	38
Discipline own members	38
Have full accountability	38
Inspect own work	25
Order material/deal with suppliers	25
Prepare own budgets	22
Hire own replacements	3

By far the most common team practice in a sample was planning, controlling and improving the team's own work processes, followed by the co-ordination of work with other departments. These practices in themselves are not particularly 'empowering' and simply demonstrate good efficient working practices. It may be that they are the easiest practices to develop without the need to change fundamentally the structure, culture or systems of the organization.

It is possible to infer, from the extent to which these practices are followed, the level of outside control exerted on teams in our organizations. In this respect it is significant that the three least common practices are related to personnel control, financial control and quality control. These less common practices are those which, if handed over to teams, would reduce the organization's ability to hold centralized control (the more common practices allow teams to contribute to the process rather than take it over).

It is also telling that only 38 per cent of our sample organizations contain teams who are accountable for what they do: this suggests that in other cases power is retained at levels above the team.

The role of the manager

Perhaps the most distinctive feature of empowerment is that a fully 'empowered' organization requires a fundamental shift in the day-to-day job of the line manager or supervisor. His or her planning, organizing and decision-making role will have been devolved to the team or individuals below; and in an organization where information from outside is processed and acted upon by those in the front line, the manager as a channel of information between upper and lower levels of the hierarchy becomes surplus to requirements. The manager's traditional role, variously described by respondents as 'hero', 'policeman' and 'technical expert' must give way to a role described by one respondent as 'willing helper'. Management in the context of empowerment involves motivating and aligning people behind organizational goals – in short, acting as a leader rather than a manager.

In those organizations which involve their managers in the process of empowerment, the involvement takes the allowing forms:

- Coaching, in which skills and knowledge are transferred on-the-job.
- Acting as sponsor for subordinate projects.
- Facilitating suggestion programmes or quality circles.
- Mentoring, in which managers offer guidance to more junior employees in a way in which is more holistic than a straightforward coaching role.
- Facilitating self-directed work teams, where the manager offers the benefit of his/her experience and expertise without directing the team's activities.
- Facilitating training events, more formal as a method of skills transfer than on-the-job coaching, but still aiding the process of passing knowledge and responsibility 'down the line'.
- Setting up job rotation schemes to broaden the experience of junior employees.
- Redesigning processes to enable more involvement by those at lower levels.
- Giving accreditation to front-line staff on the acquisition of specific competencies.
- Facilitating business planning teams.
- Taking ownership of their staff's development.

It is not uncommon for line managers themselves to become more empowered, by being involved in policy development for example. By developing a sense of ownership over a part of the process they are less likely to see themselves as transmitters of control. Several organizations in our sample use an 'empower the empowered', approach, allowing line managers to spread the word about empowerment so that the culture changes incrementally.

Barriers to empowerment

It is something of an organizational truism that everyone feels threatened by change. Certainly the fundamental shift in culture demanded by a concerted process of empowerment is likely to disrupt the homeostatic calm of most organizations. One might predict that middle management would be the most threatened by the process, seeing itself as having most to lose. Our survey supported this, 62 per cent of respondents saying that middle managers in their organizations felt threatened by empowerment. In over a third of organizations, senior and junior management also perceived some threat.

The reasons for these feelings of being threatened emerged in the extensive qualitative comments we collected. They can be clustered under the following headings:

- **Fear.** This was variously itemized as a fear of punishment on the part of the junior staff unused to the freedom to take risks; a fear of withdrawal of support from one's superior if things go wrong; the fear of failure; and, most significantly, the fear of losing one's job either because of making mistakes or through being surplus to requirements.
- **Role clarity.** This cluster includes managers who feel bypassed when power is handed from a level above them to a level below them; a general lack of understanding and direction; managers who react to the uncertainty of their new post-empowerment role by trying to increase their level of control; and a feeling of incompetence in the face of demands of a new and unfamiliar role.
- **Clinging to established ways of doing things.** Under this heading come organizations whose traditional task-oriented culture proved highly unsuited to a people-oriented process; and tensions caused by the shift from a culture in which seniority is based in the length of service to one where it is based on competence.
- **The threat of responsibility.** The consensus here was that accepting responsibility is a good deal harder than blaming others when things go wrong; some individuals also view responsibility as creating competitive situations.

In addition to specifically investigating the nature of the perceived threat of empowerment, we asked respondents to identify impediments to the success of the process. Many of the comments reinforced the findings given above, but a number of significant new topics also emerged. These impediments or barriers are listed in Table 7.3 in order of frequency of mention.

The three most commonly mentioned barriers – managers unwilling to let go, fear of the new, and risk aversion – all relate to individual or cultural attributes. These subjective, value-based factors are the most likely sticking points of an empowerment policy, and all the systems and structural alterations in the world will be wasted if the culture of the organization and the values of its people are not attuned to the desired new ways.

Table 7.3 Impediments to empowerment (percentage of sample)

Managers not letting go	50
Fear of the new	32
Risk aversion	22
Lack of skills/confidence	19
Lack of involvement/co-operation	19
Lack of understanding	16
No clear standards	13
Cost of training/lack of resources	13
Communication/IT system	9
Short-termism	6
Compensation systems	6
Hierarchical structure	6
Size/spread of organization	6

Measuring empowerment

How does an organization know when it is empowered? The answer depends on whether you view empowermenet as an end in itself or as the means to another end (such as customer focus). Our respondents, when asked what criteria they might use to measure the success of their initiatives provided the following list, reflecting perhaps the particular benefits the organization originally anticipated:

Customer-focused indicators
• Increase in customer satisfaction.
• Decrease in customer complaints.
• Increased customer retention.
• Customer perception of difference in service/increased value.

Employer-focused indicators
• Increase in employee satisfaction.
• Exit analysis (i.e. ascertaining reasons why people leave the company).
• Degree to which employees feel in control – demand for training.
• Degree to which employees take responsibility.
• Degree of success of empowered managers in developing themselves/making themselves more promotable.

System-focused indicators
- Reduced training costs through more focused training.
- Success of TQM projects.
- Increase in productivity.

In terms of measuring the success of empowerment as an end in itself, we provided respondents with a list of qualities one might expect to see in an empowered organization and asked them to rate the extent to which these were evident in their own organizations (5 = to a very great extent; 1 = to a very small extent). The average ratings are shown in Table 7.4.

Table 7.4   Measures of empowerment – average scores

Maximization of skills	3.43
Performance/results rewarded	3.39
Sense of purpose and commitment	3.22
Achievements recognized	3.14
Contribution linked to organizational success	3.14
See end results of work	3.07
Ongoing feedback	3.00
Managers facilitate/coach/sponsor	2.76
Everyone accountable for own contribution	2.73
Acceptance of responsibility	2.72
Equal opportunity to make input	2.69
Commitment to customer-focused indicator	2.68
Individual autonomy	2.41
Work teams develop processes	2.35
Job security	2.30

The most achievable step towards empowerment appears from these figures to be providing individuals with appropriate training or coaching to maximize their skills. The least achievable is ensuring that employees feel secure in their jobs. Organizations should perhaps not be over hasty in attributing a lack of job security to external factors: not one of the organizations in the survey operates a job guarantee scheme, and most have a significant proportion of employees whom they have identified as threatened by the empowerment process. These two qualities epitomize the fragility of any empowerment initiative. The need to entrench a two-way commitment cannot be overstated; providing skills training is not enough if a job in which to use these skills is not assured.

It is interesting to note that the seven highest scoring qualities (from maximization of skills down to ongoing feedback) could all potentially be true of an organization in which managers operate in their 'traditional' roles; while three of the four lowest scoring statements (the exception being job security) can only be true of an organization in which individuals are given ownership and the freedom to make decisions about how to approach their tasks. Accountability and responsibility also score comparatively low. These figures illustrate the fact that the passing of autonomy and accountability to lower levels of the organization is a difficult process to achieve; they may also illustrate a lack of willingness (for whatever reason) on the part of the organizations to achieve this final step towards full empowerment.

Conclusions

Without exception, the organizations we spoke to when conducting our survey regard themselves as on the path to, but some distance from, full empowerment. Whether they will achieve it is open to question. Despite the ever growing body of knowledge in this country, the case histories which are shared at conferences and in magazines, empowerment retains the mythical status of the holy grail. But why should such a well documented sought-after process remain so elusive? Our research suggests some reasons for this.

The main reason why empowerment is a somewhat fuzzy issue is that ultimately, its success relies on the acceptance by every individual in the organization. Thus it must preach its benefits not only to individuals with different personal value systems, but to different groups of stakeholders. Those front-line staff who value the opportunity for greater autonomy may run head first into the entrenched attitudes of managers who fear the consequences of relinquishing their decision making and controlling role. Those managers who see the empowerment of front-line staff as the key to efficiency and flexibility may fail to convince workers who are wary of taking risks when they have consistently been punished for failure in the past. And senior managers who see it as a way of reducing costs may be at loggerheads with those who see the necessity of investing in new systems or new training.

Empowerment is expensive. Developing competence in front-line staff to handle new responsibilities takes time and costs money. Changing the behaviour of managers whose roles need to change may tie up those managers in a long process of coaching and counselling. And in a time of recession, how many organizations really have the resources to commit to a process whose benefit is almost impossible to measure objectively?

The complexities of introducing empowerment as a full-scale organizational initiative call above all for consensus, commitment and focus. Everyone throughout the organization should know why empowerment is being introduced and what it means to each individual. The need for internal marketing is paramount. Any individual presented with a major change in working style is bound to ask 'What's in it for me?' and the organization must have an answer.

Business survival may be the obvious reason, but the countless employees who fear losing their jobs as a result of initiatives such as this may not be comforted by the thought of being sacrificed for the good of the company. This is one reason why some form of job guarantee scheme may be crucial for the success of such an enterprise.

Empowerment is, in many ways, a leadership issue. One aspect of this is the need for those at the top of the organization to send a clear message about the purpose and the nature of the process to be followed. The role of individual managers, too, must change from ' organizers' to 'aligners' – team leaders who provide the focus, motivation and support for their newly empowered work units. Leadership is necessary because of the need for courage in facing new and potentially threatening ways of working. Isolated management development initiatives can always help, but changing the way people work is more likely to succeed if a network of 'leaders' engender commitment on an individual basis.

The overwhelming message from our survey was that, if empowerment fails, it is very likely to be because of difficulties in changing the organization's culture. Those organizations we spoke to whose path to empowerment seemed straighter and smoother were those who – whether because of the nature of their industry or because of a long history of being employee-centred – already had a culture in which individual autonomy was a familiar idea. The organizations whose paths were the most tortuous and pot-holed appear to be those who have the most entrenched 'command and control' systems of management.

Such an organization, however flattened and flexible it has managed to make itself, inevitably has the harder job because it must convince every single employee that trying and failing will suddenly no longer be a serious offence; that having no decision to make will no longer make a manager surplus to requirements; that putting people together in a team means they are there to share talents and accountability, not to carry out the instructions of others. It is not enough to tell people they are empowered – they must have evidence.

Empowerment inevitably involves a two-way traffic, and organizations must remember that. The individual is given autonomy and ownership in return for a commitment to act in the interests of the organization. The organization gets more out of each individual in return for supporting and training him or her to increase his or her ability to perform efficiently.

Finally, there is no easy way to empower an organization. This is because empowerment is a risk, and organizations are not over-fond of risk-taking. Those organizations which play safe – by limiting those aspects of empowerment which decentralize control and accountability, for example – will find their initiatives foundering. Empowerment will then be accused of not working. On the other hand, those organizations who have a clear focus in terms of what they want empowerment to achieve for them will know whether it works or not, because they will be able to measure the extent to which their goals are being achieved. If that sounds a rather obvious statement, it is a fitting conclusion to a topic which is often accused of being obvious and simplistic – until, that is, people actually try to do it.

Empowerment through organizational transformation

Earlier we read the presentation on how empowerment enabled Miliken to achieve its quality goals. Next is the case example which illustrates **how empowerment can be maintained through organizational change**. It is the case study of restructuring in Digital as presented by David Allen-Butler of Digital Equipment Co.

... In presenting Digital as a case study let me stress that I do so in the spirit of sharing with you our successes and disappointments and not as some kind of paragon with all our challenges safely behind us...

In the dictionary, empowerment is defined as 'Authorize; license; give power to; make able'. These are, however, what I would describe as a layman's definition and not adequate for the purpose of the case I present to you. These are all words that can best be described as inputs. And I don't see empowerment as an input. I see empowerment much more as a result, an output from a system that is both complex and difficult to define.

Working in an empowering environment, 'Doing the right thing'

To understand where my argument is leading to, it's necessary to go back a few years. Digital started over 36 years ago, as a computer technology company of three employees headed by Ken Olsen. Ken was later to be labelled by Time magazine as 'the ultimate entrepreneur'. He set up the company in August 1957, in 8500 square feet of converted woollen mill in Maynard, Massachusetts. The first fiscal year saw sales hit $94 000.

After ten years we had grown to a revenue of $38m and 2500 employees. By the end of the second decade we had achieved an annual revenue of $1bn with 36 000 employees.

I joined the company in 1987, its thirtieth year. Digital had made it into Fortune's list of the top 50 US companies, at number 44. Employees exceeded 120 000 and revenue was heading for $12B. By 1989 revenue had exceeded $12.7bn. We were employing nearly 126 000 world-wide.

In 1990 we were at Fortune's number 27 position. We had become the US's second most successful company of the decade, with an annual compound growth rate of 21.7 per cent. In 1991 our revenue hit $13.9B. Digital was number two after IBM.

… What was not apparent was the looming problem this growth was creating. After all, employees are our greatest asset and our biggest expense. 1990 was the year when things changed!

That's when the market took a dramatic turn. The bottom seemed to fall out of the world economy. The US IT market was devastated. Europe was beginning to follow the US. Asia-Pacific and Eastern Europe were still relatively undeveloped and not growing at a rate that would compensate for the drops being seen in Europe and the US. IT companies were collapsing, WANG being a painful example.

In 1992 Digital lost $2.79bn. Yes that's nearly three billion dollars. Fortunately, that was against the backdrop of a very strong balance sheet. But no balance sheet can stand that sort of hit for long. Some of us wondered if it was coincidence that we changed the colour of the corporate logo to red at this time!

That's enough about the environment in which we were operating. Let's look at the principles on which the company was founded, and the culture that developed from them.

Ken had a unique management style. He was strongly religious and a had a fundamental belief in people. The 'founder culture' that evolved from his leadership can best be described as a valuing of the individual. Digital invested enormous amounts of time and money in the development of its employees. Ken also believed in the principles of honesty and trust. He believed that each employee would 'Do the right thing' – a catch phrase that became synonymous with Digital. This philosophy worked well, and the company grew rapidly, as I've already summarized.

A substantial people management and human resource philosophy evolved. Digital's current (1994) corporate human resource philosophy states:

> People will be energized and create a competitive advantage for the company when they:
> • have a sense of purpose;
> • are treated with respect, dignity and fairness;
> • apply their skills to meaningful work;
> • are encouraged and are able to contribute;
> • have opportunities to grow;
> • are able to integrate their work with the work of others;
> • embrace change with confidence and openness.

However, the company was also growing more and more complex, our customers were becoming confused, our employees were becoming confused. Like most of the big IT companies, we had evolved a complex, world-wide, multi-layered, national and international sales and management structure, heavily matrixed. And that means duplication of work and effort.

Everyone was 'doing their own thing'. With the wisdom of hindsight, it is clear this is not the same as that meant by 'doing the right thing'. What the company lacked was a sense of purpose and a clarity of direction. Ken even stimulated competition between lines of business, putting one product line directly against another. He believed this would generate healthy competition, instead it caused infighting and inefficiency. Individual employees did not have a single context in which to operate and did not share a common vision about the future, decisions were often taken in isolation.

To help you to understand how this freedom to act played itself out I will cite a few examples. There is a project review process in Digital called the 'Phase Review Process'. Over the years it evolved into a separate process for each of the engineering groups. The result was 15 similarly intentioned, but differing, processes within one function. Another example, in sales we have counted as many as 32 different forecasting processes. A more recent example of this 'diversity' is the fact that last year Digital Equipment Company Ltd made six entries in the DTI handbook. Each was sponsored and funded by a different part of the business (with different fees being negotiated), and the messages were different, even contradictory. Another example of our complexity, we discovered we had 34 0000 part numbers in multiple and complex catalogues. We discovered that only 14 000 sold in quantity and the vast majority could be consolidated and rationalized.

This complexity was not just apparent within Digital. A customer needed as many as eighteen phone numbers to track down the required service.

The stock market also saw the writing on the wall. As recently as 18 April, Louis Kahoe's editorial in the Financial Times had the leader 'Digital Equipment losses raise question of control'. From a high of $198 in September, 1988 we hit a low of $19 in April 1994.

A so-called empowering culture had created a confused, confusing and inefficient organization. What may have been right for a small growing company in more profitable times, in a growing market, was almost certainly not right for our customers, who need simplicity in their dealings with us. Operating in the highly commutative world of IT, Digital needed to change and change fast.

Centralization versus decentralization

But what does it need to change to, and how? There is a big debate raging about the benefits of centralized organizations compared to decentralized organizations. Words associated with each of these organizational types can be seen as positive or negative, depending on one's stance. Digital has experience of both, but historically seemed to favour centralisation from a business and technological perspective and decentralization from an employment perspective, tailoring employment conditions to the local labour market. In the past this has worked well. In 1990, Digital UK reorganized its selling organization into what it called the entrepreneurial model. This gave the account management organization substantial autonomy. However, we did not set any parameters or guidelines. The result was a climbing headcount, increased expense base and discontinuity. A virtual anarchy existed, which is not surprising when you consider we released fifty entrepreneurs on to our unsuspecting customers! We learnt that giving freedom to act without providing rules, guidelines or parameters leads to chaos.

The appointment of Robert Palmer as president and chief executive of Digital in July 1992 created an expectation of clearer direction setting and business focus. Bob took over the reins at a time when Digital was in the middle of a major restructuring of its business. This restructuring, started in mid-1990, had the intention of returning the company to profitability.

The challenges are threefold:

- To drastically restructure and downsize the business in order to remain competitive. (Some benchmarks suggest that Digital should be half the size it currently is, for the revenue it generates.)

- To retain many of the values on which Digital was founded and the reason so many employees were attracted to Digital in the first place (we were founded as a people company and wish to retain that philosophy).
- To reset expectations and establish new standards of working for the future. (What was acceptable yesterday is no longer adequate today and will certainly be inadequate tomorrow. Continuous improvement is necessary, just to survive.)

As soon as Bob Palmer took over, he created a clarity of purpose, previously lacking in the 'old order'. However, his decisiveness and need to manage the changes quickly created a potential risk – that of having everything decided centrally and creating lack of ownership for the changes, by the employees. However, Bob saw the advantages of involving employees as outweighing the disadvantages, especially in these times of dramatic change. I have now arrived at the nub of my presentation.

Let us relook at Digital's human resources philosophy. Employees had lost sight of any purpose we might have had. The company was still attempting to treat employees with dignity and respect but we had set an expectation over thirty years that employees had a job for life. That expectation was dashed by round after round of redundancies.

Growth potential has apparently disappeared overnight. Instead we were perceived to be removing opportunity. For example, we made 100 out of 400 managers redundant in December. People were becoming isolated from each other. They were unclear about how their work related to the work of others. And if we were confused, then our customers were certainly confused.

However, we had got some of our act together. On the technological side, innovation has been a key market differentiation for Digital. We have always held a unique position in the marketplace with our proprietary technology, the VAX. This will continue with our Alpha chip – the world's first 64-bit processor and the most powerful – developed as a world-wide initiative. Our technical capability has always been a relative strength. The resetting of our technical strategy to embrace Alpha, was a corporate decision implemented world-wide. But, whilst we have been driving our technological development from a central strategy, we have been less clear about other aspects of our business, especially marketing. This has caused considerable confusion with managers, employees and ultimately our customers and suppliers. The common cry from employees is 'Where is the leadership in this company?'. Again with Alpha, we undertook a world-wide marketing campaign, co-ordinated centrally, but with local implementation.

Bob Palmer was implementing a new management strategy: central direction setting, and establishment of ground rules with local implementation design and delivery.

Managing through rapid change – what of empowerment now?

In the last three years, up to December 1993, Digital has reduced its world-wide population from over 126 000 employees to around 85 000. That's a 30 per cent reduction. The UK business had also reduced its size by a similar proportion from 7000 to 4300. Continuing lack of profits and a need to re-align business direction meant a further world-wide cut in 1994. In the UK this meant a further 800 employees: another 20 per cent. We had to achieve this in six months.

So, in January, it was decided rather than undertake across-the-board cuts we would re-engineer the whole of the company, in line with the new world-wide vision and a defined corporate organizational framework. But we needed to do this in a way congruent with our human resources philosophy. This required leadership and participation. New territories were established by corporate management, each territory comprising a group of countries. For example, Europe's fifteen countries were reformed into five territories. Amongst other things, this involved a substantial reappraisal of the senior management structure. However, although the territory structure and organizational size were decided centrally, each of the territories was tasked with managing their own restructuring locally. This overall corporate setting, coupled with local decision-making, was a major part of the strategy for maintaining local ownership and motivation and driving the revitalization of the organization.

In the UK we adopted a restructuring approach called process re-engineering. The managing director, Chris Conway, set up a restructuring task force. This small group comprised a customer business unit manager, a process re-engineering consultant, the UK sales administration manager and myself. The company was designed from the customer back. This involved looking at the needs of the customer (we talked with customers, researched them and looked hard and long at what the market wanted and what we are offering), evaluating each internal process and how it contributed to the value chain. This is turn resulted in a major simplification of the whole organization.

But how does this relate to the empowerment of employees, you ask? All parts of the organization contributed to the discussion and were able to make suggestions about how the work could be done in a simpler way, without duplication. Over 200 people were directly involved in the re-engineering with the vast majority of employees represented by at least one person in the design work. The direct involvement ensured that all of the 'old' organizational groups could contribute to the creation of the 'new' environment. But all this was done within a defined framework set down by the task force: the customer value chain.

This freedom in decision-making with defined guidelines allowed us to work quickly and enabled us to exceed the corporate benchmarks for headcount reductions, in a shorter time frame.

Clear leadership, decisiveness about the business we were in – and in the businesses we weren't in – clarity about what was 'negotiable' and what wasn't, and the setting of precise targets and deadlines, enabled us to involve employees in the redesign of the UK business and to over-achieve our goals.

Regeneration, optimism and energy

The future brings two certainties. Business will be impacted by continuous change and to survive, let alone grow, business will need to undertake continuous improvement.

Digital is building a new organization to address the challenges of the future, whilst doing everything it can so as not to create an environment where problems grow and become difficult to address. We have learnt that giving employees substantial degrees of freedom may appear to be a way of showing that the company values the human resource, but in reality this has proved to cause virtual anarchy, which ultimately has a major negative impact on a substantial number of employees. Anarchy in a business leads to chaos which in turn leads to demoralization and a sense of failure.

Japan has been over quoted in the last decade, but the truth is it underwent a major revitalization after the Second World War, radically changing the way workers approached their work. Digital has started to tackle the same problem.

Digital is designing an organization that has a single vision and purpose, that is clearly defined, simple processes; where employees have the ability and freedom to make decisions; where continuous improvement is a way of working; where excellence in people management is a given; that it is an energizing and rewarding place to work; where leadership exists at all levels in the organization.

This then takes me to my opening comments. These were that it is very difficult to define empowerment, but one thing that's clear is that we know it when we see it.

Many of you have heard the saying: 'Power corrupts and absolute power corrupts absolutely'. I would like to leave you with my version:

Empowerment makes businesses
Absolute empowerment makes businesses obsolete.

... Digital is a learning organization, and learnt a costly lesson. The future is positive, thanks to participative re-engineering and employee commitment.

A number of organizations talk about the importance of empowerment in bringing about corporate renewal and transformation in a competitive business climate. The degree of freedom, involvement and commitment depends on the type of organization and on the calibre of top management. Empowerment is guaranteed to fail if there is a lack of courage and trust from top management and lack of conviction on the side of employees.

The three most important success factors of empowerment are ability, opportunity and motivation. For empowerment to succeed employees must:

• be able to make a decision,
• have an opportunity to make a decision, and
• be wanting to make a decision.

By way of example, if top management want their employees to play pianos then first they have to provide pianos (opportunity), secondly the staff have to be able to play the pianos (skill and training) and finally they have to want to play pianos (motivation). If employees are asked to perform beyond their ability, this will result in imbalance between actual performance and expected performance which will then result in stress at work.

For empowerment to succeed it has to have SMART dimensions:

S It has to receive full **support** from the top management.
M Staff have to be **motivated** to 'take' power.
A **Authority** has to be aligned to strategic direction.
R **Responsibility** is the core component of empowerment
T **Trust** in individuals and teamwork is essential.

The key success factors of empowerment: how to empower

- There must be information sharing, including sensitive information.
- There should be an appropriate leadership that can facilitate empowerment.
- There is a need for team-building.
- Employees should be trained to behave as 'entrepreneurs'.
- Employees should understand the challenges facing their businesses.
- The top management should trust their employees.
- Employees in turn should give their full commitment.
- Organizational culture should 'allow' employees to make mistakes.
- Leaders should be honest and give effective performance information.
- There has to be strong leadership in order to provide structure and direction.
- It is important to establish parameters.
- Managers should the assume the role of a coach and help people to achieve their goals.
- Employees should make operational decisions consistent with strategic decisions.
- The organization should make 'finger-pointing' obsolete. If you find a problem you own it.

Selected reading

William C. Byham (1988). *ZAAP: The Lightning of Empowerment.* Development Dimensions International Press.

Mark Brown (1988). *The Dinosaur Strain.* Element Books.

Stephen R. Covey (1992). *The Seven Habits of Highly Effective People.* Simon & Schuster

Ed. Oakley and Doug Krug (1991). *Enlightened Leadership.* Fireside.

Richard Pascale (1989). *Managing on the Edge*. Penguin Books.

Noel M. Tichy and Stratford Sherman (1994). *Control Your Destiny or Someone Else Will*. Harper Business.

8 The horizontal organization

A form without substance is like an egg shell without a yoke.

African saying

Summary

- De-layering the organization has been the 'management speak' of the 1990s.
- The hierarchical organization and functional specialism.
- Journey from the pyramidal organization structure to the matrix structure.
- Attributes of the horizontal organization.
- Shaping the horizontal organization: McKinsey's consultants' views.
  – Organize around process not tasks.
  – Minimize non-value adding activities.
  – Assign ownership of processes.
  – Link performance objectives to customer service.
  – Form teams.
  – Combine managerial and non-managerial activities.
  – Treat multiple competencies as a rule, not the exception.
  – Inform and train people.
  – Maximize supplier and customer contacts.
  – Reward individual skill development and team performance.
- The horizontal organization – beware of overdoing it!

The hierarchical organization

The flat or horizontal organization is presented as the organization of the future. The traditional vertical or hierarchical organization is based on the classical approach to management. The focus of attention was on division of labour, hierarchy of authority and span of control.

Division of labour led to the grouping of key activities and allocation of roles to individuals. Hierarchy of authority was based on the degree of authority delegated at each level of management. Authority is vested in the manager by the upper echelons of the organization. Span of control relates to the number of individuals reporting directly to one manager.

The organizational function of management involves developing a structure by bringing together many aspects and elements of business into a structured whole. Positions of each person or a group of persons are defined in the structure (Figure 8.1).

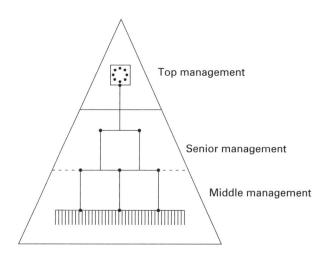

Figure 8.1   The pyramid structure

Hierarchy is based on a 'scalar chain of authority'. This relates to the number of levels in an organization and comes into existence whenever an individual is made the subordinate. The number of subordinates reporting directly to one manager is known as the 'span of control' and this in turn affects the shape of the organization. The larger the span of control, the flatter the pyramid.

Some companies today are still organized around such a structure which some writers refer to as the 'command and control' model. Such a model thrived in a stable competitive environment.The basic principle of organization structure is that a subordinate should not report to more than one manager at a time. There must be a 'unity of command' (no conflicting demands).

Throughout history, organizations had to face up to a number of issues about the kind of structure that will best sustain the success of their business. For almost a century the popular structure of the organization was based on functional specialization. Such a structure divides management into such areas as manufacturing, marketing, production and finance; see Figure 8.2.

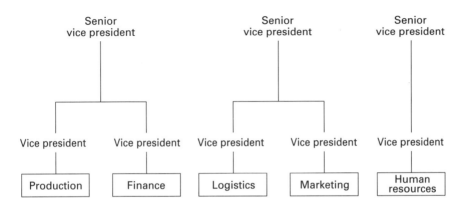

Figure 8.2   Functional specialization

How did the hierarchical structure develop?

While the greatest management thinkers like Henri Fayol and Frederick Taylor were expounding the theories on management and organization of work, a German sociologist Max Weber (1864-1924) was formulating the concept of 'bureaucracy' which defined roles within a hierarchy where job holders were appointed on merit, and were subject to rules. According to Weber, bureaucracy is a structure based on conformity to rules, correct procedures and clearly defined jurisdictions.

As the economy developed and international trade began to grow, many businesses developed structure to suit their operations. Some structured their organizations round the product range (see Figure 8.3) and others based their structure on geography (see Figure 8.4).

Figure 8.3   Structure based on product

Which structure?

Gradually as more branches and subsidiaries began to open overseas and businesses entered into the arena of mergers and acquisitions, debates evolved round the centralized structure, where all activities are controlled from the head-quarters, or the decentralized structure, where subsidiaries were given some degree of autonomy while headquarters maintaining senior functional managerial responsibility for corporate planning, corporate finance, company law and personnel.

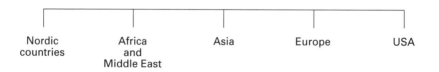

Figure 8.4   Structure based on geography

Academics and consultants were constantly debating the issue of the organizational structure following the corporate strategy. Structure, they say, should follow strategy. Organizations should be capable of making strategic adaptation, and for this they needed structure that was not rigid. The hierarchical structure was rigid. Within such a structure rules became important in their own right; relationships became depersonalized; specialization and standardization became the norm. What was needed was structure that was geared to task orientation.

The matrix structure

The late 1970s and early '80s saw the development of the matrix organization. In such a structure, projects are based on cross-functional bias and employees report to their functional boss as well as to a project manager or leader. Such a structure promotes flexibility within the hierarchical structure and a good understanding of other functions and their role within the organization.

The matrix was initially developed in the aerospace industry where organization had to be responsive to markets. Now the matrix structure is being used in a variety of organizations in the private and public sectors.

Matrix structure was the hottest innovation to hit industry since Taylor's principles of scientific management. Some critics felt that the matrix organizational structure created conflict and confusion (see Figure 8.5).

Figure 8.5   Matrix management

The matrix structure is useful when an organization wants to focus resources on a particular product or project. However, the matrix structure still operated within the context of the organizational pyramid. The structure, therefore, becomes very difficult to manage because lateral relations require special inter-personal skills and in practice some organizations found it difficult to integrate lateral processes into the vertical information flow.

However, the organizational pyramids prevailed and the matrix structure still operated within the pyramidal structure. Some have argued and still argue that the great pyramids of ancient Egypt have withstood the test of time. The same can be the case with the traditional structure of the twentieth-century organization.

As we have seen in Chapter 1, the world of business is changing fast and dramatically. As the year 2000 approaches, the corporations leading the way will be those that not only can delight their customers but are agile enough to respond to the changing environment. To do so, processes have to be re-engineered, people have to be empowered and structures have to be adapted. Information technology will also have a radical impact both on the process and the structure of organizations.

Adapting structure to meet market needs

An adaptive organization must develop a structure that will allow it to be not only reactive but also proactive. On 6 October 1995, James A. Unruh, chairman and chief executive officer of Unisys Corporation, announced 'the current Unisys matrix structure will be replaced with the streamlined decision processes, accountability and dedicated resources characteristic of stand-alone business. We will be faster and more aggressive in executing our strategy of providing technology, applying technology and servicing technology in focused markets.'

Organizations that have adopted cross-functional teams but remain too large are 'demerging' in order to be more competitive and proactive in a continually changing global business environment. AT&T stunned Wall Street in September 1995 by announcing its intention to split into three companies. The chief executive officer had taken this action at a time when the telephone and cable TV industries are about to be deregulated.

Many writers now argue that modern organizational structures are too costly, too slow to adapt and unresponsive to customer needs. Many companies are beginning to experiment
with a new model of organization by de-layering the levels of
the organization and working within the horizontal organizational structure. In such a structure there are no functional
managers any more. Organizations have redefined their roles
and responsibilities.

Instead of a hierarchy of structure, organizations now create a hierarchy of teams to respond to customer and competitive needs. Such hierarchy is driven by corporate strategy
to satisfy customers (see Figure 8.6).

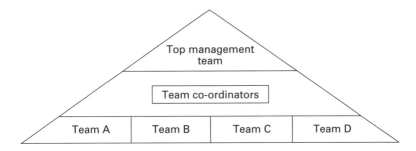

Figure 8.6   Hierarchy of teams

If we take the example of Royal Insurance, they have
reduced ten layers to five layers of management. These are
general management, senior specialists, team co-ordinators,
team leaders and service providers. There has been a move
from 'jobs' to 'roles'.

Attributes of the horizontal organization

Many organizations are now reducing the layers of management and adopting a horizontal structure. It is argued that
this will be the shape of the organizations of the twenty-first
century.

- Fewer levels of management.
- Customer-focused.

264   *Total Management Thinking*

- Process-driven.
- Self-performing teams.
- No functional 'silos'.
- Effective communication.
- Faster decision-making.
- Empowerment.
- Innovative leadership.
- Work flows designed across the organization.
- Continuous performance improvement.
- Team relationships.
- Speed, simplicity and self-confidence.
- Commitment and involvement.
- The essence of the horizontal organization is the re-orientation of a company around its core processes.

The horizontal organization – the views of consultants

This article, written by Frank Ostroff and Douglas Smith, appeared in *The McKinsey Quarterly* in 1992.

An ever more demanding competitive environment requires ever higher levels of corporate performance. The trouble is that needed performance improvements often remain stubbornly out of reach for companies organized in the traditional 'vertical' fashion: hierarchically-structured, functionally-oriented. By contrast, there is real performance leverage in moving towards a flatter, more horizontal mode of organization, in which cross-functional, end-to-end work flows link internal processes with the needs and capabilities of both suppliers and customers. The practical question, of course, is how to build such organizations. From the experience of many of the pioneering companies that have, at least in part, gone horizontal, this article distils the key design on which this alternative mode of organization depends.

The senior managers at Technocom knew their organization no longer made any sense. Post-Cold War military spending was dropping fast, and the government was scrutinizing product and service quality more closely than ever before. Moreover, the company's commercial customers were reeling from intense competition and a poor economic climate. The problems ran so deep, in fact, that the top group of managers agreed to discuss them only among themselves in a series of sessions devoted to redesigning the company.

Many months into this top-secret effort, however, after endless debates over whether to centralize or decentralize and whether to organize Strategic Business Units around products or markets, they'd gotten nowhere. Everyone agreed how the new company had to act customer-driven, total quality focused, with an empowered workforce for continuous improvement. But no could generate a credible picture of what Technocom's version of such a company would look like or of how it would work in detail.

Many top managers share the anxieties – and the frustrations – of these executives. Asking traditional organizational questions does not produce convincing answers to their most pressing performance challenge: how to build customer-driven companies that continuously improve and innovate. But neither does looking for practical guidance from the many 'organization of the future' design approaches that urge today's companies to become 'networked', 'clustered', 'self-directed', 'orchestra-like', and 'flat and flexible'. The terms may be suggestive, but no one really knows as yet how to translate such aspirations into actionable designs.

Indeed, practitioners who have tried know that these approaches raise many more questions than they answer. Who goes where in these organizations? What do they do? After de-layering, what's left? What's the role of hierarchy? At the level of the individual work unit, some pieces of the puzzle are clear. Self-managing teams, for example, do make a lot of sense. What's missing, however, is a comprehensive understanding of what the whole company will look like when it's over – and of the design principles on which such a picture must necessarily be based.

From the vertical …

With traditional vertical organizations, the picture is already in focus. They divide work into functions, then departments, then tasks. The primary building block of performance is the individual and his or her job; the chain of command goes up the functional ladder and the manager's job is to match the right individuals with the right tasks and then to measure, evaluate, control and reward their performance.

When things go awry, managers can turn to a familiar repertoire of design-related considerations:

- Whether to organize by product, customer or geography.
- Which functional resources to centralize or decentralize.
- Which committees and/or forums to use to integrate across func-

tions or units.
* How to optimize the roles of line versus staff.
* How many levels and what spans of control to use to co-ordinate tasks and departments.
* How to align individual roles, responsibilities and accountabilities with functional and/or organization-wide performance objectives.
* How best to plan, budget, review, measure and reward individuals, department, functions and SBU performance.

Years of experience have shown that the crucial advantage of vertical organizations is functional excellence. But their central defect is co-ordination – across tasks, across departments, across functions. Because so many of today's competitive demands appear to call even more on co-ordination than on functional excellence, it is no surprise that vertical organizations have a hard time responding to the kinds of challenges faced by Technocom and hundreds of companies like it. A different basis for design is needed.

... to the horizontal

In this alternative form of organization, work is primarily structured around a small number of business processes or work flows, which link the activities of employees to the needs and capabilities of suppliers and customers in a way that improves the performance of all three. Work and the management of work get performed more by teams than by individuals, and these teams assume real managerial responsibilities. In fact, flatter, but still hierarchical, arrangements of teams replace the steeper, more vertical hierarchies of traditional functional management.

At the same time, the evaluation, decision-making and resource allocation aspects of management shift toward a focus on continuous performance improvement. That means information and training get provided just-in-time – on a 'need to perform', not a 'need to know' basis. Career paths follow work flows: advancement goes to people who master multiple jobs, team skills and continuous improvement. Compensation rewards both individual skill development and team performance.

These new design objectives which add up to what we think of as 'horizontal' organization, provide a robust and actionable alternative to the vertical model. We describe and discuss its key design principles in the pages that follow. We do not, however, mean to suggest that the vertical organization should be written off as irrelevant to the needs of contemporary managers. Indeed, many of the critical performance challenges facing them and their companies still demand the creative and insightful use of vertical design. This is not an either/or choice.

Today, as always, each company must seek its own unique balance between the vertical and horizontal features needed to deliver performance. But finding that balance, and getting it right, puts managers on the spot to develop as good an understanding of the design principles of horizontal organizations as they have of those associated with the traditional vertical model. Here, then, is our working list of the ten principles at the heart of horizontal organizations.

1. Organize around process not task

Vertical organizational structures work functionally. When they seek to do things better, the focus of their efforts is on function-specific improvements. Managers can, however, shift the focus of performance by organizing the flow of work around company-wide processes that ultimately link to customer need, instead of around functions, departments or tasks.

In practice, this means selecting a few key performance objectives based on customer needs and tying them to work flows. This can be done within the confines of a single function – or by cutting across functions. In its fullest application, it means identifying the company's three to five 'core processes' – its flow of activity, information, decisions and material – that deliver against these objectives. Such processes might include, for example, order generation through fulfilment, new product development, integrated logistics management or brand management. Redesigning these processes appropriately can produce one-time performance gains and, more important, lay the basis for continuous innovation and improvement.

Focusing on core process

Based on a customer-driven analysis of its competitive environment, a major securities firm took a hard look at its 'client services' core process, which included such activities as stock distribution, dividend payments, and account maintenance. What it found was a jumble of services, fragmented authority and multiple points of customer contact. Sales administration authorized service, maintained account records and handled billing and client inquiries. Operations verified delivery instructions for service authorization, checked duplicate accounts, and answered questions about transactions' status. Finance and accounting reconciled customer accounts. The result: high cost and unacceptably poor customer service.

Clearly, redesign was in order – with the ambitious goal of cutting variable costs by 25 per cent, improving service delivery time by 50 per cent and boosting quality. At a minimum, there was a need to simplify activities, cut out redundant or unnecessary steps, and eliminate the hands-off requirements that often created errors or rework. But this was not enough. All these functional activities had to be made part of a single, integrated, and co-ordinated process. For that to work, however, the company had to stretch further and re-organize itself around its newly-designed work flows, not revert to the familiar comfort of the old functional organization.

The new principle of organization was the establishment of multiple client-based teams, each of which would provide a complete range of services for its assigned clients by carrying out each step of the process by itself. To support these teams of generalists, the securities firm created a pool of technical experts, who would provide rapid assistance on unique or troubling issues like complex regulatory matters. The bottom line: performance improvements that surpassed both cost and service delivery targets and that supported gains in quality.

Linking work flows
This securities firm is not alone in beginning to organize around horizontal, end-to-end work flows, instead of around vertical functions, departments or tasks. Xerox takes this approach in new product development, Motorola in supply management, and a major computer company in integrated logistics. Still other companies have moved in the same direction – if only within a single, broadly-defined function or two. General Electric and Kodak, for example, in manufacturing operations; American Express's IDS division in mutual fund processing; and some Knight-Ridder newspapers in advertising sales and service.

In all these cases, the basic organization module always remains a team-based work flow, not an individual task. These work flows can be linked to others, both upstream and downstream, through a variety of mechanisms. These include:

* Appointing a leader or a team of leaders to own and guide each core process.
* Charging everyone who participates in the process with objectives related to continuous improvement against 'end-of-process' performance measures.
* Establishing measurement systems for each process that tightly integrate overall performance objectives with those of all work flows within the process.
* Reaching explicit agreement on the hands-off requirements between upstream and downstream activities.
* Creating process-wide forums to review, revise, and syndicate performance objectives.

Relying on teams

Motorola's Government Electronics Group (GEG) used many of these linkage mechanisms in shifting its supply management activities to the horizontal. This was an important change because purchased materials account for more than half off GEG's cost of doing business and underpin its ability to produce hundreds of different electronic products and systems for NASA, the US Department of Defense, and other governmental and commercial customers.

Prior to the redesign GEG followed a decentralized functional and hierarchical approach to supply management. Each of the key departments – purchasing, supply quality assurance, reliability/components engineering, and bidding/estimating – existed at both the group and the divisional levels. In fact, seven organizational levels separated the head of supply management from front-line employees. The objectives from each department were to purchase at the lowest possible price and to have no bad parts. To meet these objectives, the 700 people involved were assigned to – and measured on – a variety of individual tasks ranging from purchasing to inspection to record keeping.

This arrangement made available to each GEG division what seemed like better service than a centralized group would have provided. It also developed people who were very good at specific tasks like understanding the range of materials and supplies available, getting the lowest price and policing suppliers. But, at the same time, it was responsible for excessive redundancy costs, poor co-ordination, narrow skill and career development, adversarial relations with suppliers, lack of shared perspective on quality, and lost opportunities in pricing.

GEG's managers feared that merely centralizing these activities would help in some areas (volume purchasing, for example) but hurt in others, like responsiveness to the needs of the divisions. So they decided to try a different approach – one built on a view of supply management as an end-to-end process that transforms the contributions of suppliers into the satisfaction of customers, both internal and external. Getting all customers what they needed when they needed it at the lowest total cost meant paying attention not just to price, but to the cost of bad quality, delay, and non-value-adding activities as well.

To do this, they knew they had to move away from an organization that managed only orders and price. The relevant performance objectives also had to include percentage of rejects, number of corrective actions, late deliveries and cycle time. The way they chose to institutionalize this new perspective was to organize around front-line teams charged with executing all the tasks of the supply management work flow needed to meet these performance objectives.

The redesigned GEG organization resides only at the group level, has fewer than 500 employees (down nearly 30 per cent) and just two levels between the head of supply management and the teams. Team leaders, as well as technical experts, form the leadership group, which provides overall guidance in translating company-wide goals into specific objectives and action plans.

The only remaining functionally-organized department, quality parts and analysis, has been charged with eliminating its inspection role by transferring it to the teams or to suppliers themselves.

2. Flatten the hierarchy by minimizing the subdivision of work flows and non-value-added activities

Hierarchy emerges from the division of labour. In vertical organizations, it ties together business units, functions, departments, and tasks. In horizontal organizations, it links work flows with each other. If all of the company's core processes could be 'owned' and performed by a single team, there would be no need for formal hierarchy at all – just the meritocracy that emerged inside the team itself. But that is not possible.

Effective teams rarely exceed twenty or thirty people, far fewer than the hundreds or even thousands who must contribute to core processes at companies like Motorola. And there are, of course, human limits to multiple competency. So even in horizontal organizations, some amount of hierarchy will exist. But that amount can be held at a minimum.

The way to flatten hierarchy is to combine related but formerly fragmented tasks, eliminate activities that do not add value or contribute to the achievement of performance objectives (unnecessary inspection, for example), and reduce as far as possible the number of activity areas into which each core process is divided. As a rule, the broader and more integrated the work flow assigned to a team, the greater the scope within which it can solve problems and innovate. The greater the scope, the smaller the number of teams needed to perform the entire core process. And the smaller the number of teams, the less hierarchy needed to tie them together.

Although horizontal organizations are almost always significantly flatter than vertical ones, the goal is not to flatten for its own sake. It is, rather, to shape an organization such that every element directly contributes to achieving key performance objectives. For most complex organizations, that means some hierarchy is both inevitable and good – so long as each level truly adds value to those above and below.

3. Assign ownership of processes and process performance

The need for leadership does not disappear in horizontal organizations. It is as important as ever, starting with the assignment of a team or an individual to 'own' each core process and be responsible for its meeting performance objectives. These process leaders must deliver against a demanding charter.

Consider, for instance, the self-named 'Zebra Team' at Kodak, who oversee the 1500 employees in the manufacturing 'flow' organization responsible for producing 7000 different black and white film products. At Kodak, all of manufacturing has been organized into six flows, of which black and white is one. Each flow consists of end-to-end manufacturing processes or 'streams', all of which are supported by technical experts. The explicit mission established by the Zebra Team for its streams is to produce high-value products that can 'delight their customers'. But the team has also to set an implicit, emotionally powerful mission of re-establishing black and white film as a first-class citizen within Kodak, where colour film has held the limelight.

In addition, they have specified performance objectives regarding cycle time, work-in-progress, inventory, total production costs, on-time deliveries and customer satisfaction, and they have dedicated themselves by building capability, teamwork, and open communication throughout the flow. They have charged each stream with taking the front-line, problem-solving initiative required to meet its overall objectives. And they have made it clear that the Zebra Team is there to step in to remove obstacles or resolve hands-off issues within the streams themselves. This is the essence of horizontal leadership.

4. Link performance objectives and evaluation to customer satisfaction

Managers can reinforce the shift from vertical to horizontal by making customer satisfaction, instead of profitability or shareholder value, the primary driver – and measure – of performance. This does not, however, mean that shareholders get lost in the shuffle. As more and more companies are discovering, enhancing customer satisfaction depends on boosting many of their dimensions of performance, including company profitability. But this is a by-product of good performance, not the proper measure of it.

Vertical organizations tend to equate performance with financial results and focus attention on each function's contribution to the bottom line. By contrast, horizontal performance measures focus on customer satisfaction. Indicators like market share, growth and penetration are important only to the extent that they measure relative position vis-à-vis common sets of customers and competitors. Improving such positions depends on identifying – through focus groups, surveys, joint customer-company development projects, third party ratings, or whatever – and then filling the gaps between customer expectations and customer experiences.

As teams develop a clear understanding of what they need to do to keep a core process on track, they often find it useful to think of each activity area as the internal customer of the one before – that is, as an essential link in a chain leading to the satisfaction of a company's external customers. In this way, Motorola's GEG supply management organization, like parts of Kodak, GE, IDS, Xerox, and dozens of other companies, uses customer satisfaction to drive, step-by-step, all relevant dimensions of performance.

Every employee of GEG supply management, like every Motorola employee, carries a card in his or her wallet stating that 'our fundamental objective and everyone's overriding responsibility is total customer satisfaction'. There is a 'customer advocate' on every team to help ensure that customer needs are both articulated and met. All team members perform regular surveys of internal as well as external customers to collect data on quality, timeliness, cost, communications, overall performance and suggestions for improvement. They are also evaluated on the extent to which their own activities contribute to customer satisfaction.

5. Make teams, not individuals, the principal building blocks of organization performance and design

Managers who want to organize around work flows instead of functions or tasks treat teams, not individuals, as the principal building blocks of performance. Teams regularly outperform individuals because they can direct a larger set of skills, perspectives and activities against any problem-solving challenge – and can do so in a way that reduces delays and difficulties with hands-offs. Moreover, for most people, working in teams is more personally rewarding than working alone.

Calling a group a 'team', however, does not make it one. A real team, as opposed to a mere group of individuals with a common assignment, usually comprises between two and twenty people with complementary skills – people who are committed to a common purpose and to specific and measurable performance goals for which they hold themselves mutually accountable. This definition is important because every horizontal organization with which we are familiar is critically reliant on real teams at all organizational levels, but especially at the front lines.

General Electric's Salisbury, North Carolina plant, for example, which makes electrical panel lighting, is organized horizontally. Its people fall into only two groups: self-managing teams and technical advisors. Those on teams are cross-trained so they can perform each of the tasks necessary to the entire manufacturing process. They measure themselves against the plant's overall goals for cost, quality, speed and flexibility. They set their own performance targets, production and work schedules and hold themselves responsible for plant-wide concerns like housekeeping, safety and communications. They are the plant.

6. Combine managerial and non-managerial activities as often as possible

Most companies that rely on teams aspire to make those teams self-managing. This makes particularly good sense when teams are organized horizontally around work flows. The people who do a certain kind of work know best how to improve it. Through their experience, they have seen it all before, through their proximity, they are positioned to experiment with seeing it in new ways. Moreover, as problems or 'bottlenecks' appear, decisions need to be made, self-managing teams can take action in real time, without interrupting critical work flows.

Self-management can range across a wide spectrum of activities. Not all teams do all of them. As mentioned above the GE Salisbury teams set schedules, evaluate themselves, improve processes and have broad purchasing authority; the Kodak teams set their own missions and specific performance goals, do planning and continuously problem solve, and the Motorola teams are responsible for goal setting, scheduling, peer evaluation, and job description. Over time, however, horizontal organizations strive to build in as many self-managing activities as their teams can absorb.

Vertical organizations short-circuit the benefits of self-management by limiting the scope of front-line jobs to tasks instead of work flows and by strictly dividing managerial from non-managerial responsibilities. The people who know best how to change and improve their job performance are denied the authority to do so. By design and policy, they must seek permission to try new techniques and approaches, a circumstance as degrading and demotivating as it is ineffective. And when an experiment goes beyond the scope of a worker's own task, the situation is even worse: the permission of several layers of management is often required.

Workers are not the only ones affected. Most managers in traditional organizations, 'decision-making' is a synonym for 'action'. What managers do is make decisions. Continuous improvement, however, requires something else – a kind of 'learning in action' that blends hunches, reflection, analysis, experimentation, adjustment, measurement and gut feel in the real time pursuit of well-defined goals. In this kind of pursuit, distinctions between managing and working are more artificial than helpful.

Horizontal organizations combine, not separate, managerial and non-managerial activities as much as possible. Indeed, this is the design principle most essential to the empowerment – and the accountability – of the teams on which they depend. To be effective, however, these teams, not their managerial supervisors, must have the authority, training, information and motivation to evaluate and change when, how and with whom they do their collective work. Teams who do real work must also do real management.

7. Treat multiple competencies as the rule, not the exception

Horizontal organizations know that the greater the number of skills or competencies each individual brings to a team and the richer that person's understanding of the relevant core process, the greater the problem-solving capacity the team will have. By contrast, vertical organizations emphasize task specialization in the service of functional excellence. This does not, of course, mean that core processes can ignore the importance of functional excellence: horizontal organizations must have people – accessible people – at the cutting edge of the specialities critical to their overall goals. No pharmaceutical company can flourish without leading biochemists.

But for most employees in most organizations, the cutting edge standard of specialized task expertise is illusory. Whether they are front-line workers or executive vice presidents, most people contribute more to customer satisfaction by understanding, even if åt a moderate level, a large number of the tasks required to produce satisfaction than by being extraordinarily good at only a few. And even where specialists are needed, they too must be skilled at problem-solving, process understanding, team behaviour and customer/supplier relations. Otherwise, even the best insights have a terrible time getting translated into action. Sheer brilliance can occasionally win the day; but it cannot sustain continuous improvement and innovation.

GE's Salisbury plant provides an excellent illustration. In order to make and deliver more than 70 000 product variations, every worker on every team in the plant knows how to operate every machine in the plant. They also understand the purpose of each machine, the

P&L implications of its successful operation, and the interpersonal skills needed for effective plant performance. These multiple competencies help them solve problems in real time, keep the tightly-integrated operations up and running and respond smoothly to changing customer needs.

In addition, much of the perceived sacrifice of functional excellence may itself be illusory. First, companies need to distinguish between functional excellence to be maintained versus functional biases that do not add value. Second, as companies become more horizontal, they develop a number of approaches to preserving and deepening technical competences. For example, Kodak has formed teams composed of key personnel and managers from technically complex operations and charged them with developing and diffusing technical knowledge. These teams are evaluated on the basis of ideas generated and adopted by others.

Another company has established a Technical Center of Excellence responsible for developing and transferring knowledge to cross-disciplinary product development teams. At their best, such approaches encourage experts to join teams on an 'as-needed' basis, and, when finished, to focus on further developing their own special expertise.

8. Inform and train people on a 'just-in-time to perform' basis, not on a 'need to know' basis

Vertical organizations have traditionally used information to make decisions and exercise managerial control, not to inform the front lines or support their efforts to improve performance. Indeed, for control reasons, information has been withheld from the front lines and passed only to those managers with a demonstrable 'need to know'. Moreover, the functional hierarchies in such organizations inadvertently destroy information through their elaborate 'up-over-down-back' flows of interpretation, communication and decision making. Even when they seek to provide training, the approach usually reflects the convenience of the trainers, not the real time needs and problems of the users.

It does not have to be this way. Horizontal organizations make information available on a 'just-in-time to perform' basis. Information gets provided directly to those who implement the actions needed to improve performance – and relates directly to the performance issues in question. Nor is any 'official' interpretation added to the information. Recipients interpret the raw data themselves, supported by the training they receive in basic economics, management frameworks and analytic techniques like root cause analysis.

Experience shows that adults learn best by doing, not by sitting in classrooms, and are best motivated to learn when their performance depends on it. At Motorola, for example, employees can consult a telephone book-sized compendium of training offerings and sign up for any of them at any time. Similarly, employees of Kodak's flow organizations can access an on-line menu of course offerings and technical experts for immediate assistance. In neither company do employees have to wait for scheduled courses. When they have a pressing need, they can find the right materials or instructors to provide immediate help.

An important benefit of this just-in-time approach is that employees understand how to modify their own behaviour to improve performance and how their new behaviour affects desired business results. This helps lock in a positive feedback loop. The professional film flow at Kodak provides a good example of what happens when teams have direct access to information about their performance against waste, quality, cost, efficiency and other performance measures; are routinely trained in the full business context of their activities, including what determines customer satisfaction and total costs; and receive instruction in a variety of techniques like Pareto analysis, flow charting, root cause analysis and statistical process control.

Charged with aggressively cutting waste, a Kodak team found a strong inverse correlation between waste and machine utilization rates. Applying various analytical techniques, the team identified reduced machine set-up time as a key way to increase machine utilization and then successfully altered its procedures to improve set-up time – and, ultimately, to reduce waste.

9. Maximize supplier and customer contact

The horizontal approach encourages companies to bring their employees into direct, regular contact with suppliers and customers. Such first-hand exposure enhances the quality of insight and sense of participation that help sustain continuous improvement and innovation. As these companies have discovered, people understand their work better and draw more out of it when they see, talk with and directly get to know the people who use the products and services they create.

There are many ways to nurture such contact. Employees of the Rockingham plant of Sealed Air Corporation, a maker of packaging materials, meet regularly with employees of their major customer, a chicken processing plant, to discuss each other's needs. At General Electric and Motorola, teams are encouraged to involve customers and suppliers in joint problem solving. Kodak's black and white flow organization has a special programme, the 'Road Runner', that empowers any employee in the flow to do whatever is needed to satisfy urgent customer needs and to learn whether the service met expectations and how to improve it in the future.

Contact can be increased still other ways. Many companies use surveys. Motorola's GEG supply management organization regularly asks its suppliers a detailed series of questions to find out how good a customer Motorola has itself been. Some companies, including Motorola, go even further and include supplier or customer representatives as full working members on their own in-house teams.

Even in horizontal organizations, however, managers sometimes resist these contacts because it takes front-line workers away from production schedules or because they do not trust their own people with suppliers or customers. But the evidence of those who have overcome such resistance is compelling: expanding horizontal contacts is a powerful means for strengthening customer-driven performance.

10. Reward individual skill development and team performance, not just individual performance

Suitably defined, the reward systems and career paths in horizontal organizations can do much to reinforce the skills, values and behaviours necessary to boost company performance. Their emphasis on expanding an individual's role within a team and, more broadly, within a core process is markedly different from the focus on 'chimney-like' paths and narrow job classifications that characterize vertical or functional organizations. 'Pay for knowledge' approaches, for example, reward those who gain competence in multiple tasks as well as in problem-solving and various relationship-based skills. The key point is that such recognition advances, rather than undercuts, team-based effort.

For teams to be effective, their members must hold themselves mutually accountable for agreed purposes and goals. That is why horizontal organizations try to measure and reward team performance. Even gainsharing and other performance-oriented compensation devices can be made to reflect team contributions to performance at least as much as, if not more than, individual performance.

In addition to their traditional wages and salaries, the people at General Electric's Bayamon, Puerto Rico, plant are rewarded for gaining competency in job tasks, communication, and business understanding as well as for total team and plant performance. Similarly, the team members in Motorola's GEG supply organization evaluate their peers on a list of ten criteria, including customer satisfaction, technical skills and efficient use of resources.

Getting there from here

What will the companies be like that prove to be winning competitors in the decade ahead? There is a broad agreement on at least some of their most important characteristics: vision-driven leadership, empowered workforces, dedication to customers, total quality, and continuous improvement and innovation. Building such companies, however, will require managers to move beyond their traditional focus on functional excellence, the hallmark of the vertical organization. Instead, they will have to develop the organizational forms that leverage the cross-functional co-ordination of their own in-house activities, as well as link them closely with those of suppliers and customers.

Not surprisingly, many have become frustrated trying to create such organizations by modifying functional organizations at the margin. They have found that you can't get there from here. At either the unit level, or an entire company, you have to start in a different place – with the building blocks of the new horizontal mode of organization, which shifts the focus of organization performance from functional excellence to customer-focused improvement and innovation.

This is neither armchair theory nor airy speculation. Enough companies have moved away from their vertical past, at least in part, to convince any responsible managerial jury that significant performance gains do follow the shift to a horizontal organization. In the two years since Motorola's GEG supply management organization made the change, for example, deliveries and requisition cycle time have fallen by a factor of four, supplier quality has increased by a factor of ten, and headcount has plunged by 30 per cent. At the same time, there has been a dramatic growth in a wide variety of both individual and team-based skills. These results are not unique. Kodak, IDS, General Electric, Knight-Ridder, and others have had much the same kind of experience.

As we noted at the outset, we are not arguing for the wholesale replacement of vertical organizations by horizontal ones. Indeed, neither a purely horizontal nor a purely vertical approach will serve any company perfectly. Each company must find its own proper mixture of horizontal and vertical design. Balance is the key.

But finding the right balance will take careful experimentation and adjustment and tinkering. There are no certain rules or formulas. Still, the ten design principles outlined above have been widely enough tested and often enough applied that managers can confidently give them a try. They are not 'the' answer. But they are a reliable place to begin.

The McKinsey article highlights the following key aspects:

- The traditional vertical organizations lack co-ordination across tasks, departments and functions.
- Each organization must seek its own unique balance of vertical-horizontal design.
- Organizing around processes can produce performance gains.
- Many organizations like Xerox, Motorola, General Electric and Kodak are beginning to organize around horizontal, end-to-end work flows.
- The basic organization module remains a team-based work flow, not an individual task.
- Front-line teams are charged with executing all the tasks and decision making.
- Each team should 'own' each core process and be responsible for its meeting performance objectives.
- There should be an open communication throughout the work flow.
- Horizontal performance measures focus on customer satisfaction.
- Horizontal organizations combine managerial and non-managerial activities as much as possible.
- The horizontal approach encourages companies bring their employees into direct, regular contact with suppliers and customers.

The McKinsey article, which was written in 1992, was a classical article on the nature and the benefits of the horizontal organization. Many companies took on board the principles articulated to build the horizontal organization. However, as the article says, this is not a question of either/or design.

In 1994 The Boston Consulting Group published an article entitled The Myth of the Horizontal Organization. The article, written by Amouyal and Jones, adds another dimension to organizational restructuring, namely, a set of core disciplines.

One of the messages of re-engineering is that companies, once structured as hierarchical pyramids, now need to be 'turned on their sides' and restructured as horizontal organizations. The logic for this restructuring flows from the logic for re-engineering: if processes, not functions, are the correct way to organize work, then horizontally must be the correct way to organize a company.

It seems obvious. And it is wrong.

There are no great horizontal organizations, nor are there likely to be any. One company has experience with this new organization, but is now unwinding it. This two-billion-dollar heavy-equipment manufacturer re-organized around its product lines, pulling engineering, marketing and manufacturing people together into customer-centred units, one for each product line. The payback to the company was immediate – its people, cut loose from old department loyalties, began to work much better together, and customers noticed the difference.

But when the next generation of equipment was needed, there was no one to design it. The best design engineers were busy coming up with incremental new applications that current customers wanted. In addition to breaking up the core engineering group, the engineering effort had redesigned performance evaluation measures and incentives to reward engineering and marketing people for today's customer satisfaction. For the first time, engineers were getting good bonuses and could relate them to the work they were doing. In this environment with both customers and employees so happy, the president found it hard to mobilize his organization around the future.

Processes and disciplines

Horizontal organizations won't survive because they address only half of a company's needs – its process: managing transactions with the customer from order to delivery, giving better service, developing new products. Today, companies are spending millions on engineering these processes – and they do need to be fixed. For most companies, breaking old habits and power structures takes a big push. But, ultimately, good enough in the horizontal process is good enough. Like quality in the 1980s, 'best practice' processes are table stakes for doing business today. A company can't simply declare victory once it puts its horizontal processes in place.

The reason is simple: great horizontal processes don't make companies great. In telecom transmission equipment, NEC is extremely customer responsive with typical Japanese process excellence. But AT&T poured greater effort into creating new technology and is gaining market share against NEC with more truly innovative products. In pharmaceuticals, other competitors have spent more on processes, but it's Glaxo that is envied for its cleverness in defining research priorities and deploying its scientists.

The other half of what companies need is a set of core disciplines. The engineering skill to design state-of-the-art products; the technical expertise to invent out-of-the-box information systems; financial brains, like those at GE Capital, who create the accompanying financial services that differentiate the equipment GE sells. These vertical disciplines replenish the horizontal processes. They provide the professional excellence that elevates a company's processes from best practices to competitive breakthroughs.

In fact, disciplines are the company's seed corn for its future. While the processes focus on today's customers, the disciplines are inventing the products – and the customers – of tomorrow. And, despite the brave vocabulary of re-engineering, there will always be hand-offs – from creators to implementors, and from the centre to the field.

The horizontal organization isn't the answer because it tries to create what every general manager wants today – the fast-moving, responsive company – through organizational structure. Structure alone cannot do it. In the past, matrix organizations didn't solve the problem. Nor will the horizontal one today. The real challenge of building better companies is to intertwine and reinforce the horizontal and vertical dimensions. Achieving this new organization isn't really about structure. It's about infrastructure. Infrastructure is what your people see and feel every day and which tells what really matters: role models, location of people, distribution of rewards, flows of information and a sense of membership.

Creating the infrastructure

Companies that build both thriving processes and disciplines do not make it simple for their key people; instead they make it rich. They go beyond structure to infrastructure. They ask their business unit heads, senior functional people, and key programme and process managers to lead the way in integrating the horizontal and vertical dimensions. They follow five ground rules:

- Build tensions into objectives. Having the industry's fastest customer-delivery lead time will contribute to growth for a couple of years. But beyond that only innovation will continue the growth. All your key people need to be driven by objectives.
- Give senior executives dual roles. Each functional department head should either be responsible for one product line's new product development process or the health of a business. Our conven-

tional organization charts have made too many key, able people too one-dimensional. Let each senior person wrestle with both dimensions of the organization rather than sit comfortably on just one side of a matrix organization.
- Emphasize roles along with positions for every manager. Positions are what you are directly and formally accountable for. Roles cover what you can influence – one steps up to roles.
- Visibly reward people who contribute in both dimensions. Don't let rewards be driven wholly by formula incentives. The notion that 'you get what you pay for' is one of re-engineering's more sterile maxims. It's not that simple. Your best people want to contribute in both dimensions and in uncharted ways. So reward people who step up to new roles for which there are no measures or incentive formulas, and more people will step forward.
- Remove the one-dimensional barons. Some want to stay inside their old functional domain. Others get so hooked on the new horizontal world they lose touch with their home base. Both need to get the message they are jeopardizing the company's performance.

UK companies are improving their horizontal business performance dramatically. Re-engineering is paying dividends by removing obstacles and highlighting interfaces between functions. But it shouldn't try to dominate or eliminate functions. Re-engineering is spawning some well-intentioned but simplistic ideas – the horizontal organization, pay people on what you can measure, eliminate all hand-offs, and more. If re-engineering doesn't recognize what it can and can't do, it will become just another adventure in short-term performance boosting.

McKinsey's article comprehensively deals with various dimensions of horizontal organization and it lays the guidelines for organizations wanting to restructure their businesses. In advocating a team approach the article argues for the integration of processes and core disciplines.

The horizontal organization is the structure of the twenty-first century. It is the home of the 'knowledge worker'. For the next few years most organizations will be moving towards a hybrid structure but in the long run the horizontal organization will be a business reality because customers experience a company horizontally and not vertically. When a customer, for example, buys a forecasting report from the Economist Intelligence Unit, he or she does not consider going through the order department, production department, fulfilment deaprtment, invoicing or finance department. The customer orders a report and he or she expects to receive it from the company as an integrated whole.

Competitive strength in the 1990s is derived from the knowledge, skills, speed, quality and service levels provided to the customers. Companies who still stick to 'command and control' structure and principles (and there will be some) will be the dinosaurs of the twenty-first century.

Beware of causing damage

However, there is a danger of becoming too enthusiastic about flattening the structure completely. Organizations will need at least three layers in order to be managed on behalf of all the stakeholders unless of course, it was an entrepreneurial organization owned by an individual or group of individuals.

Secondly, to flatten the structure effectively the organization has to invest heavily in information technology to underpin its strategy and operational activities, train all its employees to make key decisions, and constantly update its core capabilities to respond to market needs. Structure and infrastructure changes must take place concurrently.

In early 1990 one of the big oil companies appointed a dynamic chief executive officer who was passionate about the horizontal organization. As soon as he was appointed he formulated his strategy and issued memos to all his employees informing them the organization structure will be flattened and that there would be a need to make thousands of workers redundant. Those who remain would have to work in teams and make decisions to meet customers' needs.

The employee development department was created within the human resource function to plan training for the empowered employees. Unfortunately such a decision created a lot of uncertainty and many key employees left the company. The effectiveness of employees who remained in the company decreased because they found it difficult to cope with their new roles and training for the new roles at the same time. Eventually the business as a whole began to suffer but the

chief executive officer was confident this was only a temporary situation and that performance would improve once
change initiatives begin to settle down. However, various
stakeholders and the majority of the board members began to
feel so nervous that they lacked the courage to persevere with
their chief executive officer, who was asked to leave the company.

Flattening the organization requires a strategy that incorporates advanced planning as far as training and teaming are
concerned, and enlightened and tolerant leadership to manage the transition and the anxiety of the various stakeholders.

Selected reading

Steven F. Dichter (1991). The Organization of the '90s. *The
   McKinsey Quarterly*, No. 1.
Robert Duncan. (1979). What is the Right Organization
   Structure? *Organizational Dynamics*, Winter.
G. S. Hanson and Christopher Meyer (1994). Horizontal
   Management. *Mercer Management Journal*, No. 3.
Tom Peters (1992). *Liberation Management*. Macmillan,
   London.

9 The learning organization

If you think knowledge is expensive, try ignorance.

Unknown

To feed a man for a day give him a fish; but to feed him for life teach him how to fish.

Old saying

Summary

- Why the learning organization is in vogue.
- Peter Senge, guru of the learning organization.
- Attributes of the learning organization.
- Barriers to the learning organization.
- How do organizations become learning organizations?
- Self assessment as a route to the learning organization. Case studies: TSB and Lucas Management Systems.
- David Garvin on the relationship between quality and the learning organization.
- Guide to becoming a learning organization.

The learning organization is another buzzword which has crept into the field of management. Organizations, big and small, have been learning to survive for a long time. The concept of learning as such is not new, even when applied to businesses. Many academics and consultants have been writing articles on the learning organization for a number of years.

The learning organization guru

The person who is presented as a guru on the learning organization is Peter Senge who published a best selling book, *The Fifth Disciple – the Art and Practice of the Learning Organization* (1990). Peter Senge is director of the Systems Thinking and Organizational Learning Programme at the Sloan School of Management, Massachusetts Institute of Technology.

The learning organizations, according to Senge, are places 'where people continually expand their capacity to create results they truly desire, where new and expansive patterns of thinking are nurtured, where collective aspiration is set free, and where people are continually learning how to learn together'.

The attributes of the learning organization

According to Senge :

* The concept of the learning organization is a vision.
* The learning organization is continually expanding its capacity to be creative and innovative.
* Learning has to be intrinsically motivating.
* Learning is about acquiring new knowledge and enhancing the existing knowledge.
* Learning has intellectual (thinking) and pragmatic (doing) dimensions.
* Learning requires commitment and responsibility.
* Learning is about developing core competencies.
* Open and frank communication is one of the pre-requisites to learning.

Senge's theory enjoyed immense popularity. In 1995 he published another book, entitled *The Fifth Discipline Fieldbook*, which is a more practical guide to management. He argues that to avoid company conflict, involvement in the learning organization needs to be intense and has to go beyond a team.

As far as corporations are concerned, Senge recommends taking time out for reflection. Re-engineering and downsizing are depriving corporations of that time as remaining workers work under pressure. But taking time out is important.

Barriers to the learning organization

Many organizations have learning disabilities. Some say learning disabilities are tragic in children, but they are fatal in organizations. These are some of the reasons why organizations are slow to learn or do not learn:

- Difficult to forget past habits.
- 'If it ain't broke don't fix it' attitude.
- Lack of recognition and awareness.
- Unable to transfer skills and experience.
- Cultural resistance – 'we do not want to do things the Japanese way'.
- It is unsettling to disturb the 'status quo'.
- The culture of 'getting it right first time'.
- Lack of resources to update core competencies.
- Lack of conviction and commitment on the part of organizations and individuals.

The concept of learning is very common and all readers are familiar with it. Babies learn as they grow. Initially most of the learning takes place through parents or families. Gradually various institutions make their contributions. Various norms are injected in individuals as they grow through life. This process is known as socialization.

Our behaviour is guided by the norms and the values of the societies we live in. As we grow older we acquire more competence to adapt ourselves to the environment. As we meet other people and travel we observe the differences and we assimilate values and norms that fit our needs and aspirations. In most cases learning takes place as we grow up.

However, in order to realize our aspirations to become whatever we wish to become, we make a focused effort to acquire a specific form of learning. To acquire new competencies we become competitive or collaborative or dependent. This is important if we want to fulfil our aspirations. Organizations learn as they conduct their operations in the business environment. But to acquire a 'best practice' they have to go in search of best practice. Like people they also learn in different ways. Some companies learn by being competitive, some by being collaborative, some by being dependent while others prefer to be independent.

Most organizations are habit-driven organizations. Habits are learnt but once acquired become resistant to unlearning and thus inhibit future learning. As Tom Peters often says 'The most difficult thing for many organizations is to forget old habits.'

The learning organization is an adaptive organization. It is willing to benchmark against the best practice and learn to be adaptive. It is willing to empower its employees and change the organizational structure to facilitate delivering service excellence. It has a tolerant culture to allow its employees to make mistakes and learn from them.

In practice most organizations do not have the courage to allow their employees to make mistakes. Talkland, a cellular telephone company, converted losses into profits by asking employees what was going wrong. In *The Fifth Discipline*, Senge gives the example of the founder of Polaroid. The inventor of instant photography had a plaque on his office wall which read: 'A mistake is an event the full benefit of which has not yet been turned to your advantage'.

In an article in *The Times* of 19 August 1993 by Desmond Dearlove, he wrote 'Mistakes made at work are important in the corporate learning process'. He presents two schools of thought on management, namely the 'sweep-it-under-the-carpet' school and the 'learning organization'. These are represented in Figures 9.1 and 9.2.

How to become learning organizations

If we go behind the sweeping metaphors and grand schemes we will find that organizations adopt the following avenues in order to become creative and acquire knowledge in order to adapt to the changing environment:

- **Benchmarking.** Many organizations now benchmark their new product development process, human resource practices, marketing activities and customer service in order to adopt 'best practice'. Benchmarking has become one of the powerful tools of improving core competencies and becoming 'best in class'.

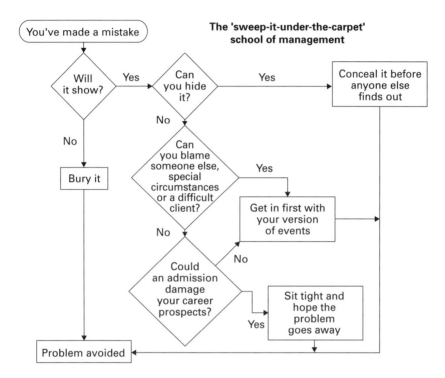

Figure 9.1   The sweep-it-under-the-carpet school of management. © Times Newspapers Ltd, 1993

- **Total quality management.** Total quality management is one of the effective approaches to accelerate organizational learning. The Deming cycle of plan-do-check-act is a cycle of continuous learning.
- **Focus on customer service.** Re-engineering processes and de-layering organizational structures in order to be responsive to customer needs has enabled organizations to 'unlearn' old habits and become innovative and creative in managing a new way of doing business.
- **Empowerment.** Those who have truly empowered their employees and introduced a tolerant culture of facilitating entrepreneurial behaviour have become learning organizations as long as they do not get distracted from continuous learning.

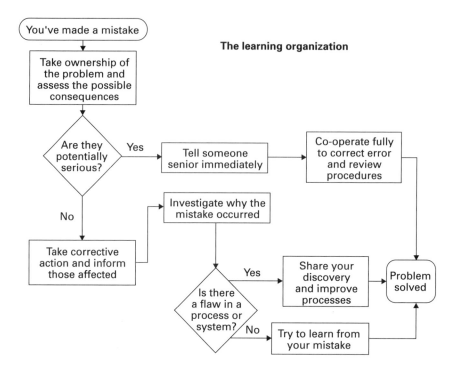

Figure 9.2 The learning organization. © Times Newspapers Ltd, 1993

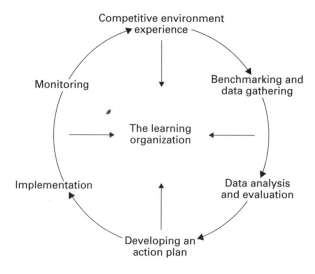

Figure 9.3 The learning organization cycle

To become and remain learning organizations, companies have to stick to five disciplines:

1. continuously monitor competition,
2. benchmark to adopt best practice,
3. have courage to adapt organizational structure,
4. empower their employees, and
5. do not take your eyes off the customers.

Self assessment as a route to learning

TSB – a case study

TSB is one of Britain's leading financial institutions acting in retail banking, insurance merchant banking, investment services and a number of commercial businesses. The TSB, with seven million customers, served by over 1300 branches and over 23 000 staff, is one of the best known names in the British high street.

The executive stated their commitment to total quality at the end of 1990. This was supported by the Bank's mission statement and reflected in the TSB quality policy:

> We shall provide defect free products and services to our internal and external customers which meet their agreed needs. We shall do so on time, first time and every time. Only by doing this will we achieve our mission to be the UK's leading financial retailer.

The first objective in the programme was to obtain a consistent awareness and language throughout the business. The approach used was an intensive training programme using the Philip Crosby Associates methodology. This involved a direct spend of over £7m and over 100 person years in training all staff. This exercise was completed successfully in early 1993 and provided a firm foundation for other initiatives that had to be introduced to support this, the largest single European management development initiative.

With the training programme underway, eighteen quality improvement teams were established to represent all business areas. Each team consisted of about ten members. Their responsibility is to manage the quality improvement process for their respective business areas.

Why self assessment?
A mechanism was needed to support the quality improvement teams to ensure that the skills and knowledge acquired from the training were being applied.

Several methods of quality audit were considered, but third party assessment seemed to conflict with the no blame culture encouraged by the training. Although other self assessment tools were considered, the European Quality Award model seemed to meet all requirements with the added bonus that TSB is eligible to apply for the EQA in future years.

What is our approach?
As no form of self assessment existed in TSB, it was felt that the approach must be simple and non-threatening.

The approach decided on for the first round was facilitated workshops delivered to the eighteen quality improvement teams. Manuals were produced based on the European Foundation for Quality Management guidelines customizing the 'areas to address'.

The workshops last one and a half days. The first session provides a background to the model; the reason for using it, an explanation of the scoring system and a self assessment of the leadership.

Individually, participants are asked to identify the strengths and improvement opportunities for each of six sub-categories and provide a score for each one. Once this is complete, individual scores are displayed on a flip chart and form the starting point for the group discussion.

The person with the highest score is asked to share their strengths with the rest of the group. These are recorded on the flip chart. After others have contributed to the list of strengths, the person with the lowest score is asked to identify some improvement opportunities and these are also recorded. This generates group discussions and gives participants the opportunity to review and change their original scores and reach a consensus score for each of the sub-criteria.

Prior to the second session, each participant undertakes a self assessment on the remaining eight categories for subsequent group discussion.

Once all categories have been covered, a prioritization process is undertaken using sticky dots. The prioritized improvement opportunities formulate the basis for an action plan. A scoring matrix was developed and is used to show the results of each team compared to the average. This will also be used to monitor progress in subsequent years.

What lessons have we learnt?
The methods used provide a good basis for the first self assessments and, from feedback received, have proved valuable for all users. As the process was new, some of the scoring was a little subjective. It is emphasized that the scoring is not as important as identifying oppor-

tunities for continuous improvement.

Although self assessment provides the improvement opportunities to formulate an action plan, continuous improvement will only occur where the actions are implemented, monitored and regularly reviewed.

What have been the benefits?

The use of self assessment process has provided significant benefits to the quality process within TSB. The introduction of the common framework has been effective in focusing the organization; it has confirmed to the organization that they have only just started on the quality journey, and it has been the catalyst to developing ambitious goals for improvement in the future.

Finally, the self assessment has been effective in generating real ownership for quality amongst senior managers in the business because it forced them to examine their own activity and develop their own plans for their own areas, in their own ways.

What are our future plans?

The basic workshop method appeared to be the correct initial approach. TSB now need to develop this further in future years by moving to assessments carried out by internal teams from other parts of the business and, eventually, by preparing a written report for external assessment.

Towards the future

The group believe they have gained significant individual value from sharing between their organizations and some themes have emerged that appear common to all companies. They believe:

- Self assessment should be an important element in any organization striving to achieve total quality.
- The approach selected has to take account of the organization's maturity, its culture, its particular business environment and strategic issues. Thus what is right for one company may not be appropriate for another.
- The various self assessment processes that the companies have developed and deployed in their organizations are all identifying opportunities for improvement and providing them with an effective means to prioritize them.
- For greatest effectiveness self assessment has to be positioned and introduced as an integral part of the business process and not a separate and potentially short-lived initiative.

The benchmarking framework established by the group has been a powerful tool for them and has helped them to gain maximum value from their interaction. They hope that what you have read in this short report has perhaps given you some ideas and that you can see the potential benefits of self assessment in your own organizations.

If the way the group came together seems to have been casual, well it was. The lesson they have learnt as individuals is that any such group with a common interest can start and get benefit without waiting for any external stimulus.

Source: Business Improvement through Self Assessment. European Foundation for Quality Management, EFQM Brussels Representative Office, Avenue des Pleiades 19, B-1200, Brussels, Belgium. Tel: 32 2 775 35 11. Fax: 32 2 775 35 35.

David A. Garvin, professor of business administration at Harvard Business School, gave an interview to *European Quality* in which he described the relationship between quality in practice and the concept of the learning organization.

The article, Beyond Buzzwords – A Realistic Approach to Total Quality and the Learning Organization, appeared in Vol. 1, Number 2 (1994) and is reproduced with the permission of the editor, John Kelly.

Garvin on why learning is in vogue

We have shifted from an economy where the greatest asset is resources to an economy where the greatest asset is knowledge. If there is one lesson of the Japanese success story it is that resource co-ordination has been dramatically successful in open competition. Japan is famously short of natural resources, but they succeed by adding value through knowledge: through just-in-time systems, through understanding the customer, through research, development and design. Another reason why learning is suddenly so important is that the rate of change has increased dramatically. Product cycles are much shorter. New technology has broken down the boundaries that protected industries in the past. Formerly separate industries like telecommunications and computing are now converging at great speed. All of a sudden, your knowledge base needs to be much wider and you need to assimilate new ideas much quicker than before. The landscape is changing, in some cases literally, day by day.

At the same time researchers and consultants have struggled with the vocabulary of learning. It has been really difficult to describe the process as it applies to an organization. Without doubt, 'learning organization' is one of the worst buzzwords yet devised. Its resonance is even more 'new age' and mystical than 'quality management'. It is essential to arrive at a basic definition which avoids such airy ambiguities. Stated simply, a learning organization is skilled at creating, acquiring and transferring knowledge, and at modifying its behaviour to reflect new knowledge and insights.

In order to learn, you need new ideas, otherwise you simply repeat old practices. Learning organizations are unusually skilled in problem solving, experimenting, creating, acquiring and using knowledge – as distinct from companies with data gathering resources but no processes to apply them. All too often, organizations take old practices, give them new names and end up repeating the same thing. If you gather new knowledge, but you don't change the way you work and act, you cannot consider yourself a learning organization. For example, universities are enormously skilled at creating and acquiring knowledge, but unusually cool on the idea of changing the way they act, in an administrative and business sense.

Garvin on the three Ms

In the past, definitions of learning have tended to sweep past the gritty details of practice and waft about on waves of philosophy and grand themes. The trick in the learning organization is to be extremely 'nuts and bolts' about how learning is acknowledged. Apply the three Ms test to your organization: meaning, management and measurement. You can define its effectiveness and qualifications in the learning sense:

- **Meaning.** You need a plausible and clear definition of a learning organization which must be practical and easy to apply.
- **Management**. You need to put in place guidelines for practice, filled with operational advice rather than theory.
- **Measurement**. You need tools to assess an organization's rate of learning, otherwise you cannot tell whether new knowledge has been accepted and assimilated.

Once these principles are in place, the real business of learning should be rigorously encouraged. You have to adopt a systematic problem-solving approach. You cannot rely on assumptions. You need to distinguish unique events and chance occurrences from the kind of variation which requires action and is a symptom of a problem requiring a solution. Management must allow time for learning to happen. You must carefully nurture attitudes over time. But there are some obvious steps which anyone familiar with quality processes will recognize – like using brainstorming techniques, problem solving, strategic reviews, benchmarking and systems audits to stimulate knowledge gathering. Make the process of learning important, and encourage a shift away from continuous improvement towards a commitment to learning. This way, knowledge will move higher up the organizational agenda.

You must move away from past experience and ask yourself: 'How do we know that this is true?' This calls for constant experimentation. There is a certain amount of mythology in the practices which managers follow on a day-to-day basis. Replace the statement: 'Of course we know that's what our customers want', with 'How do we know that's what our customers want?' and see where it leads. You may have market research; but is it up to date? You may have three new competitors since the last time you made a market analysis. Most managers are carrying around an invented set of assumptions. The way to break out is to keep asking yourself: 'What's the basis for this?' Doing this requires a combination of empiricism and rigorous reason, and above all, you need diagnostic procedures. The danger in not having these is false positives, false negatives and thinking you're right when in fact the data doesn't support your arguments. You must relentlessly search for the facts.

Garvin on the need for best prototyping

Sometimes the options or the alternatives are neither obvious nor well defined and the only alternative you have is to create experiments. Test new knowledge by prototyping new products and new approaches to manufacturing or service processes. Test the concept. If it looks promising, then generate an experimental design, commission market research, see what the reaction is then see if you can manufacture it. But log your findings at every stage of the process in an empirical way. That is what best prototyping is all about. Experimentation should be just as rigorous as diagnostic problem solving. You should systematically go through the processes, start with opposites and ideal situations and attempt to steer a way to a conclusion. But remember, when many companies think about experimentation they think only about experimenting on the deliverable, on the product, the service, whatever it is that the customer wants. They don't always think about experimenting on the processes, the system, the organization, the way we get there, and increasingly that's where the advantage comes. Think back to the Japanese. The lesson of the Toyota production system is one of careful experimentation with alternative machinery, with the notion of just-in-time. Over the course of two or three years in real time they radically changed factory procedures. Obviously it took time to refine and perfect that system, but it stands as a prime example of experimentation – not on the product, but on the way of doing things.

Garvin on the dangers of company folklore

The past is important, but you must separate company myths from fact. The famous philosopher George Santayana said: 'Those who cannot remember the past are condemned to repeat it.' All too often we see companies with exactly the same problems as they had in a previous cycle repeating the strategies that failed them before. Since they never understood why, under what circumstances, for what reason, with what people they made the earlier mistakes, they are powerless to change the present and drift into the future. As a learning organization, you don't discard the past: the trick is to understand it. You look at new product successes within your own organization, and you systematically work out why they worked. What was the difference? Was it the people, the structure of the assignment, the amount of contact with customers? From the successes you try to work out what you did right and from the failures what went wrong. And then you repeat what you did right and avoid what you did wrong.

To summarize, there is a great danger in accepting wholesale what happened rather than using careful analysis to discriminate. Much of the task is trying to understand what is a truly unique competitive advantage that you cannot afford to lose, and distinguishing this from the common skills you happen to be good at.

Garvin on techniques of acquiring knowledge

New ideas do not come about without hard work and application. You need constantly to search for new sources of knowledge in all sorts of directions. You can acquire knowledge by literally buying another organization, or sometimes by a study mission. Xerox invented benchmarking back in the early 1980s as a way of understanding what its Japanese competition were doing. Rank Xerox in Europe use benchmarking, but then they're a global organization and benchmarking is part of their ethos, but most European companies find the idea difficult to come to terms with.

First you need to solve the obvious problem of gaining access to benchmarking subjects. The rule of thumb is never ask for something that you wouldn't be prepared to give yourself. You should only be prepared to embark on a benchmarking study if you are willing to welcome the other company inside your door. That resolves about 90 per cent of the problem. It is surprising how co-operative other companies are when there is clearly a mutual benefit. You don't necessarily invite a competitor in to see everything. Nobody should reveal their competitive advantage, the features which keep them head and shoulders above anybody else. That's giving away the keys to the kingdom. The principle behind benchmarking and the learning organization is that you uncover best practices which theoretically make the whole business of selling things to customers easier. It is really creative borrowing. Miliken, winners of the Baldrige Award (and the 1993 European Quality Award) call it SIS or 'steal ideas shamelessly'. But joking aside, benchmarking requires real discipline. It is almost impossible to absorb someone else's policies in a wholesale manner, and this should not be an objective. You typically have to make some changes, and you cannot do that unless you first carefully study and understand your own processes and problems.

In some ways benchmarking is an exercise in humility. You must be capable of admitting that you do not have all the answers. This admission in itself is a benefit, because any company that thinks it has all the answers probably won't be around for very long. And benchmarking is certainly not 'industrial tourism'. It is a careful study, calibrating your own performance and then going out and doing the same thing at one or more other companies. The biggest error in benchmarking is made by companies whose objective is to find out who has the highest number of repeat orders, or the lowest defect statistics in their industry group, and then relentlessly pursue their figure. The answer is in the process, and this is a combination of skills disciplines, attitudes, people, philosophy and sometimes even a small amount of happenstance. So you must study processes and ways the work gets done in order to understand the results.

Garvin on knowledge transfer

Once you have got knowledge in one place, the hardest part is to spread it throughout the organization. This is an area in which companies have the least creativity. There are tremendous opportunities for knowledge. What you want to do is take advantage and there are lots of ways to do it but the easiest ways are typically the least advantageous. Typically, hordes of people are brought in to write up the findings in a report. One thing we know about learning is that the best results come about through participation. So it is desirable to make the process of spreading knowledge, of compiling findings, and the business of discovery itself, a team effort.

Companies can design education and learning – you can either apply what you have learnt while you are taking the courses, or immediately thereafter, and have some feedback to make sure that people track whether you've learnt anything. You can move knowledge around by skilfully relocating the source of that knowledge. Take the savvy first-level supervisor and send him or her to another factory. Take the division manager or brand manager and move him or her to another branch. Even better if you can combine these two.

One of the most effective knowledge transfers that I ever saw came from Proctor & Gamble. They found a very successful plant manager who had developed a highly innovative work system, built around sub-management teams. He had spent three years designing, developing and running it. They made him a resource manager, with a key assignment as the development of a training programme, designed for all first-level supervisors in all their other plants. Personnel rotation, properly managed, and backed with an educational training programme, will transfer the knowledge of one or two outstanding workers to hundreds of first-level supervisors who will in turn pass on everything they have learnt.

Garvin on the difference between a learning organization and a total quality process

While there are obviously very strong parallels between the continuous improvement methods of the quality management profession and the learning organization, the methodology of quality is continuous improvement with a hint of a results focus, while the explicit focus of a learning organization is improvement by learning and by modifying your behaviour to take into account what you have just done. The result is the same – continuous improvement – but in quality management, the idea of learning, of how we achieve the improvement, is much less transparent.

The learning organization concept is not a rejection of quality management. The measurements and disciplines of quality management are part and parcel of the learning organization's activities. But quality management in too many cases has lost itself in endless definitions. I can speak far more authoritatively about the USA than Europe, which I guess is about two years behind the key changes, but it is generally true that the quality movement ran for four periods. The first was in the 1970s, the Deming era, when all of a sudden people saw quality as the secret of Japan's success. There was a period of tremendous creative turbulence, which delighted the quality experts and held back factionalism while the paw prints of quality cost and continuous improvement were laid down.

The factionalism set in and with it, dual definitions. The quality world split into Crosbyites, Demingites, Feigenbaumites, Juranites, and a few of the others. Each one rejected the other's claim to knowledge. The issue was further clouded by those who saw certification and standards as the solution to all our problems. Then there was a third period of consolidation where factionalism was set aside in favour of a larger integrated perspective. Companies like Motorola and Xerox put their own stamp on quality. They all started with some mishmash of textbook theory, but went beyond it with a holistic, systemic view. Now we are just entering a new phase, that of the visionists.

In the first phase, quality was oversell: people were told it was going to solve all our competitive problems, and it hasn't. In the second phase, people tried it and it didn't work. This group never really got into quality in depth, and really don't believe it. An element of the problem was that we never worked through the techno-babble to a clear statement of what we were supposed to accomplish. People who are suspicious of trends took a good hard look at quality and were not convinced that it works.

Now you have a very extreme split where there are a group of people who do not understand the criticisms. Xerox doesn't think it would be in business today if it hadn't done quality management. Motorola achieved pre-eminence through quality, but the people who never got anywhere with quality are scratching their heads and saying: 'What next, what do we do?' The lessons of quality movement must be learned and better ways of communication must be encouraged if we wish to avoid repeating the cycle with the learning organization.

The learning organization concept no doubt contains some questionable terminology – it is a little too new-wave for most managers. But you have got to ask, what's learning all about? Learning is about change. And all of these organizations are saying: 'That's us!' Change is the norm in the world today and, where quality may seem compartmentalized, learning, change and improvement seem to cover a wider prospect.

Another advantage of the learning organization is that it is very easy to understand in terms of the five main activities that you need to perform: systematic problem solving, experimentation with new approaches, learning from your past, learning from the best practices of others, and transferring knowledge. You can ask: 'Do we or do we not run experiments?' You do not need a new technology to answer that question. I think the reason for the appeal of this new frame is that it gets you beyond the technical aspects of quality, which I think to some extent have derailed the movement. Learning says: 'Forget the technology, are we getting better? Are there new ideas in this organization? Here are the five activities. Either we are doing them or we're not.'

Extract published by kind permission, © 1994 European Quality Publications Ltd. Beyond Buzzwords – A Realistic Approach to Total Quality and the Learning Organization. Volume 1, Issue 2.

A learning company is an organization that facilitates the learning of all its members and continuously transforms itself. The concept is not new; it goes back to Moses. Organizations have grown from very small entrepreneurial businesses to become, over time, national and multinational companies. Experiments have also been done such as changing organizational structures in order to be responsive to customer needs. Management gurus like Taylor, Galbraiths, Burns, Lippit, Peters, Drucker, Argyris, Pascal, Senge, etc., have been telling us how to manage businesses in turbulent times and how to manage our business in order to beat the competition.

Every time a crisis develops the 'new' management thinking is born. As long as organizations do not behave like dinosaurs and are willing, with the help of their people, to become adaptive to the external environment, they can call themselves learning organizations.

Key success factors

- All departmental or divisional activities should be aligned to corporate strategy and objectives.

- At corporate level new knowledge should be taken on board to adopt corporate strategy.

By focusing on these two aspects, the benefits are accrued at corporate level. As Senge puts it '... well focused actions can produce significant, enduring improvements, if they are in the right place'. Systems thinkers refer to this ideas as the principle of 'leverage'.

Learning is a key aspect of communication process. People learn by interacting with one another and by sharing knowledge and experience. The impetus for continuous learning must come from within.

Starting to learn

There are various ways of initiating a learning process. In the case of TSB the organization decided to adopt the European Quality Award model. They undertook self assessment within the structure of this model. Lucas Management Systems, who have also decided to adopt the self assessment route, have adopted the Malcolm Baldrige National Quality Award model.

Lucas Management Systems – a case study

Lucas Management Systems is in the business of helping companies operate more productively and profitably by providing planning and control 'Artemis' software, consultancy and support services. Formerly Metier Management Systems, it was founded in 1976 and has more than 1200 clients world-wide. It has development centres in the UK and USA, distribution channels in over 20 countries, and employs 600 people world-wide.

The executive stated their commitment to total quality in the mission statement and in Lucas Management Systems' total quality policy:

In pursuit of this team's commitment to evolve and sustain a total quality culture by continuously improving our organization and products, we will:

- focus the organization on client satisfaction

- empower every individual to contribute to the continuous improvement of every aspect of our business
- foster an environment where ideas can be developed openly, honestly and without fear
- set the standards which others seek to follow

thereby achieving growth and profitability through continuously exceeding client expectations and anticipating their future needs.

Lucas Management Systems' investment in total quality is made to improve business effectiveness and profitability for the benefit of clients, shareholders (Lucas Industries) and staff. The quality programme '20/20 Vision' focuses these quality investments in the following critical business areas:

- Client driven new product development and introduction.
- Client satisfaction with sales, consultancy and after-sales support.
- Client response to operational effectiveness and efficiency.

Why self assessment?

In order to achieve a quick start to measuring the company's overall progress and to drive improvement, the company used the criteria suggested by the Malcolm Baldrige National Quality Award model (MBNQA). The major advantage of seizing on the MBNQA criteria in the early stages was that it set the agenda for the 20/20 Vision programme.

Total quality for Lucas Management Systems would involve leadership from the top, management through information and analysis, total quality as part of the strategic planning process, human resource development and management, measurement of process quality, evidence of consistent total quality results, and very importantly a focus on client satisfaction.

What is our approach?
At the meeting of the executive and senior managers in Orlando in 1991 the key presentation was of the first overall programme for total quality, 20/20 Vision. 20/20 Vision was coined by the executive during an earlier team building workshop. It stemmed from the desire to add operational quality measures to the more academic Baldrige measures. Since the Baldrige-based questionnaire measures were scored out of 1010, giving equal weight to operational factors would yield a score of 2020; add a little imagination and 20/20 vision is the result. (20/20 vision is the measure used by UK opticians for eyesight which 'needs no improvement'.)

Six workshops were held, each one led by one of the executive directors who took ownership of one of the categories, and each one considered the most effective ways in which they could improve their rating in each of the Baldrige categories through existing improvement efforts, task forces, improvement groups and so on.

The method used to establish the Baldrige score was via a standard questionnaire sent to 25 per cent of the company's employees each quarter. This was coupled with 'awareness' presentations to outline the 20/20 Vision approach. The questionnaire replies were analysed and a rating calculated for each category; for each geographical region, each division, and overall on a quarterly and annual basis. These results were fed back to the executive to identify areas for improvement and to provide a measure of progress.

What lessons have we learnt?
It was recognized from the outset that this method provided a fast start-up. The result of using the questionnaire was that it measured employee opinion of our progress rather than an objective measure. This proved to be a valuable communication tool, significantly raising the visibility of 20/20 Vision throughout the company. A major drawback, however, was that the questionnaire was not specifically designed for this purpose and was often difficult to understand, particularly for non-native English speakers. In addition, the results were seen as a passive measure of our progress rather than a driving force for improvement.

What have been the benefits?
Self assessment today has benefited Lucas Management Systems primarily by raising the awareness of, and setting the agenda for, quality. In the future, it is hoped that further benefits will be gained through using additional methods of self assessment through the EQA criteria.

Future plans
For the future, it has been proposed that the model used for self assessment is the EQA model. It was agreed that the Baldrige survey be replaced with an employee opinion survey to measure and provide a drive for improvements in 'people satisfaction' for each business unit. This survey, along with the existing client satisfaction surveys and a checklist of additional information (for example business results), will provide input to a broader assessment using the EQA criteria. This will give a more objective view of progress, will indicate areas on which to concentrate improvement efforts, and will provide an overall performance indicator. Ultimately these tools will be used by each business unit of the company to assess their own progress and drive improvements.

Source: Business Improvement through Self Assessment Report. European Foundation for Quality Management, EFQM Brussels Representative Office, Avenue des Pleiades 19, B-1200, Brussels, Belgium. Tel: 32 2 775 35 11. Fax: 32 2 775 35 35.

Organizations learn through their people. Individuals learn through various stimuli in their environment, their experiences and their state of mind. One of the key factors inhibiting learning is the climate of de-layering, restructuring and downsizing. Even business process re-engineering has become synonymous with job cuts. According to some writers some key companies in undergoing corporate transformation have caught a potentially lethal disease called 'corporate anorexia'. Such a disease has two key attributes:

* Organizations have lost the ability to be creative which is very important in the changing competitive climate.
* Employees work in a climate of uncertainty and hence find it difficult to give their best and help their organization become learning organizations.
* Employees in such organizations have also acquired 'initiative fatigue'.

Christopher Bartlett and Sumatra Ghoshal writing in *The Sloan Management Review*, Autumn 1995, issue, referring to the twenty large US, European and Japanese companies' experiences in transforming themselves, said, 'some companies have woken up with little to show except a massive hangover ... Not only have the organizations become too physically strained and emotionally exhausted to maintain the momentum of improvement, but employees' day-to-day behaviour has reverted to old, familiar patterns'.

Other companies such as 3M, Intel and Kao of Japan have developed a favourable climate of entrepreneurship, collaboration and learning. According to Bartlett and Ghoshal, trust and support accompanied with discipline and stretch are the key characteristics which provide a remedy for corporate anorexia.

Learning by coaching

Another way to facilitate learning is by introducing coaching. In some organizations managers act as coaches and help their staff to improve performance and use their skills effectively. Task-oriented coaching is based on a coach showing how a particular task should be done and taking a trainee through different procedures of completing a task. This was the job undertaken by supervisors and managers.

The learning organization adopts the concept of coaching differently. A coach facilitates in bringing out the best performance from his staff. He provides an environment where the staff give their full commitment and expertise. He facilitates knowledge sharing among staff. Coaching in such organizations is developmentally based rather than being just instructional.

Again whether coaching is going to succeed or not will depend on the culture and the intention of the organization. Employees have to perceive that there is trust and commitment at the top management level. Without such a perception the learning process will be hindered.

On your way to becoming a learning organization

- Free up information within your company. Information is knowledge.
- Be tolerant when mistakes are made. Getting it right first time does not facilitate learning.
- Provide resources to show commitment.
- Do not send everyone on training courses without understanding what capabilities are required to gain and maintain competitive advantage.
- Learning must also take place at the top. Remember we talk about a bottleneck meaning a hindrance. If you look at a bottle the neck is at the top!
- Introduce performance measures that focus on qualitative and quantitative indicators.
- Performance assessment or appraisal should identify and

facilitate individual development.

- Make sure that all operations throughout the organization are aligned to corporate strategy and objectives.
- Regularly scan the environment within which your business operates.
- Learning cannot take place without commitment and a desire to want to learn.
- There must be an environment of continuous improvement within an organization, when asking becomes the sign of strength rather than weakness.
- The organization has to provide self-development opportunities for all its employees.
- Learning benefits all the stakeholders of the organization – top management, all employees, investors and society.
- Finally expressing corporate vision and making patronizing statements are not enough. There has to be action throughout the organization, starting from the top.

Selected reading

John Burgoyne, Mike Pedler and Tom Boydell (1994). *Towards the Learning Company*. McGraw-Hill.
Peter Senge (1990). *The Fifth Discipline*. Century.
Peter Senge (1994). *The Fifth Discipline Fieldbook*. Nicholas Brealey.

10 Teaming for business success

Know how to give without hesitation, how to lose without regret, how to acquire without meanness.

George Sand

Summary

- Many organizations now work with teams.
- Teams go through stages of development. It is very important to understand these developmental stages.
- Differences between teams and groups.
- Factors affecting the effectiveness of teams.
- Teams and culture.
- Roles of teams in organizations.
- Team performance.
- Career development.
- Twenty-one questions organizations must ask when forming teams.
- Are you a good team player?

Organizational transformation

As we have seen so far in this book, organizations are under considerable pressure to improve their performance in the face of intense competition. Successful organizations are those who can respond to market needs swiftly and meet customer satisfaction. To do so has meant embarking on total quality initiatives, de-layering organizational structures, re-engineering processes, empowering employees and in some cases transforming the entire organization.

Such changes have produced many casualties and have created problems of motivation and career development. Organizations like Miliken, Rank Xerox and ICL, are continuously finding ways to leverage their employees' capabilities in order to gain and maintain competitive advantage.

In the light of all these changes many organizations have resorted to forming teams. The role of the team has become all important. Teams now form a new way of working and learning.

From groups to quality circles

In the 1960s and 1970s considerable attention was paid to the formation of groups at work. Research findings have indicated the existence of 'informal groups' and their influence on employee behaviour and productivity. Formal groups were constituted in the shape of committees and task forces to address 'ad hoc' business issues. Then came the formation of quality circles in the 1980s to improve quality and combat Japanese competition.

A quality circle consists of about five to ten volunteers who work under the supervisor, meeting once a week to identify and solve work-related problems. The growth rate of quality circles during the 1980s was phenomenal. It is estimated that in the early 1980s there were one million quality circles and ten million members.

By the mid to late 1980s the quality circles began to lose their enthusiasm and excitement. The reasons for their failures were as follows:

- Lack of resources needed to make such groups successful.
- Some companies introduced them as a flavour of the month or as a 'quick fix'.
- Suggestions for improvements were not considered seriously by the top management.
- Supervisors or circle leaders were not trained in facilitating such groups and in group dynamics.
- People were expected to make contributions outside their work hours.

Some organizations who are cynical about teams and team-approaches to decision making cite the examples of the failure of the quality circles without understanding that a quality circle is merely a way of doing things. What matters in the end and in practice is the way such groups are managed.

When you bring a group of people together in any situation the important thing is to understand group dynamics. Group dynamics show how people interact in groups. At the interpersonal level individuals have to be assured of the role they are expected to play, role conflict that may arise, status, power and group-decision making processes.

Stages of group development

Understanding the stages of group development is also important if groups (whatever they are called) have to achieve their objectives. Groups go through certain stages of development during their formation. These stages are sequential and are categorized as forming, storming, norming and performing. Other organizational development experts have given different names to different stages and highlighted more than four developmental stages.

Forming

When people are put together at a very early stage they require guidance and direction. At this stage they are dependent on facilitators and other members and this is the stage of gathering impressions, identifying similarities in expectations, values and note the differences. The focus at this stage of group formation is towards tasks to be accomplished.

Storming

At this stage competition and conflict develop. 'One upmanship' games are played and group members desire some structure. Questions such as 'Who is going to be responsible for what?', 'What's in it for me?' and 'What are the rules and what are the rewards?' often crop up. This is the stage of the 'testing and proving' mentality.

Norming

Values get established and synchronized at this stage and group members begin to gel together and group cohesion develops. Members within the group begin to acknowledge each other's contribution and the 'let's give it a try' attitude develops. At this stage expectations, values and ideas are shared and inter-personal communication becomes effective.

Performing

The group gets into problem-solving mode and group loyalty and pride come into play. This is the most productive stage of the group formation and there is a support for experimentation. This is also the 'I'm OK, you're OK' stage.

Understanding of group developmental stages is very important. Group cohesiveness does not come into existence over night. Many groups have been abandoned while at storming stage. The signals from group members were misunderstood.

Teams are groups of individuals who cluster together to perform common tasks. Quality circles were specific types of teams. Charles Handy in his book *Understanding Organizations* suggests ten major purposes for which organizations use groups or teams.

1. To bring together sets of skills or talents with a view to distributing work.
2. To manage and control work.
3. For problem-solving and decision-making.
4. For processing information.
5. For getting ideas and information.
6. For testing decisions.
7. For co-ordination and liaison.
8. For increased commitment and involvement.
9. For negotiation and conflict resolution.
10. For investigation.

Attributes of teams

Many experts make a distinction between groups and teams. A **group** becomes a **team** when the following attributes are taken on board:

- There is a trust among team members.
- There is a common purpose and vision.
- Sacrifices in individuality are demanded.
- There is discipline and a guidance to what is acceptable and what is not acceptable.
- There is a specification of goals and associated performance indicators and measures.
- There is group accountability.
- There is sharing of experience, knowledge and communication.
- There is unrestricted interpersonal communication.
- There is commitment and involvement.

These attributes give rise to 'teaming' within the groups. Teams per se are not important; it is the relationships and dynamics, in other words teaming, which are important and which matter in practice.

Apart from the existence of these attributes, the effectiveness of teams depends on structure, tasks, environment and process.

Structure

The size and composition of teams matter very much. In one recently privatized industry the top management decided to form a team of 230 people. They subsequently came to the conclusion that teams will not work in their organization. With such a number, group dynamics become very difficult to manage and group developmental stages get extended. Apart from the size the composition is very important. In order to form multi-skilled teams, one telecommunications company formed teams which embraced all skills, irrespective of whether all the skills were appropriate to the tasks to be performed.

In other cases some skills are left out in multi-skilled

teams because they may be scarce and in some cases specialists join teams at a very late stage. Again no regard is given to group dynamics.

Tasks

Teams, like organizations, have to have missions and objectives. These have to aligned with corporate mission and strategy. It is also important to identify the nature and complexity of the tasks involved so that proper direction and guidance may be provided. The leadership role in such circumstances has to change in providing coaching, supporting and training teams.

Environment

Organizational effectiveness depends on internal environment (structure, culture, management style, competencies), and external environment. The effectiveness of teams will also be influenced by the external and internal environment. In a hierarchical or bureaucratic structure, teams perform less well than in an empowered climate. Equally there has to be appropriate and adequate capabilities within the teams in order to enable their organizations to be responsive to the changing external environment.

Process

Teams take time to form, storm, norm and perform. This fact is often forgotten. Whether you form multi-cultural teams or cross-functional process teams or self-managed teams, facilitating free communication, providing appropriate support and direction and motivating team members all accelerate the development of effective teams.

Do not lose money on team training

In the past fifteen years and especially in the last ten years, team-building training has become a growth industry. We now have not only in-door but also out-door training courses. These courses have some usefulness but the majority of them are a waste of money and time if the organizations have not analysed the following:

- What types of teams do we have or are we to have in our organization?
- What are the team objectives?
- What skills and capabilities do we need to put together in teams?
- What is the size of the teams?
- What kind of training would they need?
- What mechanisms do we have to enable them to transfer their experience from the training field or training room to work situations?
- What role should top management play in training?

There is a tendency for many organizations to send their teams to team-building courses without seriously analysing the objectives and the pay-off.

The two other things which organizations constantly have to consider is the role of 'groupthink' which is valid in relation to teams and team maintenance. As Charles Handy said, 'Close teams can become closed teams'. Groups eventually develop their own mind and their own thinking (groupthink) and become blind to the things happening outside their groups. The role of leadership plays a key part in not allowing 'groupthink' to develop. This is done by cross-team meetings, flow of information, and the use of outsiders as catalysts. The other point to consider is team maintenance. After a while team enthusiasm may sag and it is the function of leadership to motivate and maintain the team spirit.

Teams and culture

It can be difficult forming teams and demanding team work in societies grounded in individual values and beliefs. Very often the rapid transfers of management techniques and thinking collide with the deeply rooted mentalities of other cultures.

In forming multi-cultural teams (globalization has encouraged the formation of such teams), it is important to take some time to ponder over cultural differences that exist in social and management thinking. Being aware of different attitudes, values and beliefs will facilitate smooth formation of teams and effective resolution of conflict at the 'storming' stage of development.

In the studies entitled *Organizational Change and Cultural Realities – Franco-American Contrasts*, the authors make the following points:

- Americans and the French seem to favour different approaches concerning the way change should be introduced into the organization.
- The nature of organization is perceived very differently on either side of the Atlantic. Americans seem to perceive the organization as a system of tasks to be accomplished and objectives to be attained. French managers tend to share a personalist and social model of the organization which is perceived as a collective of persons to be managed.
- In the American model authority is conceived of as a way of seeing that tasks are accomplished; in the French model activities and tasks become a prime way of establishing one's authority. Americans would ask 'who is responsible for what?' whereas the French would ask 'who has authority over whom?'.
- The American manager perceives his role as that of a co-ordinator of resources and activities. The French manager considers it very important to have precise answers to the majority of questions he might be asked by subordinates.

In the report *Managing in Britain and Germany* (1994), published by the Anglo-German Foundation, the following are selected highlights of the differences in management behaviour and style that are relevant to teaming processes and working in teams:

- German middle managers exhibit a more technical orientation towards their jobs, while their British colleagues stress the general management tasks of their jobs.
- Communication of German middle managers with their subordinates is predominantly task oriented, while that of

their British counterparts concentrates on motivation, reaching agreement on targets and getting policies implemented.

- German middle managers spend more time alone than British middle managers.
- In order to enlist support, British middle managers rely first of all on persuasion and networking. Their German colleagues trust that they can convince others primarily by the content of their arguments, not the presentation.
- Managers in Britain and Germany hold different sets of values which give them different perspectives and lead to different ways of behaving. These value systems have an impact on motivation, satisfaction, patterns of interaction and so on.
- The German cases studied put emphasis on *Kollegialitat* (team spirit among colleagues), *Zusammenarbeit* (co-operation, working as a part of a team) and *gutes betriebsklima* (good working environment).
- In Britain managers systematically took the individual as their focal point, whether responding to questions about job satisfaction, expectations of bosses and subordinates or job priorities. Typically, the British managers wanted freedom to adopt their own approach to the job; they liked work which gave them a personal sense of accomplishment and what they wanted from their bosses was recognition of their personal contribution.

Cultural dimensions

Geert Hofstede, professor of organizational anthropology and international management at the University of Limburg, The Netherlands, identified four cultural dimensions relating to different countries. These dimensions are:

- the degree of integration of individuals within the groups,
- distribution of power in society,
- uncertainty avoidance, and
- differences in social roles of women versus men (endorsement of masculine or feminine qualities).

These dimensions affect the way the organizations are structured and managed. He shows how organizational practices and theories are culturally dependent (Hofstede, 1991).

Another person who has made his mark on the relationship between culture and organization is Fons Trompenaars, a Dutch economist and consultant. Trompenaars' research revealed seven dimensions of culture (1993). These dimensions provide the most practical way for managers to consider how cultural differences influence their organizations and the behaviour of individuals within organizations. In every culture, he says, phenomena such as authority, bureaucracy, creativity, good fellowship and accountability are experienced in different ways. Understanding such differences will lead to effective management. Such differences are very important to consider when practising empowerment or facilitating teams. He says 'culture is like gravity: you do not experience it until you jump six feet into the air'.

Cultural diversity promotes creativity and minimizes 'groupthink'. However, forming or facilitating a multi-cultural team requires a different management style than that needed to facilitate a uniform or mono-cultural team. For example, it takes longer to establish inter-personal relationships in multi-cultural teams than in mono-cultural teams. Team leaders in multi-cultural teams have to be trained to handle prejudices, stereotyping, differences in values and attitudes and expectations.

Americans generally speaking adopt an instrumental approach to working in teams. The teams are there to achieve certain results. So let's get on with it. Arabs, Latin Americans or Japanese for example, want time to build relationships. At the 'forming' and 'storming' stages, relationship building is more important than results.

Managing teams

The developmental stages of teaming differ in duration and management depending on whether one is dealing with mono-cultural or multi-cultural teams. The factors to consider in forming and managing teams are as follows:

- The mission and the objective of the team.
- The nature of the team and the time scale of achieving results.
- Cultural mix.
- Trust building.
- Integrity and communication.
- Development stages of team-building.
- Historical hang-ups. Previous failed attempts, for example.
- Ways of surfacing differences.
- Identifying cultural blind spots.

The role of teams in organizations

Competitive tracking

In one chemical company based in the UK, the marketing department decided to form functional teams to carry out competitor intelligence. One team was responsible for tracking financial indicators and analysing the performance of identified competitors by looking at their financial performance in relation to one specific group of stakeholders, namely, shareholders.

The other team were asked to analyse the product portfolio, the product development process and the cost of research and development. Other teams track customer service, labour relations and marketing and distribution channels.

These were project teams based on functions. The analysis of the competitor's performance was done in cross-functional teams and the report incorporating an action plan was subsequently presented to top management.

Quality

We have already examined the formation and role of quality circles. Some companies, bearing in mind the causes of failure, still work with quality circles in order to maintain the ethos of continuous improvement.

Process re-engineering

A bank, in order to re-design its branch's operations, formed multi-skilled teams to examine overall workflows and the physical layout of the branch from the customers' perspective.

In a pharmaceutical company teams consisted of a sponsor, process owner, facilitator and team members. Various teams were formed to examine different processes required to reduce 'lab to market' time.

Teams are becoming a way of life in many businesses. Federal Express and IDS boosted productivity up to 40 per cent by adopting self-managed work teams. At Land Rover, delivery of all new products since the mid-1980s has been via project teams.

At AT&T there are four types of teams. They are quality councils, process management teams (PMT), quality improvement teams (QIT), and task teams. An improvement in the billing process, for example, will be examined by the process management team, an improvement in cycle time will be done by the quality improvement team and database improvement will be undertaken by the task team.

Project-based teams

In an article entitled The End of the Job, published in *Fortune*, 19, 1994, the author wrote:

> Study a fast-moving organization like Intel and you'll see a person hired and likely assigned to a project. It changes over time, and the person's responsibilities and tasks change with it. Then the person is assigned to another project (well before the first project is finished), and then maybe to another still. These additional projects, which also evolve, require working under several team leaders, keeping different schedules, being in various places, and performing a number of different tasks. Hierarchy implodes, not because someone theorizes that it should but because under these conditions it cannot be maintained. Several workers on such teams that Tom Peters interviewed used the same phrase: 'We report to each other'.
>
> In such a situation people no longer take their cue from a job description or a supervisor's instructions.

Signals come from the changing demands of the project. Workers learn to focus their individual efforts and collective resources on the work that needs doing, changing as that changes. Managers lose their 'jobs', too, for their value can be defined only by how they facilitate the work of the project teams or how they contribute to it as a member.

Special tasks

Many organizations form special teams to tackle various tasks. Such teams come into existence and are then disbanded once they finish their assignments or projects.

A Japanese electronics manufacturing company constituted a special team to conduct a joint venture project with an American company. The Japanese team consisted of 32 members whereas the American team consisted of 7 members. The teams on the both sides did their homework on cultural differences and associated behaviour as a result of which the negotiations were completed successfully. When teams of different cultures meet it is very important to balance duality – power of analysis against power of synthesis; a sense of reality against imagination; rational thinking against entrepreneurship; vision against reality; action against reflection and flexibility against focus.

Team performance

Team performance needs to be measured. The right measures help teams excel. The following factors need to be considered in formulating team performance measures:

- Consistency of team objectives with corporate objectives.
- Planning of adequate resources required to do the job.
- Quality of decision-making.
- Interpersonal effectiveness.
- Sharing of information.
- Team morale.
- Levels of skills and capabilities.

- Measuring the effectiveness of the process.
- Achievement of output targets.
- How innovative the team has been?
- Assessing individual performance by peers.

Consideration for employees

The big debate over the past few years has been the reward and incentive scheme based on the team approach. There is also the question of career path. When organizations remove layers of management in order to be responsive to market conditions, they create hierarchies of teams to make the best use of the skills, knowledge and capabilities of their people. Organizational pyramids become progressively flat. Career ladders in the traditional sense disappear and the issues of career development arise. Most of the organizations still have not come to terms with satisfying entirely their employees' aspirations when organizational structures get flattened.

When Rofey Park, a management training centre, conducted a study of flatter structures in 1994, it found that for most employees de-layering is seen as a cost-cutting exercise which results for the majority in lower morale, more work and few promotions.

Individuals are increasingly told to take responsibility of their own careers. Sony, UK, for example, have a range of self development and skill-related courses which they make available to their employees. Individuals are increasingly expected to take the initiatives for themselves. We are also told by management development experts that employees are moving away from career success associated with title and status to being involved in things that give them satisfaction

Other organizations have appointed 'mentors' whose main objective is to provide information and direction for employees to build their skills. Other organizations, by way of financial incentives, are encouraging their staff to move horizontally in order to gain long-term employability. Individuals in many organizations now have to come to terms with the 'new order' and respond to the challenges of a changing business environment. People are now moving from doing jobs to performing roles. To perform various roles individuals will need to plan a portfolio of skills. Career development is about building such portfolios.

Career development – the lateral alternatives

Paul Davies, human resource development manager of 3M Europe, made the following presentation at the conference on 'Managing the Horizontal Organization' organized by the Economist Conferences in London in March 1995.

Career development – the lateral alternatives

Introduction and background
Many people have heard about 3M and know a little about the company's products. There is generally less knowledge about the true breadth of the product range and the extent of the international presence of 3M.

3M has operations in 58 countries, most of which are wholly owned subsidiaries of the American parent company based in St Paul, Minnesota. Some 42 countries have their own local manufacturing facilities, very often at more than one location. In 1994 world-wide sales totalled just over $15 billion with profit after tax of over $1.3 billion.

Perhaps the most unusual characteristic of 3M is the product range in excess of 66 000 items. Quite recently Fortune magazine named 3M as the fifth most admired US corporation in terms of annual profits.

Organizational issues in career development
The structure of the company as large and diverse as 3M is complex and continuously evolving. Fundamentally, throughout the world 3M businesses are grouped together into three market sectors – industrial and consumer, information and imaging and life sciences. Each sector is organized into three or four groups which are further structured into a number of divisions.

In Europe the company has more than 18 000 employees, sales in excess of $4 billion and operations in 20 countries.

Three fundamental trends appear to be influencing the career development picture at the organizational level.

Firstly, the scope or role development is significantly increasing within the new rapidly changing and multiple networking structures, in particular at the senior professional level. Role development is achieved by extending responsibilities into broader geographic, functional or multiple business situations. When we look at job changes at middle and senior professional and management levels we see significantly more positional growth in recent times.

Secondly, we are seeing a need for greater flexibility and creativity in the way that jobs are valued within the organization. There are more requests to recognize the uniqueness of a particular role and the potential contribution of a new position. Role complexity and potential impact are seen to be more critical. This trend places a significant challenge on traditional hierarchical job evaluation systems.

Thirdly, we see a structure developing that has much larger incremental steps between job levels, not only as a consequence of the consolidation of management positions but also because of the tendency for role growth already described.

The overall result of these trends is to produce an organizational structure that has a significant amount of opportunity, much of it centred on developing individual expertise and as a consequence much of it unpredictable. In addition, the tendency for larger steps to develop between levels presents some challenges and real dilemmas for our development processes.

Individual issues in career development
There are no certain answers for the individual seeking career progression in today's organizations. This is probably less of a dramatic change from the reality of the past – what is different is that companies are now openly declaring that it is neither practical nor desirable to attempt to manage career development in the manner of an organizational chess game.

This apparent loss of predictability and precision in career development has many benefits for employees. There are some clear action steps that individuals can take to position themselves in the best possible situation for future opportunities even when these are continuously evolving.

An obvious one is that of breadth of experience. Moving laterally across an organization to develop a portfolio of functional and business experience does not depend on the availability of hierarchical opportunities. People who are successful in achieving this pattern of development almost always benefit in the longer term. A broad range of experiences can be an individual's competitive edge when selection decisions are taken for tomorrow's key positions.

We encourage our people to play a full part in the human resource planning processes – performance appraisal, development planning, job information and career workshops. We sponsor networks to exchange information and share expertise and encourage cross-functional teamwork.

We also place great emphasis on individual ownership for personal development and look for a high level of commitment to both the current role and development for broader responsibilities. This aspect is reinforced in a tangible way by our sponsorship of formal education programmes which may often relate more to a future role than to and individual's current responsibilities.

Mechanisms for career development
In common with our peer companies we have seen deteriorating trends in employee perception levels relative to career opportunities in recent years.

Our response to this has been to concentrate on defining the new scenario through communication and education in order to re-position the career development issue. We have put in place a company-wide information system to publicize available job opportunities. We have studied ways to encourage more lateral movement. Later this year we plan to redefine our remuneration guidelines for lateral assignments to allow greater recognition for career broadening moves.

We have also built on the professional career ladder experience of our technical and sales functions and extended these to other key groups, e.g. finance and customer service.

Other areas of attention include the 'Job Swap' idea where two individuals are encouraged in their roles for a defined period of time often in a different function or location.

These mechanisms have been successful in stabilizing employee satisfaction in this area and we believe, over time, will lead to higher levels of employee satisfaction.

Roles in career development
As indicated earlier in the summary there is now much more emphasis on the role of the individual in career development at 3M. Individuals are seen as the owners of their own career development plan and accountable for any defined action.

The manager is positioned as the coach in a supporting role, able to provide visibility and recognition and to remove barriers to progress. This contrasts sharply with the more traditional view of the manager's role, i.e. responsible for 'making it all happen'.

The company or organization's role is defined as the provider of appropriate structures, information and processes and the most conducive environment for personal growth. In addition, the company is responsible for intervening when and if succession planning for key positions is judged to be fragile or inadequate.

The fine balance between these ideas is a key factor in our overall career development strategy.

Mobility in career development

The final issue in this summary of key influencing factors in career development relates to employee mobility. However effective may be the formal training and development activities in an organization, it is clear to us at 3M that most individual development takes place in and around the job.

We are a global organization operating through more than 50 business divisions, in 58 countries, making 66 000 products with 20 functional centres of expertise. The scope for personal development and growth in such an enterprise is virtually limitless. One possible limiting factor could be restricted employee mobility. We have worked hard to minimize this potential barrier to personal development by putting in place relocation policies at local, European and global levels. Relocation is an expensive business with many associated problems. Some companies have given up on the relocation front seeing it as too complex, too disruptive and too costly.

At 3M we have continued to provide a series of alternative relocation programmes that enable any individual with the right skills, motivation and capability to work in any 3M organization world-wide. Several hundred 3M employees are on the move at any one time to new positions in their own countries or around the globe. Of course this is not for everyone and most people in our company will spend their entire careers at one location or within their own country. The key issue for us is that we have the scope and flexibility for these career development options. The benefits far outweigh the costs. The assignment process acts as an accelerator for management development. A simple analysis of the background and expertise of the company's top 100 managers provides a solid testimony to the effectiveness of this strategy.

Summary

In summary, we see some clear trends that are impacting our organization today and that different individual strategies are required to maximize the likelihood of achieving sustained personal growth and the full realization of potential. At 3M we have found that specific organizational initiatives have worked well in influencing employee perceptions and that the shift in focus to individual ownership for career development is a key factor. We value the acquisition of broad experience through lateral assignments and see the need to provide more recognition for these moves. Finally, we recognize the strength of our diversity as a catalyst for personal growth and the importance of providing the appropriate employee mobility policies to maximize the impact of our diversity or career development.

Conference paper presented by Paul M. Davies, manager, HRD Europe. 3M United Kingdom PLC. © 1995 3M United Kingdom PLC.

In flatter organizations and in organizations where teams and teamwork exist, the issue of individual aspirations and career development have become important considerations. The question of individual performance appraisal is partly answered by the introduction of the 360° feedback system but the question of individual career development and rewarding individuals within the team environment still need to be thought out very carefully.

Putting people together in a team does not mean they will work together as a team. Getting people to work effectively in teams is difficult and has to be managed properly.

Twenty-one questions organizations must ask in forming teams

1. Why do you want to form teams?
2. What type of teams do you want to form?
3. Do you have adequate and appropriate resources to staff the teams?
4. Have you formulated smart, meaningful and attainable objectives?
5. Have you established the time-scale for task or process objectives?
6. Do these objectives stretch the capabilities of team members?
7. Do the team members understand why they have been formed into teams and have you clarified their roles?
8. What type of training are you going to design and deliver for team members?
9. Do your training programmes cover technical, personal and inter-personal dimensions of team work?

10. How much time are you going to allow for teams to form, storm, norm and perform?
11. How are you going to promote team maintenance?
12. What should be communicated within the team, to whom, by what method, when and how?
13. What kind of direction are you going to provide to the teams?
14. Have you appointed a coach or a facilitator or a team leader?
15. What actions are you going to have in place to avoid the formation of 'groupthink'?
16. Have you designed performance measures for the teams?
17. Are the performance indicators and measures appropriate to team-work and team objectives?
18. How are you going to update the capabilities of team members?
19. Have you given consideration to career development of individuals?
20. How are teams and individuals within the team going to be rewarded?
21. How are you going to introduce changes to the teams?

Having answered all the questions one can then proceed to forming teams. It is also important to regularly monitor the teaming process (see Figure 10.1).

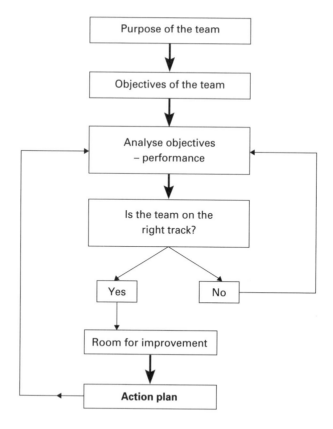

Figure 10.1   The team analysis process

Are you a good team player?

1. I am a competent and caring person.   Agree/Disagree
2. I like to communicate my ideas freely.   Agree/Disagree
3. I seldom question the usefulness of our
   decisions.   Agree/Disagree
4. I go along with what others say in order to
   avoid arguments.   Agree/Disagree
5. I do not like to say what I really think.   Agree/Disagree
6. I do trust my manager.   Agree/Disagree
7. I do not trust all the members of the team.   Agree/Disagree
8. I like working in the team because I do not
   like to make decisions.   Agree/Disagree
9. I do not like to be criticized.   Agree/Disagree

10. Teams are a nice way of fudging the issues.   Agree/Disagree
11. I do not like to give my views on the
    performance of my colleagues.   Agree/Disagree
12. I do not feel strengthened by my colleagues.   Agree/Disagree
13. I like to question the way we operate.   Agree/Disagree
14. I believe tighter supervision produces better
    results.   Agree/Disagree
15. Working in teams is a waste of time.   Agree/Disagree
16. I like to defend my function when I am in a
    team.   Agree/Disagree
17. I make an attempt to understand the views of
    others.   Agree/Disagree.
18. I like to be consulted.   Agree/Disagree
19. I am not prepared to express my beliefs openly.   Agree/Disagree
20. I do not like raising delicate issues.   Agree/Disagree
21. I like thinking of new ideas.   Agree/Disagree
22. I am ready to face temporary unpopularity if I
    can improve the situation.   Agree/Disagree
23. I like talking very much.   Agree/Disagree
24. I am over-responsive to the team atmosphere.   Agree/Disagree
25. I have an aptitude of influencing others.   Agree/Disagree
26. I get very angry and frustrated if I do not get
    my way.   Agree/Disagree
27. I like working in groups.   Agree/Disagree
28. I work better on my own.   Agree/Disagree
29. I am not good at getting my points across.   Agree/Disagree
30. I get bored very easily.   Agree/Disagree

Answer: You are a good team member if you agree to 1, 2, 6, 13, 17, 18, 21, 22, 25 and 27, and disagree to 3, 4, 5, 7, 8, 9, 10, 11, 12, 14, 15, 16, 19, 20, 23, 24, 26, 28, 29 and 30.

And finally in the words of Charles Savage, the author of *Fifth Generation Management:*

Our challenge is not just to build teams, but to master the dynamic teaming process of combining different constellations of capabilities within the context of concrete business opportunity.

Selected reading

William Bridges (1994). The End of the Job. *Fortune*, 19 September.

Brian Domain (1994). The Trouble with Teams. *Fortune*, 5 September.

Geert Hofstede (1991). *Cultures and Organizations*. McGraw-Hill.

Ralph L. Kliem and Irwin S. Ludin (1992). *The People Side of Project Management*. Gower.

Christopher Meyer (1994). How the Right Measures Help Teams Excel. *Harvard Business Review*, May-June.

Fons Trompenaars (1993). *Riding the Waves of Culture*. Nicholas Brealey.

11   The knowledge era: computers and communication systems

In a time of drastic change it is learners who inherit the future. The learned find themselves equipped to live in a world that no longer exists.

Eric Hoffer

Summary
- Use of computers – from data processing to information management.
- Use of computers in business.
- Computers and organizational transformation.
- Computer and Porter's competitive forces.
- Some businesses use computers wrongly.
- Creation of the information society: initiatives in the USA, Japan and Europe.
- The information society: one business executive's view.
- Enter the knowledge era: the organization of the twenty-first century.

Knowledge is information + intelligence

From being the learning organization and working with empowered multi-functional teams, organizations now believe that their strategic and competitive advantage lies in the leverage of knowledge. Computers and communication systems have played a key role in enabling organizations to transform themselves into knowledge-based organizations.

Computers and communication systems

In the 1950s and the 1960s computers were used to process data and to focus on financial and administrative tasks. Computers enabled companies to gather and store data and convert data into information.

Gradually the computer's impact grew with its scope of application and the depth of its capability. SABRE, the American Airlines travel agency reservation system, began as an internal reservation system in the 1950s. In the mid-1970s it was linked to travel agents. Computers became the most effective competitive weapon in the airline industry. The SABRE system enabled American Airlines to build up a detailed database of people's travel habits, their destination, how they travelled and so on.

Computers in business

There are numerous examples to show how businesses are using computers to improve communication with their customers and suppliers and innovate their products.

- American Hospital Supply's ASAP order-entry and inventory control system generated huge sales increases for the medical products.
- Computer-aided-design (CAD) and computer-aided-manufacturing (CAM) became very prominent in the 1980s.
- British Telecom after privatization achieved significant benefits and improved its efficiency by adopting an executive information system (EIS). The software takes raw data and presents it in a very user-friendly form.
- Some companies have reduced their order lead time by as much as 90 per cent by computerizing their operations.
- Some have given their distributors electronic access to their inventory files in order to improve and overcome

scheduling problems.

- Many hospitals send pricing and other information to their purchasing agents via a computerized system.
- 'Hole in the wall' automated teller machines (ATMs) were introduced to provide better service and cut the costs of processing cheques and other transactions.
- In retailing, computers are used to inform retailers what they are selling and in what quantities. They can get information on how much they are selling of each product line, who their customers are and so on.
- In the 1970s supermarkets installed EPOS (electronic-point-of-sale) systems. EPOS records each sale using a laser scanner which reads the barcode on the product.
- The story of success of Wal-Mart is the story of how this business used computers creatively. Wal-Mart set up computer links between each store and the distribution warehouses through electronic data interchange (EDI); it also hooked up the computers of the firm's main suppliers.
- Wal-Mart also uses computer modelling incorporating over 2500 variables to customize its assortments for particular stores.
- Many businesses are now controlling their supply chains via computer networks.
- Mrs Fields Cookies relied on its retail operations intelligence system to build a nation-wide chain of 400 outlets without headquarters bureaucracy.
- Otis, the elevator company, installed the OTISLINE computer system to improve service offered to its customers. According to Index Group (consultancy) OTISLINE revolutionized customer service and it also gained a 6 per cent additional market share.
- Many businesses are linked by computers to carry out functions such as order processing and payments and reducing scheduling problems and inventory overheads.

Today businesses are driven by three success factors – quality, time and cost. Computers have become an enabling technology and many companies are using computers as a strategic tool to improve overall management and market performance.

Ask not what computers can do for us but what we can do with computers

- Enabled businesses to process information and its functions, ranging from data management to transactions processing.
- Converted information into knowledge and enabled knowledge-sharing among companies.
  - Helped integrating various businesses and managing complex operations.
  - Changed 'the way we do business' attitude and promoted 'out-of-the-box' thinking.
  - Questioned the fundamental assumptions of business.
  - Opened up various strategic options.
  - Made relationship marketing and database marketing possible and effective.
  - Enhanced core competencies of businesses.
  - Underpinned various change initiatives.
  - Enabled teleworking.

The list is not exhaustive. Every day one reads about a new application. The arrival of cheaper computer systems have also provided opportunities for small companies to configure their businesses and use information to compete effectively. Experts are predicting that within the next few years sales of PCs will break through the 100 million level, thus exceeding annual sales of television sets for the first time.

Each new generation of microprocessor brings more power and businesses are not slow in seizing opportunities to explore and exploit the greater use of value-added communication services in order to enhance business communications and improve competitive positioning.

The computer and competitive forces – some comments

The use of computers has had a significant impact on all competitive forces with the result that companies have to be constantly on their toes to survive in the competitive arena.

Porter's competitive forces

(1) Barriers to entry
- Information technology in the form of computers and telecommunications continue to penetrate and transform every aspect of business.
- Barriers to entry are constantly being eroded due to the development of electronic highways.
- Information technology has made the economies of scale arguments redundant.

(2) and (3) Bargaining power – supplier and buyers
- Computer technology, used creatively, can help companies capture, satisfy and retain customers.
- Companies consider their suppliers as 'partners' and give them access to their inventory files.
- Customers have electronic access to pricing and other information in relation to certain products and companies.
- Computer technology has enabled companies to link with suppliers and customers globally.

(4) Substitutes
- Customers can now book flights on almost any airline due to computerized reservation systems.
- The microcomputer revolution has enabled new products to come to the market in a very short period.
- The significant advances of computers have created a wide spectrum of new strategic options.
- Computer technology has accelerated product and process innovation.

Computers that listen and talk are beginning to dominate businesses. There are graphical user interfaces driven by the use of icons and the mouse, notepad computers that can be written on with a pen and so on. The 'interface revolution' has given many the taste of user-friendly screens.

Companies' mechanisms of control and management as well as communication are changing immensely as we pass into an era of the Internet, information superhighways and computer software. Employees are becoming skilled with their workstations and move between systems without extensive training. Computers are becoming as familiar a part of the business environment as telephones.

Why do some businesses lag behind in computer technology?

* Computer technology changes 'the way we do business' attitude. There is, therefore, resistance to embrace computer technology wholeheartedly.
* Some use computers as a window-dressing exercise in order to impress their boards of directors.
* Some do not understand the capabilities of computer technology.
* Some companies have failed because of a complete misunderstanding of users' needs.
* In some cases system development and implementation have proved very costly.

Computer technology and business transformation: beware!

* The misuse of technology can reinforce old habits and block re-engineering by reinforcing old ways of thinking.
* A company that cannot change the way it thinks about IT can not re-engineer.
* Computer technology should be used innovatively and creatively.
* Computer technology cannot offer solutions if businesses are not capable of identifying problems.

Computers, communication systems and national initiatives

The information society

The USA, Japan, and Europe independently but in close concert during 1993 and 1994 launched separate information society programmes. According to G. Russell Pipe, of the Global Information Infrastructure Commission, based in the USA, the shared information infrastructure objectives of these initiatives can be summarized as follows:

- 'exploring opportunities offered by advanced computer and communications technologies, new products and services;
- improving quality of life by offering new working life styles; greater personal interaction, reducing environmental problems caused by energy overuse;
- raising efficiency and productivity, stimulating economic growth and trade competitiveness;
- modernizing all aspects of society;
- addressing environmental problems by more efficient use of resources and energy.'

The main objectives for the USA, Japan and Europe for constructing national information infrastructures (NII) are as highlighted below:

The USA
Network of communication networks; computers, databases linking homes, businesses, schools and libraries to a vast array of electronic information resources and creating commercial opportunities.

The NII task force has been set up to work on ways to materialize these objectives.

Japan
Fibre optic information communication networks to every business and household for an intellectually creative society able to meet social and economic restructuring in the twenty-first century.

Japan is advocating a 'shift of perspective in which the goods- and energy-oriented twentieth century gives way to the information- and knowledge-oriented twenty-first century based on info-communications infrastructure'. According to the Telecommunications Council of the Ministry of Posts and Telecommunications, 'In the intellectually creative society based on high performance info-communications of the twenty-first century, great importance will be attached to the free creation, circulation and sharing of information and knowledge as social and economic assets'.

Europe

Creation of an information society based on trans-European networks and liberal telecommunications markets to create jobs and strengthen competitiveness.

An action plan for planning 'Europe's Way to the Information Society' was presented to the European heads of state meeting in Corfu, Greece in June 1994. The plan was designed by a high level working group chaired by EU Commissioner Martin Bangemann. The core principles of the EU action plan are to:

• Strengthen industrial competitiveness.
• Create new jobs.
• Promote new forms of work organization.
• Improve quality of life and the environment.
• Respond to social need.
• Raise efficiency and cost-effectiveness of public services.

In February 1995, a G-7 ministerial conference took place in Brussels. The conference served two purposes:

1. To confirm that the leading industrialized nations are committed to national information infrastructure pro-grammes leading to information societies.
2. To provide actual demonstrations of a whole array of applications.

In preparation for the ministerial conference, a group of business leaders headed by Mr Carlo Benedetti, President of Olivetti, prepared a draft policy paper entitled Building a Global Information Society – A Call for Government Action.

A similar request was also heard at the Asia-Pacific Economic Co-operation (APEC) ministerial meeting held in Seoul in May 1995.

The information society: one business executive's view

The following is the view held by Henri Aebischer, director, European R&D, Apple Computer, Inc.

Surviving with data in a voice-oriented world ...

To say, today, that the communications, computing, and consumer electronics industries are converging is as to say that the earth is round. In this context, we have chosen four questions offering a specific perspective from a computer point-of-view:

- What will be the impact of the computer industry on the voice-focused telecom industry?
- When will data traffic outweigh voice traffic?
- When will wireless telephony support video signals?
- What will be the 'killer application' in the telecom arena?

What will be the impact of the computer industry on the voice-focused telecom industry?
Mutations
Figure 11.1 was originally developed at Harvard University to track the size and convergence of the various information industry segments. The interesting areas are where the segments overlap or influence each other because it is where most opportunities exist for value and profit creation.

Digital engines
It is generally accepted that the new landscape emerging from this convergence will comprise three main types of companies: contents, conduit, and user devices. The **digitalization** of all forms of information gives **computers** a predominant role in this landscape. Computers are invading all levels of the global information infrastructure the same way that microprocessors have become embedded in virtually all electronic devices, in vehicles, in credit cards, etc.

View of the past
This transformation of information into bits on a superhighway makes the question of survival with data in a voice-oriented telecom world obsolete. We can soon forget about pie charts segmenting telephony, networking, or telecom markets where, as an afterthought, 5 to 10 per

cent are 'left' to 'data' applications. We will see later that data already represents far more than 10 per cent of the traffic on the well-established public telephone network.

However, the transition will take years. As an example, the 9600 bps left for data on sophisticated digital systems such as GSM are already too tight compared with the 28 800 bps V.34 modems offer to Internet surfers today.

View of the future

So, the future is this now almost infamous information superhighway that makes headlines in publications of all sorts. Yet, today, we see just the tip of the iceberg. The full impact will occur when television will join, one way or another, after completing its digital mutation.

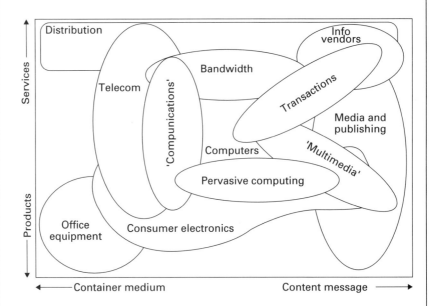

Figure 11.1   Information industry battlegrounds

The vicious circle

In any case, computing (data) and communications (voice) need each other because they are locked in a vicious circle.

With the widespread adoption of graphics/mouse-based user interfaces, personal computers have become easier for everyone to use. Their increased performance has spurred the development of more powerful applications giving these systems more obvious benefits.

Paradoxically, the telephone seems to have followed an opposite

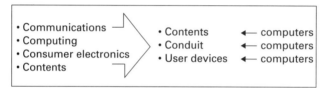

Figure 11.2   New landscape from convergence

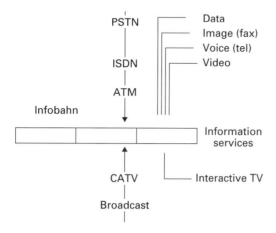

Figure 11.3   The information superhighway

path. While anybody knows how to use a 'normal' telephone, a mobile handset requires some training. And, remembering all the functions of a desktop telephone connected to a sophisticated PABX makes, by comparison, programming a VCR child's play.

Computers need communications to become more **useful** by offering immediate access to masses of digital information. Reciprocally, telephones need computers to become more **usable** by offering intuitive access to network intelligence.

With the exponential growth of information in digital form on one side, and of computing power on the other side, communications become increasingly important to give computer users access to this information and to make computers more useful.

At the same time, the intelligence and the functions in communications networks are also growing exponentially. Current telephones make it very difficult for users to tap into this intelligence. The intelligence of computer technologies – especially those related to the user interface – can certainly solve a major part of this problem.

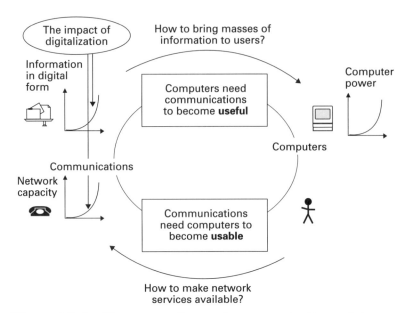

Figure 11.4   The computing and communications vicious circle.

The telephone industry already makes extensive use of computers for transmission, network management, and especially switching. Manufacturers of modern electronic switches already master the most complex and reliable software systems in the world. It shouldn't be complicated, for people who manage a world-wide network of over 500 million endpoints, to integrate software that has grown out of Californian garages.

Today, computers at both ends (and in the conduit) are required to explore the Internet. By comparison, the French Minitel, though extremely useful, clearly shows the limitations of dumb terminals at the user end.

The virtuous spiral

A point of view is worth 80 IQ points.

A. Kay

We have already started to come out of this vicious circle. The modem was the first step to conceptually integrate a telephone into a computer and make the computer use the telephone network for data communications and fax transmissions. The next step is to conceptually do the opposite: integrate a computer into a telephone. Several desktop telephones are being developed with integrated pen-based computer technologies.

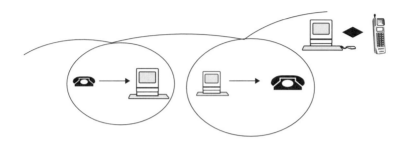

Figure 11.5 Integrating communications systems

The real potential of this integration will be, in our opinion, unleashed in the area of mobile, wireless devices where the voice and the related telephony functions will be totally integrated like any form of digital information (a.k.a multimedia). So, ultimately, the difference between computing and telephony industries will vanish as Alice in Wonderland's Cheshire cat.

When will data traffic outweigh voice traffic?
This has **already** happened in many domains and it will be more and more difficult and meaningless to measure.

Perversions
We use the term 'perversions' in its original Latin sense: per-via (detour). As an example, modems and fax machines are wonderful and useful perversions of the public switched telecoms network (PSTN) in that they use the voice band to transmit data or images. Figure 11.6 shows how technologies and applications intermingle to finally converge on the information superhighway.

Today, fax transmissions apparently represent over half of the PSTN traffic across the Atlantic Ocean and over 75 per cent of the traffic between Japan and the USA.

Furthermore, while the number of personal computers in homes is growing faster than in business, an increasing number of these systems have a modem. So, the telephone network carries a lot of 'data' that mimics voice.

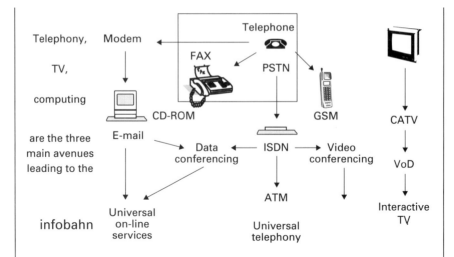

Figure 11.6   The information superhighway

Conversions

'Bits (of information) are easier to clip than atoms (of objects)', observes Nicholas Negroponte in *Being Digital*, his latest book. In a computer, it is possible to mix bits of voice-comments to a document with text bits, picture bits, and video bits. Many standards coexist to represent text, voice, sound, images and motion pictures, but since this representation is in the form of bits, computers can easily convert from one standard to another.

However, humans remain analog. The technique to convert bits into something understandable by people will be the toughest to refine. Current products implementing handwriting recognition, text-to-speech, or automatic speech recognition show consumers have difficulty accepting that a system is not 100 per cent reliable.

Figure 11.7 shows a possible combination of such conversion technologies and suggests that, as an example, one could have a hand-written document sent by fax read by a computer to a person calling this computer.

The next question, assuming that such a conversion is reliable, is whether such a function is useful. Can one have the patience to listen to a four-page fax over a telephone line? We touch here upon another human factor: the brain works in a non-linear way through approximation and intuition. As we will see later, we will need sophisticated agents and automatic pilots to help us explore the landscape at the end of the superhighway.

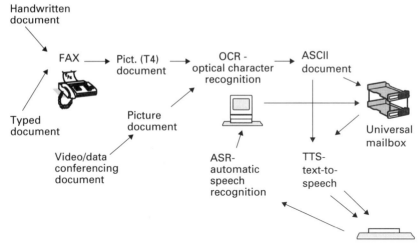

Figure 11.7   Technologies converge

Progression
Figure 11.8 shows how computers progressively take over all forms of information. Today's **on-line services** offer access to a huge mass of information and enable universal messaging.

The latest telecom adapters (modems, ISDN) **integrate computing and telephony** through an increasing number of applications such as screen-based telephony, answering machines, automatic database activation through identification of an incoming call, etc. Global standards for **data and video conferencing** are being imple-

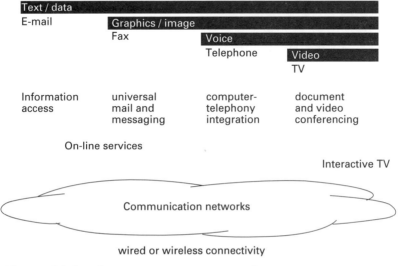

Figure 11.8   Communications networks

mented on personal computers. And the same PCs can display TV in a window. However, this is still analog TV. The integration of digital TV is the next challenge. The computer industry is in intense dialogue with the digital TV industry to maximize compatibility between both technologies (e.g. use of square pixels).

Transformation

Many trials are being conducted to understand how consumers will adapt to a mix of technologies and media and actively interact with them. Figure 11.9 is another way to show the path to the superhighway and suggests a Darwinistic perspective to the mutation we witness today.

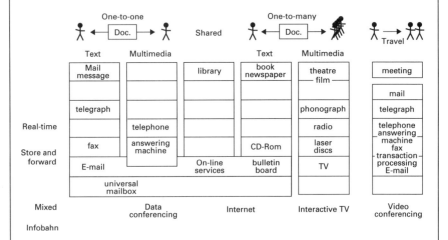

Figure 11.9   The information superhighway

When will wireless telephony support video signals?

Inversion

History has put the television and the telephone on the wrong media. Nicholas Negroponte has already pointed out that we need an inversion. Television has to use wired infrastructures to free up the spectrum for wireless communications, including particularly telephony. In other words, fixed systems such as TV sets and desktop computers should communicate over wires while mobile devices must have enough spectrum to eventually support video.

Access ramps to the superhighway

Out of 135 million workers in Europe, 33 million spend more than 20 per cent of their time away from their desk or workplace. These nomadic people want their electronic tools, telephones, computers, personal digital assistants, to be as mobile as they are. Consequently, **wireless communications** are as important as cables because users want to communicate anywhere, anytime. This has profound implications on the design of the information super-highway.

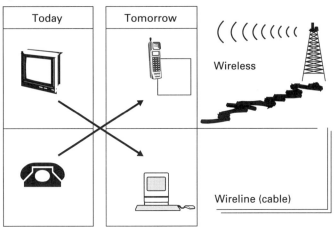

Figure 11.10   Today and tomorrow

Beyond the Model T

Today, most PCs with access to the Internet look the same while there are many kinds of different vehicles on the asphalt highways. But the success of different kinds of notebook computers (though most of them still are just shrunken desktops) and the increasing use of personal digital assistants (PDAs) in vertical applications suggest that the Ford Model T era of computing is ending.

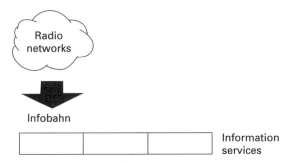

Figure 11.11   Wireless communications

Today's PCs and workstations all look the same ...

Tomorrow's users of the superhighway will probably require systems adapted to their specific needs and lifestyles just as some of them drive sports cars, some minivans, trucks, motorcycles, etc.

It is reasonable to assume that the combination of technologies such as wireless digital telephony and PDAs will spur the development of new breeds of devices where it will be difficult to distinguish the computing genes from the telephony ones. Computer architectures will dominate new generations of TV set-top boxes and we will probably see specific systems to navigate the superhighway.

TV: the last frontier

The implosion of the last analog empire – TV – creates a new 'Far West' where key players such as Disney, Time Warner, TCI, AT&T and the Baby Bells rush to take positions. We have killed the last dinosaur by preventing HDTV becoming analog and simply current TV with better screen resolution. Computers will invade STBs and visionaries already say that the TV of tomorrow will be a PC.

The convergence of digital TV on the superhighway will have far reaching consequences outlined by Apple's chairman, Michael Spindler, in a speech to the World Economic Form in Davos earlier in 1995. 'Television has the most dramatic impact on our society, to a point where some cultures and even nations appear defenseless to its influence ... In the nineteenth century the media was under the influence of politics and often under direct government control. Today the situation is the opposite. The advent of mass media has turned politics into show business...

'The TV set hasn't acquired much intelligence in the past ten years. The viewer remains a passive receiver for broadcasted media. The basic multimedia architecture and versatility of a PC may provide a better platform for a variety of user appliances including the format for future digital boxes and embedded telephony management.'

What will be the 'killer application' in the telecom arena?

For anybody with a hammer, everything looks like a nail.

Many specialists have already predicted what the superhighway killer application will be. My guess is that there will not be one major single application that will make the superhighway 'take off' as was the case for VisiCalc for the PC almost 20 years ago.

Challenges for servers

One has to note that, while the term 'highway' refers mainly to the conduit part of the upcoming information industry landscape, communications networks are only means to an end. For most users the **journey** is more important than the highway. Quite simply, users want to explore meaningful contents, acquire useful 'things', or communicate with each other. So basically, we need information servers, transactions servers, and communications servers.

The servers should **share** their **intelligence** with user devices to minimize network overload (a distributed intelligence enables some kind of infrastructure-level compression) and to maximize user control.

The servers' contents and services should be **scalable** to different network or user configurations. As an example, on Internet, a meaningful subset of World Wide Web pages should be selectable via lower bandwidth wireless accesses. And the same pages should be reformatable for viewing on lower resolution displays such as TV sets.

The **architecture** of the servers should also be compatible with the user devices because compliance to the same open standards at both ends eliminates unnecessary conversions and facilitates the navigation; and most importantly, because on 'democratic' systems such as the Internet the same device can be used both to publish user-provided information (as server) and to gather publisher-provided information.

Those are key reasons why Apple focuses on servers as much as on user devices. And that's why the Macintosh has such an important share of the multimedia contents creation market.

Challenges for user devices

The evolution of hardware performance (the world of **atoms**) is fairly easy to predict. The improvements to software (the world of **bits**) are more difficult to plan and design.

The basic challenge is to design devices that are both **usable** *and* **useful**, Usable means really easy to use, even by intuition, allowing users to focus on the expected result and not on the tool itself (when one hammers a nail, one shouldn't look at the hammer). Useful means helping users solve real problems or bringing real value for business, education, or the environment.

Manufacturers will have advantages if their devices are part of a full range of systems with a scalable architecture spanning from low-cost consumer set-top boxes to super PCs and including special systems, such as portable devices using wireless highway on-ramps.

Users will expect manufacturers of devices and developers of associated software to offer improved systems and tools for navigating the ever increasing amount of bits in the digital society. Such systems include, as an example, **automatic filters and browsers** able to adapt to specific circumstances (e.g. travel) and to users' observed needs, taste and habits. They will also require security (especially for electronic commerce) and **privacy** (we trust our current postal services to not open our mail).

Publishers and service providers have the same concerns at the server end. In addition, a big issue to solve is the one of **global copyright** and intellectual property protection.

Challenges for operators

Since networks are a means to an end, the overall challenge for the operators is to make them transparent to the users by enabling plug and play connections and providing adequate and reliable bandwidth in varying configurations.

I think that the famous **last mile** problem will be quickly resolved for technical and economic reasons when competition opens in 1998.

Another practical problem is the one of the **last meters**, i.e. how does one distribute multi-Mbps across a home in all possible locations. Many have probably seen by now the cartoon where the husband tells his wife: 'Darling, could you please answer the TV because I'm watching the phone'. This suggests we will most probably see a myriad of different devices that mix and match functions which are separated today. The vision of one single home **super information centre** connected to a multi-mega-bit-per-second fibre pipe and combining interactive TV, telephony, access to on-line services, and other functions is probably not realistic. When the first electrical motors replaced the old mills it was reasonable and economical to have one motor per factory. In computer terms, this was the time-sharing period of the 1960s. Today, microprocessors are everywhere and mostly invisible to the users. Can one imagine going to the electric motor in the centre of a house to grind coffee, shave, play a CD, or run a fan? We may have all the bits entering the home through a single fibre but **wireless** technologies and **embedded computers** will allow us to use them **anywhere, anytime**. I think that short-range/high-speed digital wireless technologies, such as ETSI's HIPERLAN could play an important role in deploying such technologies.

Operators will also play a key role concerning **security**, especially for commercial transactions. In a global system where consumers may buy goods and services in different countries, operators could become mediators and represent their customers with all their resources and influence. The same is true for **privacy** issues. Operators can promote and enforce encryption standards guaranteeing global interoperability.

Challenges for regulators

In my opinion, the government should focus on enabling develop-ment and removing barriers; not on regulating or architecting. Markets should be allowed to function unencumbered and to provide the widest availability of products and services at competitive prices. So, a global information infrastructure should guarantee interoper-ability, free market access, security for commercial transactions and personal information, privacy and intellectual property protection.

The future is no longer what it used to be.

In conclusion, let's quote again Michael Spindler's speech: 'I hope and believe that the consumers will remain the sole judge of demand and consumption and that this world will not be defined from the van-tage point of technobuffs predicting how one will 'live on the Net'. Each medium enables a unique mode of discourse by providing a completely new orientation for thought, expression and sensibility.

'We don't yet understand the real impact of a global information society. The key is to acquire 'a point of view' about our information assets, since information can't be both a blessing and a curse. We crave more information and, at the same time, feel inundated, intruded upon and out of control. We must ensure that the real user remains in control of the interaction'.

Source: Conference speech delivered by Henri Aebischer at the Economist Conferences 7th Telecommunications Conference held in Stockholm, November 1995.

There is no looking back – enter the knowledge era

The successful corporations of the next millennium will be those who are knowledge-driven with world-wide information highways, massive computer power and leadership styles that will facilitate value-added by all employees.

The twenty-first century is going to be dominated by knowledge-driven companies. Stan Davies, the author of *Future Perfect* (1987) has predicted that all businesses, high tech as well as low tech, face the choice of launching new products and services that are knowledge based.

Knowledge is rapidly becoming the most important resource of the future. Davies's latest book *The Monster Under the Bed*, co-authored with Jim Botkin, declares:

Today knowledge is often a businessman's most valuable commodity and knowledge workers are often its most valuable resource. Knowledge is an increasing portion of the value of an offering in the market place and the basis for competitive advantage.

It is said that in business information is knowledge and 'knowledge is power' (*The Economist*). Louis Gerstner, chairman of IBM said, 'Powerful networks will increasingly unlock corporate knowledge and move it to people who can use it effectively and creatively'.

The concept of knowledge is not a new one. The first learning organization to realize the importance of knowledge was IBM which adopted the word 'Think' as its motto. What subsequently happened to IBM was that thinking was not capitalized into action to respond to fast changing market environment.

The learning organizations of the 1990s will take advantage of the convergence of technologies and become networked knowledge organizations of the twenty-first century. Suppliers, partners and customers will be linked by computer technology to share skills, costs and access to one another's markets. Some say that come the twenty-first century the marketplace will be replaced by cyberplace.

What of those who lag behind or are not prepared? They should ponder upon the moral of the following story:

> Once upon a time there were two businessmen walking in a jungle. Suddenly, they heard the roar of an angry and hungry tiger. One businessman opened up his rucksack and took his running shoes out. As he was putting them on the other businessman remarked, 'You are crazy; you cannot outrun the tiger!' The other businessman replied, 'No, you are right. I cannot outrun the tiger but I can outrun you.'

And the moral of the story? Be prepared to outrun your competitors.

The last word on the role of knowledge must go to Peter Drucker. According to Drucker:

> But the modern organization is a destabilizer. It must be

organized for innovation ...And it must be organized for the systematic abandonment of whatever is established, customary, familiar and comfortable ...In short, it must be organized for constant change. The organization's function is to put knowledge to work – on tools, products and processes; on the design of work; on knowledge itself. It is the nature of knowledge that it changes fast and that today's certainties always become tomorrow's absurdities.

He goes on to write:

For managers, the dynamics of knowledge impose one clear imperative: every organization has to build the management of change into its very structure.

(Peter Drucker: *Managing in a Time of Great Change* (1995). Butterworth-Heinemann.)

Glossary of terms/ abbreviations used

Bandwidth:	The capacity of a communication circuit
Encryption:	Security system technique which encodes voice, data or image
ETSI:	European Telecoms Standards Institute
GBPS:	Gigabits per second
GSM:	Global system for mobile
HDTV:	High definition television
ISDN:	Integrated services digital network
LAN:	Local area network
Open System:	System which allows interoperability with other systems
PABX:	Private automatic branch exchange
PDAs:	Personal digital assistants
PSTN:	Public switched telecoms network
WAN:	Wide area network

Selected reading

Peter Drucker (1995). *Managing in a Time of Great Change.* Butterworth-Heinemann.

Stan Davies and Jim Botkin (1994). *Monster Under the Bed.* Simon & Schuster.

The EIU Report (1991). *Executive Information Systems.*

The Economist (1995). A Survey of Retailing. March 4.

Management Review (1995). Technological Transformation of Enterprises. *The American Management Association Magazine.* Nov.

Epilogue: Memo from all employees to the chief executive officers

To: Chief executive officers

From: All employees

Subject: Is there anyone out there listening?

....

You have indicated to us the necessity for business to improve product and quality service, to benchmark in order to adopt best practice, to re-engineer processes and businesses and to become customer-service minded. 'People are our greatest asset' you say in our annual company report. You ask us to give you full support and commitment and to understand the nature of changes undertaken by the company.

   You have our full support. You have to make special efforts to promote understanding of the various change efforts but do please make sure that we do not become 'initiative fatigued'. We would like to draw to your attention the following:

Organizational schizophrenia

In our company annual report to shareholders and to us there are numerous platitudes about us. 'People are our greatest asset', 'People are our life and blood', 'It's our people who make things happen'. And yet when there is a hint of crisis and you are put under pressure from your board and shareholders to reduce costs the first thing you do is 'downsize' the organization. Downsizing is simply getting rid of people without analysing the loss of capabilities. Getting rid of people is the easiest and the 'macho' thing to do in order to buy time or impress the board. The true character of the inspirational leader in our view is facing crisis with courage and imagination. You only get rid of people as a very last resort when everything else has failed. In a crisis situation you need to analyse the capabilities that exist within the organization and make use of them to perform strategic manoeuvres.

If you find that you have 'surplus' people in your company why not redeploy them to acquire new skills so that you do not lose their experience and loyalty? Of course, in the short run you will still have high costs and you will not be able to impress your board and shareholders but in the medium and long term if you face the crisis with courage and imagination we will give you full support and the company will come through crisis and sustain the survival instinct for a very long time to come. You will gain respect and trust from us. This is one of the ways you can win trust.

If you have to make some of us redundant as a last resort please do treat us as human beings with feelings. When you did make 100 of our colleagues redundant last time, some of them were on holiday and some of them have been asked to leave the office within a day. Our manager was asked to clear his desk within ten minutes and return the company car keys immediately. There are many horror stories of the way this company has treated people when getting rid of them.

With waves of redundancies we also find it difficult to concentrate on our work and trust your leadership. We constantly ask 'who next?' Not a very nice feeling!

What can we do for the company?

We are one of the groups of stakeholders of the business and we want the business to succeed just as you and your board do. We require leaders we can trust and who trust us. Trust has to be institutionalized and made transparent so that we feel it in our hearts and minds.

Tell us openly about our company strategy and objectives. Give us the chance to help out during crisis.

Do not respond to every management fad but when you do,

consider implications throughout the entire business. We have read that change initiatives such as re-engineering lead to 'corporate anorexia' and 70 per cent of re-engineering initiatives fail because they have not been done properly.

We are willing to change our 'jobs' and adopt different roles within the company. Give us adequate and appropriate training to become a multi-skilled workforce so that we can help the company be responsive to changing customer needs.

Empowerment

We work in teams now and we are told we are empowered. To perform key roles within the teams the human resource department has arranged for us to attend the Outward Bound course and attend team-building seminars. We have enjoyed the course and had a very pleasurable time together. But there is no one able to help us transfer the experience to the workplace. We need help to solve problems and make decisions. We believe we should be consulted on our training needs. Training should not be left to the human resource department.

Career development

We understand there are not going to be promotions in a traditional sense. We are responsible for our own career development. There is information available in our library about various courses available. We do, however, need career counselling within the company.

Our company has various schemes to promote horizontal mobility. We are seconded to other departments if we wish to acquire broad experience. This is very good idea as it gives us a chance to understand how different businesses work.

One thing, however, has not been addressed sufficiently. As we take care of our destiny as the organization structure is becoming flatter, the payment and incentive system has not changed very much. We believe the incentive and pay scheme should be consistent with the changes taking place.

We also believe the new psychological contract is developing between the employees and the top management. For such a contract to be effective you have to promise us support and give us an opportunity to acquire new skills. Employability rather than stability should be the centrepiece of this contract.

We promise to give you full support and commitment. But you have to demonstrate the courage of your conviction in us, your people. Open communication, trust and credibility should be the key attributes of inspirational chief executive officers.

Index